Economics of
Natural Disasters

Economics of Natural Disasters

Editors

Suman Kumari Sharma • Euston Quah

Nanyang Technological University, Singapore

with additional contributions by
Zach Lee

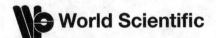

NEW JERSEY • LONDON • SINGAPORE • BEIJING • SHANGHAI • HONG KONG • TAIPEI • CHENNAI • TOKYO

Published by

World Scientific Publishing Co. Pte. Ltd.

5 Toh Tuck Link, Singapore 596224

USA office: 27 Warren Street, Suite 401-402, Hackensack, NJ 07601

UK office: 57 Shelton Street, Covent Garden, London WC2H 9HE

British Library Cataloguing-in-Publication Data
A catalogue record for this book is available from the British Library.

ECONOMICS OF NATURAL DISASTERS

ISBN 978-981-4723-22-0

For any available supplementary material, please visit
https://www.worldscientific.com/worldscibooks/10.1142/9791#t=suppl

Desk Editor: Sandhya Venkatesh

Typeset by Stallion Press
Email: enquiries@stallionpress.com

Printed in Singapore

DEDICATION

I dedicate this book to my husband, Mohan Sharma, for his immense faith in me and my work whose continued love and support throughout made this possible. Also, the value of honesty, integrity and faith in humanity that I share with him were my initial motivations to work in areas aimed at reducing peoples' pains and sufferings caused by disasters. I also dedicate this book to my two daughters, Ava Sharma and Sima Sharma, for their constant support and encouragement.

Suman K. Sharma

I dedicate this book to the memory of all those who have suffered or perished in natural disasters. I also dedicate this book to the memory of my mentor and teacher, Professor E.J. Mishan of the London School of Economics who taught me much on the value of wisdom in addition to knowledge. Finally, the love for my family who understands and supports my endeavours, as always.

Professor Euston Quah

PREFACE

Natural disasters are not only catastrophic and often damaging to lives and property, they can also displace people's livelihood and job options. Major catastrophic events usually result in lost productivity and can exert severe adverse impacts on the affected economy. Intangible damages such as psychological pain and suffering, and emotional stress are often underestimated.

In recent times, natural disasters' adverse consequences are seen to be more severe where societies and peoples' lives and livelihoods are more and more connected. Furthermore, recent disasters' consequences have extended over regions, time and sectors depicting that major catastrophic events can disrupt economies far beyond the local ones largely in terms of global infrastructure and interconnected supply chains and markets. Consequently, the growing need to understand natural disasters' impacts cannot be emphasized enough. Comprehending disasters will not only help understand the underlying financial risks but also enable the policymakers and development actors to devise and implement effective disaster risk reduction policies and strategies aimed at mitigating risks and minimizing potential disaster threats and building resilience.

Much has been written on the devastating impacts of natural disasters and the resilience of countries and societies. However, there is a paucity of work on the economics of natural disasters. This book attempts to fill in this much neglected gap, and hopefully, the examples of various types of natural disasters occurring especially in Asia can help to understand better and enrich the literature.

The topics covered in this book range from Poverty and Natural Disasters, Impact on Growth, Government Budget and Depth, International Trade and Financial Flows, Human Capital and Political Economy, Quantification for Economic Losses, Risk Exposure to Extreme Events, to Impacts on Residential Property Values to disaster risk reduction policy agenda, government planning and building resilience.

Detailed case studies of natural disasters such as the Great Hanshin-Kobe Earthquake are also discussed.

It is perhaps ominously coincidental that one of us (Euston Quah), had experienced first-hand, the June 19, 2018, Osaka Earthquake when he was visiting Kobe University. The magnitude of this earthquake which reached 6.1 on the Richter scale struck Osaka at 7.58 am, and reached its neighbouring city Kobe at 8 am. Awakened by the big jolt of the earthquake, the entire hotel (Sheraton Kobe Bay) shook and swayed for almost two minutes before normalcy returned. It was emotionally distressing, and thoughts of this present book being prepared quickly met reality.

We would like to place on record the valuable advice and encouragement throughout by Ms. Sandhya Venkatesh of World Scientific Publishing, as we worked to get the manuscript ready for publication. We have also benefitted from Luke Luldashov, our very capable and diligent research assistant.

Needless to say, all errors remain with the editors.

Dr Suman K. Sharma and Professor Euston Quah
Editors

ABOUT THE CONTRIBUTORS

Azreen Karim is an applied economist and is currently based at the Bangladesh Institute of Development Studies (BIDS), Dhaka, Bangladesh. Besides her qualitative work on establishing a conceptual framework on *disaster-development* nexus, her current research interests include environmental and disaster economics, international and development economics. Azreen's articles have appeared in international reputed journals namely *World Development*, *The Singapore Economic Review*, and *Review of Economics and Institutions*. In 2015, she was awarded the prestigious *Jan Whitwell Prize* for best presentation of work undertaken by a doctoral student. She had consulted and developed projects for United Nations Development Programme (UNDP), The World Bank, International Institute for Sustainable Development (IISD), International Centre for Trade and Sustainable Development (ICTSD), Sustainable Development Policy Institute (SDPI), Trade Knowledge Network (TKN) and Economic Research Institute for ASEAN and East Asia (ERIA).

Ilan Noy is the Chair in the Economics of Disasters and a Professor of Economics at Victoria University of Wellington, New Zealand. His research and teaching focus on the economic aspects of natural hazards' and disasters, and other related topics in environmental, development, and international economics. He is also the founding Editor-in-Chief of *Economics of Disasters and Climate Change*, a journal published by SpringerNature. He previously worked at the

University of Hawaii, and has consulted for the World Bank, the Asian Development Bank, the Inter-American Development Bank, UNISDR, the International Monetary Fund, ASEAN, the Japanese Government, and the Chilean Central Bank.

Jonathan van der Kamp obtained his PhD in economics from the Karlsruhe Institute of Technology (KIT) in 2017. He has been working as a researcher at the European Institute for Energy Research (EIFER) in the field of energy and environmental economics since 2009. In 2013, he was a visiting scholar at the economics department at Nanyang Technological University (NTU) in Singapore. His research covers a broad range of topics centered around the integrated assessment of environmental and health impacts of energy-related activities. He has published in well-known international journals and contributed to private and public funded research projects, amongst others to the most recent update of the German methodological convention on environmental costs.

Jonathan Neo is a UK-based management consultant in the public sector practice. His work primarily involves advising central government and local authorities on issues ranging from transport and infrastructure to regional economic development. In 2013, he was a research assistant at the Nanyang Technological University in Singapore where he focused on topics in environmental economics. He graduated from the London School of Economics and Political Science with a Masters in Development Studies (Distinction), and University of York with Bachelors in Philosophy, Politics and Economics (First Class with Distinction).

Lopamudra Banerjee teaches economics at Bennington College in Vermont in USA. Her research explores how social structural conditions shapes people's risk of exposure to natural disasters and their quality of life.

Yasuhide Okuyama is a Professor in the University of Kitakyushu, Japan. He earned his doctoral degree in regional planning from the University of Illinois at Urbana-Champaign in 1999. He also holds the master's degrees from the University of Wisconsin-Madison (urban and regional planning, 1994) and from the University of Tsukuba, Japan (environmental science, 1986). His research interests center on economic impact of disasters, regional science, input-output analysis, and urban and regional planning. He has published a number of articles in various academic journals and book chapters, and edited a book titled "Modeling Spatial and Economic Impacts of Disasters" in 2004 with Professor Stephanie Chang of the University of British Columbia. In addition, he has been contributing to research projects and consultation for organizations including the World Bank, the European Commission, the Economic Research Institute for ASEAN and East Asia (ERIA), the Japan Bank for International Cooperation, and so on.

Wasantha Athukorala, Ph.D. is a Senior Lecturer in the Department of Economics and Statistics, University of Peradeniya, Sri Lanka. He is involved in a number of studies in the fields of environmental economics and agriculture economics. He has published more than 20 research papers in well-known local and international journals and has co-authored three text books and authored two text books. He has also published 7 book chapters. In addition, he has presented more than 30 research papers in various national and international conferences. He holds a PhD in Economics from the Queensland University of Technology (QUT), an MPhil and a BA (hons) from the University of Peradeniya, Sri Lanka.

Wade E. Martin, Ph.D. is a Professor of Economics attached to California State University, Long Beach. He is an applied economist with a special interest on wildfires. He has published several papers and book chapters on this topic. Over the last 20 years he has also supervised over 20 research projects for the USDA Forest Service, Bureau of Reclamation and numerous private contracts. He is also a past editor of Contemporary Economic Policy and is currently the Executive Director of Western Economics Association International (WEAI).

Prasad Neelawala, Ph.D. has a BSc in Agriculture and MSc in Environmental Economics from the University of Peradeniya, Sri Lanka. He has a Master of Business (Economics) and PhD in Environmental Economics from the Queensland University of Technology (QUT), Australia. Currently he is attached to the ESOFT Metro Campus, Sri Lanka and is an active member of academic circles related to agriculture and social science.

Darshana Rajapaksa, Ph.D. is a Senior Lecturer in the Department of Forestry and Environmental Sciences, University of Sri Jayewardenepura, Sri Lanka. Prior to his present position, he served as a Researcher at Queensland University of Technology (QUT), Australia, Assistant Professor, Kyushu University, Japan and Agricultural Economist, Department of Agriculture, Sri Lanka. His research interests are on environmental economics, agricultural economics, climate change and natural disaster. He has published several research papers in refereed journals.

Jeremy Webb, Ph.D. is a visiting researcher at the Queensland University of Technology (QUT). He is involved in a number of studies on the effect on urban environments of 'peak car' and new forms of transport and in particular the uptake of shared electric autonomous vehicles. As a former head of the Australian Department of Foreign Affairs and Trade's Economic Analysis Unit he has been responsible for a wide range of reporting on global trade and investment issues. He holds a PhD in Economics from QUT, an MA from the University of Hawaii and a BA (hons) from the Australian National University.

Clevo Wilson, Ph.D. is Professor of Economics at the Queensland University of Technology (QUT). He specialises in agricultural, environmental, transport, tourism, ecological, agricultural, energy (renewables), and development economics with a special interest in using environmental valuation techniques, both revealed and stated. His research interests also focus on supply chain value analysis, efficiency and productivity analysis and structural equation modelling. He also undertakes cost benefit analyses. He has undertaken research and published papers in diverse topics including tourism (with a special focus on nature-based tourism and economic value analysis), aquaculture, energy and water conservation, agriculture, transport, natural disasters (floods and wildfires), impact of major projects and pollution on property values, environmental sustainability and conservation of wildlife. The work has real world applications. In 2012 he co-authored a book entitled *Nature-based Tourism and Conservation: New Economic Insights and Case Studies* published by Edward Elgar, Cheltenham, UK.

ABOUT THE EDITORS

 **Dr Suman K. Sharma** holds Masters and Ph.D. degrees from the University of California, Santa Barbara, USA. Dr Sharma has been teaching and undertaking research at the Division of Economics at the Nanyang Technological University in Singapore. Dr Sharma has extensive research and consulting experiences with the government, non-government and international organizations, such as, the United Nations, the Asian Development Bank and the World Bank. Over the years, Dr Sharma has conducted research/consultancy in a wide range of fields, though concentrating mostly in the areas of socio-economic aspects of disasters, social protection and poverty issues.

Besides working on economics of natural disasters, Dr Sharma has undertaken country studies of social protection policies, programs, and interventions, in Singapore and Malaysia in Southeast Asia, and previously on South Asia, as part of the Asian Development Bank's project on *social protection and committed poverty reduction in Asia and the Pacific*. Also, Dr Sharma has undertaken a country study of Singapore on existing social security policies, programs, and schemes as part of building the Social Security Inquiry Database of the International Labour Organisation, Geneva.

Over the years, Dr Sharma has participated as invited speaker at various regional and international conferences including the annual Social Experts' Meetings of the OECD/Korea Policy Centre, organized by the OECD, Korea Policy Center, ADB and ILO. For instance, during the most recent *Social Experts' Meeting Asia-Pacific*, held in Seoul, South Korea, Dr Sharma presented Singapore case study on '*Informal Workers in Singapore and Social Protection Coverage*'.

 **Professor Euston Quah** is Head of Economics at the Nanyang Technological University (NTU), Singapore, and an Adjunct Principal Research Fellow of the Institute of Policy Studies at the National University of Singapore (NUS). He was formerly Chair, School of Humanities and Social Sciences at NTU; Vice-Dean, Faculty of Arts and Social Sciences; Deputy Director of the Public Policy Program (now called the Lee Kuan Yew School of Public Policy); and headed the economics department at NUS. A prolific writer, Professor Quah had published over 100 papers in major internationally refereed journals and opinion pieces. His most recent works include a paper in an international publication on cost-benefit analysis for Oxford University Press, 2013; a Lead Journal Article in World Economy in 2015; a Commentary in the Asian Economic Policy Review in 2016; an Invited Paper in the Macroeconomic Review in 2017; and a forthcoming paper in the Annual Review of Resource Economics, 2018. Two books on Cost-Benefit Analysis was published by Routledge, UK in 2007 and 2012 respectively. His work on Cost-Benefit Analysis (with E.J. Mishan 5th edition, and 6th edition due in 2019) was recommended for reference by the US White House, Office of Management and Budget for use by Government Agencies applying for project grants. He was co-author of an Asian Edition of the best selling Principles of Economics text with Gregory Mankiw of Harvard University, now a second edition in 2013. The Third Edition will be published in 2019.

Professor Quah advises the Singapore Government in various Ministries and was a Member of the Prime Minister's Economic

Strategies Sub-Committee on Energy and the Environment. He had served on the Boards of Energy Market Authority, Fare Review Mechanism Committee of the Ministry of Transport, Board Member of the Energy Studies Institute at NUS; and presently sits on the Government's Market Compliance and Surveillance Committee; the Singapore Medical Council's Complaints Committee; the Advisory Panel of the Ministry of Finance; and the Competition and Consumer Commission of Singapore. In 2016, Professor Quah was appointed a Member of the Social Sciences Research Council of Singapore. He is also a Review Panel Member for the Bill and Melinda Gates Foundation project hosted by the Overseas Development Institute, London; and in 2015 was inducted as a Fellow Member of the prestigious learned society, European Academy of Science and Arts. Professor Quah is Editor of the Singapore Economic Review (since 2002), and the President of the Economic Society of Singapore since 2009. He has been invited by Stanford University, Princeton University, the USA Inter-Pacific Bar Association, WWF for Asia, UNESCAP, Earth Institute of Columbia University (Asian Meetings), ADBI and ADB to speak at their functions and conferences and he is one of the most highly cited and influential university economists in Singapore.

CONTENTS

Dedication   v

Preface   vii

About the Contributors   ix

About the Editors   xv

Chapter 1. Introduction and Overview   1

Chapter 2. The Empirical Literature on Poverty
           and Natural Disasters   15

Chapter 3. Economic Losses from Natural
           Disasters: Quantification Approaches
           and Developments in Asian Countries   49

Chapter 4. An Analysis of Exposure Risk
           to Extreme Events in Nature   85

Chapter 5. After the Thrill is Gone: Impact
           Analysis of the 1995 Kobe
           Earthquake and its Reconstruction   119

Chapter 6. Impact of Natural Disasters on
Residential Property Values:
Evidence from Australia   147

Chapter 7. Disaster Risk Reduction and
Disaster Management in
Government Planning and Policy
Agenda   181

Chapter 8. Disaster Risk Reduction and
Sustainable Development:
Going Forward   257

Index   275

CHAPTER 1

INTRODUCTION AND OVERVIEW

Suman K. Sharma and Euston Quah
Nanyang Technological University

Natural disasters like earthquakes, typhoons, wildfires, floods, volcanic eruptions, can have consequences far beyond physical and economic damages leading to disruptions on communities, societies and peoples' lives and livelihood options. In current times, since we live in a highly globalized world where the lives, livelihoods and businesses of peoples, communities, and nations are deeply interconnected, natural disasters' adverse consequences can be profound on multiple fronts — with cross cutting implications over regions, time and sectors. One of the implications of a global economy is that major catastrophic events can disrupt economies far beyond the local ones in terms of global infrastructure, since worldwide businesses can also be impacted due to their interconnected supply chains and markets following the aftermath. As an example, the 2011 Japan earthquake and tsunami and the 2011 Thailand floods demonstrated to the world that although the events seemed to cause relatively localized damage to individual countries, they had far wider indirect economic implications through market disruptions caused by supply chain reactions, among others.

More recent events have shown that economic losses resulting from natural disasters have been continuously growing. Disaster literature frequently appears with disturbing news indicating for the most part that globally, economic damages and losses from natural disaster events have been increasing. For instance, the 2015 Global Climate Catastrophe Report stated that "in the 10 years since Hurricane Katrina, the world has seen an annual average of 260 major natural disasters, with average annual economic losses of US$211 billion and 76,000 lives lost"; while another report highlighted that the three major earthquakes in April 2016 — driven by two tremors in Japan's Kumamoto region and one in Ecuador — clearly stood out in their capacity to inflict vast economic damage as well as human suffering, ended up causing nearly $35 billion in economic losses (Aonbenfield, 2016b).[1] According to the 2016 Annual Global Climate and Catastrophe Report, globally, in 2016, a total of 315 natural disaster events caused total economic losses equivalent to USD210 billion, an amount estimated as 21% above the 16 year average of USD174 billion (Aonbenfield, 2017). To reiterate, besides the obvious economic damages, the potential chain reactions of negative economic impacts of natural disaster events can spill over to countries around the globe due to an intricately globalized supply chains and interlinked market environments, thereby threatening the adverse impacts to persist over a much longer time period.

Asia-Pacific has been labelled as the most disaster-prone region in the world where natural disasters have been more frequent, intense and disaster risk is out pacing resilience, according to the 2017 Asia-Pacific Disaster report (UN-ESCAP, 2017). The region has consistently been one of the hardest hit in the world, for instance, over the last decade, out of the top five countries that are most frequently hit by natural disasters, four are in Asia, namely, China, India, Indonesia and the Philippines (other than the United States) (CRED 2017). Furthermore, future natural disasters are likely to have greater destructive potential, for example, between 2015 and 2030, forty percent of global economic losses from disasters will be in Asia and the Pacific, while the region accounts for around 36 per cent of global GDP (UN-ESCAP, 2017).

---

[1] Aonbenfield (2016).

As such, not surprisingly, the complexities surrounding a comprehensive picture of disaster impacts are so immense that both their immediate and longer-term impacts are often far too difficult to fathom, which, in turn, compounds and complicates the tasks and processes of devising disaster management policies and plans to address the underlying issues. At the same time, it is becoming ever more important not only for businesses to understand the financial risk that catastrophes pose to their supply chains and markets across the region and beyond, and develop robust disaster plans to reduce the potential impact, but also for policymakers and development actors to devise and implement effective disaster risk reduction policies and strategies designed to mitigate risks and minimize potential disaster threats and build resilience.

This book aims to contribute to existing literature on economics of crises and disasters and further our knowledge of some of the complexities associated with understanding of disasters' impacts and consequences, and also, the policy implications aimed at disaster risk reduction. First, we begin with impacts and consequences of natural disasters, using a number of case studies based on some of the major disaster events in the Asia-Pacific region. Next, we provide a broad discussion of some of the key policy measures employed by the national governments in the region to translate their understanding of disasters into respective policy agenda to pursue a sustainable development path aimed at risk reduction and resilience building highlighting the associated issues and challenges.

Chapter 2 (*"The Empirical Literature on Poverty and Natural Disasters"*, by Azreen, Karim and Ilan Noy) begins with a comprehensive review of empirical literature on natural disaster impacts. The last few years have seen an explosion of economic research on the consequences of natural disasters due to a growing awareness of the potentially catastrophic nature of these events, which is also a result of the increasing recognition that natural disasters are social and economic events, despite the fact that they are triggered by a natural hazard: their impact is shaped as much by the structure and characteristics of the countries they hit as by their physical attributes. The chapter argues that in addition to the growing interest in the social and economic aspects of natural hazards, increased awareness of climatic change is playing an important role. Consequently, much of the discourse in the past few years has focused on potential changes in the pattern and intensity of future events due to human-induced climate change.

Chapter 2 stresses that while recent research projects on impacts of natural disasters have evaluated the impact on various aspects like growth in the short and medium-to-long terms; government budget and debt (for various time horizons); international trade and financial flows; populations (in terms of migration and fertility choices); human capital, the importance of political economy in shaping the aftermath of the disasters; and others; there is little research on the impact of natural disasters on the poor and on income distribution. These intersecting themes of disasters, climate change, and poverty are only becoming more prominent as seen through the new DRR treaties including the Sendai Framework for Disaster Risk Reduction (signed in March 2015), the Sustainable Development Goals (a successor to the Millennium Development Goals; August 2015), and Climate Change Prevention, Mitigation and Adaptation (the Paris Agreement; December 2015[2]). Chapter 2, therefore, contributes to these discussions by surveying the existing literature on the impact of natural disasters on poverty and the poor, discussing some of the limitations associated with this literature, and outlining a future agenda of investigation that can contribute to better-informed policymaking.

How does existing literature have to be approached to understand and estimate disaster impacts particularly in terms of disaster components, disaster datasets and quantification methodologies? Since major disasters tend to cause great damage, destruction and human sufferings, estimating the associated economic losses is crucial, as this information supports decision-making not only in the immediate follow-up period of disaster events, but also for the development of longer-term risk reduction and mitigation

---

[2]Falkner, R (2016).

strategies. Along this line, Chapter 3 ("*Economic Losses from Natural Disasters: Quantification Approaches and Developments in Asian Countries,*" by Jonathan Kamp and Jonathan Neo) sets out with three objectives, namely, to identify and classify those components that enable to assess the full societal impacts of natural disasters; to present associated economic quantification approaches and their limitations; and to analyze statistics on natural disasters for countries in East, South, and South-East Asia during the period from 1990 to 2015.

To achieve the objectives, Chapter 3 provides an overview of assessment approaches through a quantitative analysis of economic losses from natural disasters in East, South and South-East Asia during the time period 1990 to 2015 along with data on socio-economic factors such as population density or level of economic development into the analyses in order to allow for better informed comparisons of results. Furthermore, Chapter 3 discusses various issues and limitations related to data and methodologies in impact estimation emphasizing that as a consequence, trade-offs need to be made between what is theoretically desirable and what is practically feasible.

At the forefront of disaster impact analysis, researchers and practitioners frequently encounter a range of factors at interplay — from physical, to economic, to social and psychological — responsible for contributing to and/or resulting in the observed consequences of a disaster. Chapter 4 ("*An analysis of exposure risk to extreme events in nature*", by Lopamudra Banerjee) studies the common factors that determine people's susceptibility to extreme natural events, and explores how geographic hazards and social conditions determine the chance of disaster exposure.

Based on datasets from Bangladesh, Indonesia, and Tanzania, Chapter 4 observes that while a household's chance of experiencing exposure depend on the type of hazard (viz., flood, drought, volcano and tsunami) and its level (viz., low to high), certain common social factors that determine the household's everyday living conditions (viz., occupational mode, household size, and regional poverty), also, determine its susceptibility in exceptional times of disasters.

Focusing on the hazard and vulnerability conditions of households across various geographic regions to examine the latent factors that generate disaster risks, specifically, Chapter 4 prescribes two major findings. First, while disaster risks are higher when higher levels of hazards are present in a household's habitat, certain categories of hazards (viz., flood and tsunami hazards) entail greater risks than others (viz., drought or volcanic hazards). Second, while the chance of experiencing disaster conditions is obviously greater for households if the region is afflicted by a natural extreme, probability of exposure is lower for households that have relatively secured prior access to resources under normal conditions (i.e., in absence of disasters).

Regardless of the level and type of hazard present, findings based on Chapter 4 indicate that certain attributes of households, which ordinarily determine their access to resources under normal conditions, such as, occupation of the household head, play an important role in determining their resilience under exceptional conditions of disasters. Presumably, households that have relatively stable livelihood conditions and relatively steady flow of income have greater material ability to cope with the adverse situations generated by a disaster event. Thus, these households have greater chances of avoiding losses and bear lower risks. Risks are also lower for investment of public resources to deploy buffers may entail construction and maintenance of irrigational canals to mitigate the effects of drought and floods, that of embankments and dams to control floods, and that of roads public transport systems to facilitate evacuations in the case of volcanic eruptions and tsunami. Investment of private resources, for instance, may entail installation of pump and well irrigation systems to cope with drought, access to vehicles to assist evacuation in the case of volcanic eruptions, and so forth. Smaller household sizes entail, on one hand, lower consumption expenditures and greater access to ready savings to tide over a period of crisis, and, on the other, greater mobility for the family when the crisis situation arises. Thus, these households have greater ability to remove themselves from a potentially dangerous situation.

Chapter 4, therefore, concludes that in a divided society, where resource entitlements are conditional upon social and economic statuses of households, any deficits in the social and economic determinants of a household's material conditions under ordinary circumstances additionally constrain the household's ability to obtain private goods, and weaken its claim over public goods, in an emergency situation. These deficits generate the latent vulnerability conditions for the households, which are brought into surface when a violent environmental event occurs. The results in this chapter, obtained in context of three rather (socially and economically) dissimilar countries of Bangladesh, Indonesia and Tanzania, universally, highlight this phenomenon. They indicate that risk of disaster is neither exogenous nor indiscriminate. Rather, disaster risk can be associated with prior deterministic conditions that are already always generated through the functioning and organization of a social system, long before a violent event occurs in nature.

Chapter 5 (*"After the Thrill is Gone: Impact Analysis of the 1995 Kobe Earthquake and its Reconstruction"*, by Yasuhide Okuyama) investigates the economic effects of the 1995 Kobe earthquake — occurred in the second largest economic region of Japan — based on the empirical data using econometric technique and structural analysis method. The results indicate that the event had created statistically significant deviations from the pre-earthquake growth path of Kobe. The economic damages of the event were estimated around 10 trillion yen while in addition, the damages from the earthquake and the subsequent reconstruction activities led to significant structural changes in the regional economy, which further affected Kobe's long-run growth trend.

Through investigating the total effects of the Kobe earthquake using econometric models and structural analyses, Chapter 5 presents findings that the economic recovery from the 1995 Kobe earthquake initially surged for a few years, but declined subsequently since then. The decline was quite severe and persistent for the City of Kobe, and it appears the case that the substantial efforts and budget allotted for recovery and reconstruction were still insufficient to bring about full recovery from the event. It is, therefore, observed that both the Hyogo Prefecture's and Kobe's reconstruction plans were not intended to recover the regional economy to the pre-event state. Rather, they aimed to pursue the pre-existed long-range development plans proposed before the event and to lead to a sustained growth path with the promotion of high value-added industries and through economic structural changes to service industries. As found in Okuyama (2014 and 2015b), the production levels of these high value added and service industries fluctuated widely after the event and did not result in a consistent growth pattern, whereas most of manufacturing industries decreased the production level due mostly to the underlying hollowing-out process. Perhaps, the local governments of Hyogo and Kobe believed that this event could have accelerated this transformation to a sustained economic growth through the enormous reconstruction activities. The chapter argues that from a planning perspective, sustaining the long-range plans, even after a catastrophic event, seems legitimate, but utilizing the reconstruction from the event as a springboard to accelerate the development process is rather questionable. In the mean time, the underlying long-range development plan of Kobe assumes the target year of 2025. It might be the case that Kobe would soon return to the original development path and could reach their planned and desired targets by 2025 through the continuing and persevering reconstruction process, while the Kobe earthquake hampered the local economy's long range development plan.

Chapter 5, consequently, highlights that the long-run analysis of disaster effects provides an important lesson — solely analyzing the short-run impact and recovery would lead to the inaccurate conclusions about reconstruction process. After the Kobe earthquake, underlying structural changes have been somewhat accelerated by the reconstruction activities. The resultant structural changes were significant and extensive as seen in this chapter. Therefore, when the long-run effects of a disaster are investigated, the study should include the effects from and the process of the reconstruction activities, since reconstruction activities are the consequences of the disaster process and considerably influence the long-run trends of the regional economy. As a policy implication, in order to hinder the acceleration of or to slow down the pace of underlying structural change during reconstruction period, it is important to promote and support regional inter-industry linkages so that the ripple effect of injected reconstruction demand can be predominantly retained within the region.

Furthermore, given that population changes have had a marked influence on the decline of the regional economies, Chapter 5 stresses that the decreased population led to decreased consumption demand and, in turn, to a lower level of economic activities. While the population was restored to the pre-event level in 1999 for Hyogo and in 2004 for Kobe, the per capita income recovered in 2001 for both Hyogo and Kobe but still lagged noticeably behind the national average trend despite attempts made to promote high value-added industries. Additionally, Chapter 5 suggests that the uneven population recovery in Kobe, partly resulted from the uneven reconstruction progress over space, could become a deep-rooted problem over time. Hence, it is important and interesting to analyze the rapid changes in population compositions (age and income distributions) after the event and during the reconstruction period over time and space in order to reveal the demographic-economic interactions and their impact on regional economies after a disaster.

One of the most prominent casualties of a natural disaster is the property market. As seen through recent devastations caused by major disasters around the world, the private and social costs from such events typically run into millions of dollars. To investigate disaster impacts on property market, Chapter 6 (*"Impact of Natural Disasters on Residential Property Values: Evidence from Australia"*, by Athukorala, Clevo Wilson and others) uses a dataset on residential house prices following a hedonic property (HP) values approach.

Specifically, Chapter 6 uses datasets pertaining to before and after both wildfire and flood events, which affected Rockhampton in central coastal part of the state of Queensland, Australia. The data is unique because one of Rockhampton's suburbs was affected by wildfires and another by floods. For the analysis, three suburbs namely Frenchville, Park Avenue and Norman Gardens are used. Frenchville was significantly affected by wildfires in the latter part of 2009 and to a lesser extent in 2012, while Park Avenue was affected by floods at the end of 2010, January 2011, 2012 and 2013. Norman Gardens, which was relatively unaffected, is used as a control site. This enables to examine the before and after effects on residential property values in the three suburbs. The results confirm that in the aftermath of a natural disaster property prices in affected areas decrease even though the large majority of individual houses remain unaffected. Furthermore, the results indicate that while prices in largely unaffected suburbs may gain immediately after a natural disaster, this gain may disappear if natural disasters continue to occur in the area/region due to a flood prone stigma being created.

The results based on Chapter 6 have several important policy decisions and welfare implications. What the results show is that affected suburbs have lower property values. This means that in the case of wildfires, any avertive action taken (which lead to decreased wildfires) will result in increased property values of the suburb. Avertive action can include back burning for which a council levy for affected suburbs can be charged. Similarly, flood Levees could be constructed (have been recommended for Rockhampton) to minimize the damage from floods. Insurance companies could contribute towards mitigation efforts. What this means is that residents clearly discount the possibility of their properties being affected or they believe that they have adequate insurance, have undertaken actions to self-insure and are effectively making the trade-off to pay more to live in close proximity to green space at the risk of wildfires affecting their properties. Hence, in the absence of a wildfire insurance policy, residents will continue to pay more to live closer to natural disaster areas such as wildfires.

In the case of flooding and wildfires it is also important to weigh the costs and benefits of rebuilding. For example, in the case of flooding it might be best to convert identified areas subject to frequent flooding into green spaces. Another important policy implication stemming from the study is the importance of disclosing natural disaster affected areas to potential buyers so that the purchase price reflects the true costs of living in natural disaster prone areas. Currently, no such mandatory requirement exists but rather relies on the principle of *caveat emptor*. Given the high degree of information asymmetry that exists (and hence market failure) this is an area that is worthy of government intervention.

How effectively do the impact analyses of natural disasters contribute to policy implications such that national governments and disaster practitioners are able to reflect those into their respective planning, policy and development agenda aimed at risk reduction and resilience building? Chapter 7 (*"Disaster Risk Reduction and Disaster Management in Government Planning and Policy Agenda"*, by Suman K Sharma) aims at contributing to this discussion with a broad assessment of national governments' planning and policy agenda based on disaster risk reduction and disaster management while highlighting the associated issues and challenges commonly encountered during the implementation phase.

In recent times, countries are seen to be increasingly vulnerable to natural hazards and disasters arising from a range of socio-economic factors and other anthropogenic drivers reflecting complex linkages between those all of which, in turn, complicate the task of impact estimation. Consequently, the undertaking of policies and actions — measures considered essential — to mitigate risks and threats to hazards and disasters, can also get disrupted considerably. With the goal of highlighting issues and challenges involved in translating a development agenda driven by disaster risk reduction, Chapter 7 discusses how well the national governments fare in addressing challenges and risks associated with disaster risk management: focusing for instance on questions like: have they identified regulatory and legislative measures to mandate disaster risk reduction concerns in their planning and development agenda?; and if so, how far they have progressed? Based on the available disaster literature, Chapter 7 observes that in most countries in the region, DRM policies and frameworks are in place but at the operational level the existing policies and planning agenda are at the most partially implemented depicting a very slow progress.

Along with the broad assessment of DRR based development agenda and the national governments with reference to the Asia-pacific region, Chapter 7 discusses planning and policy agenda in the context of Indonesia and the Philippines, based on which several issues and challenges are identified considered relevant in mainstreaming the DRR development agenda in practice. Furthermore, Chapter 7 highlights the significance of resilience building essential for a successful DRR based development approach as well as the complexities associated with operationalizing the resilience concept into practice. Chapter 7 concludes with the discussions on the role of communities in disaster management followed by the issues and challenges involved in a community based disaster management model.

Although national governments in the region have employed various measures to translate their understanding of disasters into respective policy agendas and pursue a sustainable development path aimed at risk reduction, available evidences indicate that despite making significant progress, for example, in terms of identifying satisfactory level of DRR focused development programs and policy agenda, most governments still lack severely in terms of translating effectively the DRR development agenda into practice due to various issues and challenges that require immediate attention. Along this line, going forward, Chapter 8 (Disaster Risk Reduction and Sustainable Development: Going Forward by Suman K. Sharma) briefly weighs in our outlook on the status of DRR development agenda in practice, particularly, in view of our understanding of disasters and the issues and challenges, involved in operationlizing the agenda, and provides some thoughts and reflections on how best to mobilize our efforts and address the challenges through building on available supportive environments.

REFERENCES

Aonbenfield (2016). The One Brief, *The Cost of Catastrophe Assessing the Impact of Natural Disasters*. Available at http://www.theonebrief.com/the-cost-of-catastrophe-assessing-the-impact-of-natural-disasters/.

Aonbenfield (2016b). 2015 Annual Global Climate and Catastrophe Report. Available at https://www.aon.co.za/Assets/docs/publications/IF-Annual-Climate-Catastrophe-Report.pdf.

Aonbenfield (2017). 2016 Annual Global Climate and Catastrophe Report. Available at http://thoughtleadership.aonbenfield.com/Documents/20170117-ab-if-annual-climate-catastrophe-report.pdf.

Centre for Research on the Epidemiology of Disasters (CRED) Institute of Health and Society (IRSS) Université catholique de Louvain — Brussels, Belgium (2017). Annual Disaster Statistical Review, The Numbers and Trends. Available at http://emdat.be/sites/default/files/adsr_2016.pdf.

Okuyama (2014). Disaster and economic structural change: Case study on the 1995 Kobe earthquake. *Economic Systems Research*, 26(1), 98–117.

Okuyama, Y (2015b). The Rise and Fall of the Kobe Economy from the 1995 Earthquake. *Journal of Disaster Research*, 10(4), 635–640.

Robert, F (2016). The Paris Agreement and the new logic of international climate politics London School of Economics and Political Science. *International Affairs*, 92(5), 1107–1125.

United Nations Framework Convention on Climate Change (UNFCCC) (2015). Adoption of the Paris Agreement, 12 December 2015. Available at https://unfccc.int/resource/docs/2015/cop21/eng/logrol.pdf.

UNISDR (2015). Sendai Framework for Disaster Risk Reduction 2015–2030. The United Nations Office for Disaster Risk Reduction (UNISDR), 2015, Geneva, Switzerland. Available at http://www.preventionweb.net/files/43291_sendai frameworkfordrren.pdf.

UN-ESCAP (2017). Leave No One Behind: Disaster Resilience for Sustainable Development — Asia-Pacific Disaster Report 2017. The United Nations Economic and Social Commission for Asia and Pacific, 2017. Available at https://reliefweb.int/sites/reliefweb.int/files/resources/AsiaPacific%20Disaster%20Report%202017%20%28Full%29.pdf.

CHAPTER 2

THE EMPIRICAL LITERATURE ON POVERTY AND NATURAL DISASTERS*

Azreen Karim
*Bangladesh Institute of Development Studies,
Dhaka, Bangladesh*

Ilan Noy
Victoria University of Wellington, New Zealand

1. ECONOMIC RESEARCH ON DISASTER IMPACT

The last few years have seen an explosion of economic research on the consequences of natural disasters. This is likely attributable to a growing awareness of the potentially catastrophic nature of these events, as evident, for example, in the earthquake and tsunami in South-East Asia in 2004, the 2010 Port-au-Prince earthquake, and the 2011 triple earthquake/tsunami/nuclear disaster in Japan. The increase in the volume of research is also a result of the increasing recognition that natural disasters are social and economic events, despite the fact that they are triggered by a natural hazard: their impact is shaped as much by the structure and characteristics of the countries they hit as by their physical attributes.

In addition to this growing interest in the social and economic aspects of natural hazards, increased awareness of climatic change

*This chapter is an extended and updated version of a survey published in the Singapore Economic Review, Vol. 61, Issue No. 1, March 2016. World Scientific: Singapore.

is playing an important role. Much of the discourse in the past few years has focused on potential changes in the pattern and intensity of future events due to human-induced climate change. A summary of these intersecting literatures was recently published by the Intergovernmental Panel on Climate Change (IPCC, 2012).

Recent research projects on the impact of natural disasters have evaluated the impact on growth in the short and medium-to-long terms, the impact on government budget and debt (again for various time horizons), the impact on international trade and financial flows, the impact on populations (in terms of migration and fertility choices), the impact on human capital, the importance of political economy in shaping the aftermath of the disasters, and other related topics. Intriguingly, there is little research on the impact of natural disasters on the poor and on income distribution.

These intersecting themes of disasters, climate change, and poverty are only becoming more prominent as three new comprehensive international treaties under the aegis of the United Nations will be implemented in the near future: on disaster risk reduction (the Sendai Framework for Disaster Risk Reduction; signed in March 2015), on the Sustainable Development Goals (a successor to the Millennium Development Goals; August 2015), and on Climate Change Prevention, Mitigation and Adaptation (the Paris Agreement; December 2015).

Here, we aim to contribute to these discussions by surveying the existing literature on the impact of natural disasters on poverty and the poor, discussing some of the limitations associated with this literature, and outlining a future agenda of investigation that can contribute to better-informed policymaking. A companion paper, Karim and Noy (2016), generalizes some insights from a subset of the empirical research papers described here using a meta-regression technique.

2. A TYPOLOGY OF IMPACTS

Before we discuss this literature, we need to clarify what we mean by "disaster impacts," and what the methodological decisions inherent in this choice are. ECLAC (2003) distinguishes between the direct impact of sudden-onset disasters (the immediate mortality, morbidity, and physical damage) and the indirect impact on the economy, in the aftermath of the actual damage caused (including secondary mortality and morbidity, and an impact on economic activity). The World Bank, in their survey *Natural Hazards, Unnatural Disasters*, (2010) employs a different terminology that makes essentially the same distinction, between first-order and higher-order effects.

The terminology of n-order effects might be preferable in theory, since it enables one to distinguish between second-order effects (e.g., the immediate decline in production as a result of the destruction of productive capital), and third-order (or even higher-order) effects (e.g., the decline in production that results from the decline in imported inputs that resulted from exchange rate and terms-of-trade changes following a disaster).

However, these distinctions between second-order and higher-order effects are difficult to operationalize into a precise typology. We therefore refrain from using this terminology and persist in using the more coarse distinction between direct and indirect effects (Cavallo and Noy, 2011). Here, we are interested in understanding both the immediate (direct or first-order) effect of disasters on poverty and income distribution, and also the consequent indirect (higher-order) effects that have an impact on the lives of the poor and on the distribution of income and resources within a society.

Another potentially important distinction lies in the difference between natural disasters that occur regularly, and those disasters whose nature or magnitude is unusual (and therefore probably unexpected). The distribution of disaster damages is highly skewed, with the presence of very extreme "fat tail" disasters, whose costs (in terms of mortality, morbidity, and/or physical destruction) are significantly higher than the costs of an average disaster. The Haiti earthquake of January 2010, for example, led to a mortality that was at least 10 standard deviations higher than the mortality resulting from earthquakes of similar or even higher strength (Noy, 2013). The 2004 earthquake/tsunami in the Indian Ocean and the cyclone *Nargis* in Myanmar in 2008 are also examples of these fat-tail events.

Fat-tail events are typically associated with extremely small probabilities in common risk assessments, but they are nevertheless quite common occurrences on a global scale. Importantly, since the probability that these catastrophic events will occur is thought to be very small, policymakers tend to ignore them, and as a result societies are generally underprepared for them.

Our aim in this survey paper is to discuss the impact of natural disasters — both direct and indirect — on poverty and income distribution. In this description, we will distinguish between the impact of sudden-onset catastrophic events and more regular natural hazards that occur in many countries (e.g., typhoons in the Philippines or the annual monsoon floods in Bangladesh).

3. THE DIRECT IMPACTS OF DISASTERS ON THE POOR: SUDDEN-ONSET EVENTS

The direct damages from a disaster are generally unevenly distributed. Comparison between countries clearly shows that richer countries can prevent or mitigate the impact of disasters more effectively, and therefore the cost they bear (as a fraction of their economic size) is significantly smaller (Kahn, 2005). The first, and most obvious, factor driving these cross-country differences is the fact that preventive measures are normal (or luxury) investment goods, so countries with higher permanent incomes or wealth will be able to devote more resources to prevention or mitigation.

However, Escaleras *et al.* (2007) argue that a significant amount of the cross-country differences in initial impacts of similar events is attributable to corruption, and since it is well documented that corruption is inversely related to average per capita income, this may explain why differences in impacts are income-dependent. Kellenberg and Mobarak (2008) find evidence for a non-linear cross-country relationship between average incomes and direct impacts, where (for some types of disasters) the costs initially increase with incomes, and above a certain threshold (which they typically identify as the per capita income level of a lower middle-income country) they begin to decrease.

Most of the papers that identify this cross-country pattern of correlation between income levels and direct disaster impact conclude that this evidence can be interpreted to suggest a "disaster-growth curse" i.e., a country whose incomes will grow over time, will, according to Kellenberg and Mobarak (2008), initially experience higher disaster costs (measured by mortality) and then eventually, as average incomes increase further, lower disaster costs. However, the evidence supporting this interpretation is rather less clear. Hallegatte (2012), for example, points out that when these figures are aggregated worldwide, global GDP has been growing at about 4% a year in the past several decades, while disaster losses (as measured by EMDAT) have been growing, on average, at about 6% while mortality has been decreasing. This implies that as the world continues to grow, the financial cost of disasters is going to increase (relative to the world economy).

Ultimately, however, identifying the direct impact of disasters on the poor (in both absolute magnitude, and relative to the rich) cannot be done by examining the cross-country distribution of costs and economic activity, since this evidence may be more related to country-wide differences in institutional capacity and policy that are correlated with incomes, rather than dependent on incomes directly. In any case, most of our conceptions and measurements of poverty are based on national identification.

The evidence on the distribution of the direct impact of a disaster within a country on households in various income levels is less well understood; the evidence that does exist generally suggests that poorer households are more vulnerable, and will bear the direct damages disproportionately, both at higher levels and as higher shares of their households' income.

A salient feature of disaster risk exposure is the choice of millions of people to live in disaster-prone areas, and in many cases these groups of people are predominantly poor (e.g., Boustan *et al.*, 2012). Milan and Ruano (2014), in their description of the mostly indigenous highlands of Guatemala, find evidence of marginalized people forced by circumstance to live in climate-vulnerable places. In surveying the local population, they find that plausible ways of adapting to this vulnerability are limited, including only *in situ* diversification of crops, and migration opportunities away from their ancestral lands. Kim (2012) examines geographical distribution to test for the poor's exposure to natural disasters and argues that, on average, the poor are at least two times more exposed than the non-poor globally.

A more detailed effort by Baez and Mason (2008) to identify the regional hot spots of increased weather variability reveals that central and southern Peru and western Bolivia prove to be the most vulnerable to heavy rains and flood among Latin America and Caribbean (LAC) regions; these are regions that are associated with high poverty rates and high population density. Supporting evidence on other Latin American countries, as well, was documented by De la Fuente (2010). Tesliuc and Lindert (2002) present evidence from Guatemala, where the poor seem to be more exposed to natural shocks than the non-poor (though the reverse is true in the case of man-made shocks[1]). Tesliuc and Lindert (2002) additionally report that in Guatemala, 35.4 percent of the poorest quintile is affected by natural shocks, compared to 21.2 percent of the richest quintile.

A study conducted by UNISDR (2012) in Syria, Jordan and Yemen shows that poverty is most severe in rural, non-diversified economies, where agriculture is severely limited by low rainfall, degraded lands, erosion, and desertification. The study concludes that low productivity and shortage of water leads to the stagnation of rural incomes, increasing poverty in Syria and Yemen. In Jordan, these dynamics are more severe in urban areas. Rains, flash floods and snowstorms affect the densely populated areas possessing the largest share of the country's poor, particularly women. In short, while poverty is clearly associated with increased exposure to hazards, the exact causality is often country-specific, and probably quite complex.

---

[1]As coping with natural disasters is related to prior economic conditions, the average impacts of a fairly regular natural shock (e.g. periodic drought) is found to have a lesser impact compared to a sudden economic shock (e.g. financial crisis).

Neumayer and Plumper (2007) investigate gender differences in disaster-related mortality, and conclude that, generally, women are both more likely to die than men, and more likely to die at a relatively young age, especially when they come from disadvantaged socioeconomic backgrounds.[2] By one estimate, women represented 70 percent of casualties after the 2004 Indian Ocean earthquake and tsunami in Aceh, Indonesia (World Bank, 2011).

There have only been a few completed attempts to analyze the direct impacts of specific natural disasters by examining various indices of poverty, income inequality and human development; these attempts include Datt and Hoogeveen, 2003; Reardon and Taylor, 1996; Lal, Singh and Holland, 2009 and Rodriguez-Oreggia *et al.*, 2013. A full picture of these impacts is not yet within reach, and whether these impacts and their variance across events are due to direct or indirect channels is not easy to determine. Gignoux and Menendez (2016) examine the impacts of multiple earthquakes in rural Indonesia, and find short-term economic losses for affected households; however, intriguingly, these losses seem to be recovered in the medium-term, with potential income and welfare gains in the longer term. It is possible that the findings of larger and more durable losses are associated with more catastrophic events, while the events that Gignous and Menendez (2016) are smaller and more local.

4. DROUGHTS AND RAINFALL FLUCTUATIONS

Droughts and extreme fluctuations in rainfall are also frequently disastrous, with very noticeable adverse consequences for human populations. In these sorts of cases, unlike the sudden-onset cases, the distinction between direct and indirect effects is less clear-cut. In this section, we therefore focus on the overall effects of these events rather than separating their immediate (direct) impacts and the longer-term indirect impacts.

---

[2]A higher level of women's socio-economic rights appears to offset the negative effect of natural disasters on women (Neumayer and Plumper, 2007).

Despite evidence of the adverse changes in overall income in the aftermath of slow-onset natural catastrophes such as droughts, some projects conclude that these disasters do not have much impact on poverty and income distribution (and should be seen as across-the-board adverse shocks). Little *et al.* (2006), for example, find that droughts did not increase overall rates of poverty in the medium-term in Ethiopia. They suggest that this is mainly due to increasing income diversification and a reduction in the emphasis on rain-fed agriculture. However, the balance of the limited available evidence seems to suggest, if anything, that droughts and extreme rainfall volatility do increase poverty, even if poverty is also influenced by numerous other factors (see also Karim and Noy, 2016).

Several projects have analyzed the impacts of rainfall shocks and local rainfall variability on various household socio-economic indicators, including consumption growth, human capital accumulation, life expectancy, and adult and children's anthropometrics (as a proxy for health/wellbeing outcomes). These projects include Jensen, 2000; Shah and Steinberg, 2012; Asiimwe and Mpuga, 2007; Hoddinott *et al.*, 2013; Dercon, 2004; Hoddinott, 2006; Maccini and Yang, 2009; Tiwari *et al.*, 2013; Neumayer and Plumper, 2007; Thai and Falaris, 2014, and Bandyopadhyay and Skoufias, 2015.

For example, a project on the Philippines by Huigen and Jens (2006) reveals that the relative economic losses per crop on yellow corn, banana, and rice due to drought were 64%, 24%, and 27%, respectively. A recent case study on Bihar, India by Kishore, Joshi and Pandey (2015) reveals that cropped paddy area dropped by 6% and yield dropped by 22% in drought years. Interestingly, government counter measures significantly increased costs of crop farming and livestock breeding during continuous drought as evident in a case study on Inner Mongolia (Wang and Zhang, 2010). This is crucial in the context of poverty alleviation and sustainable development.

An examination of children's attendance in schools in Côte d'Ivoire revealed that enrolment rates declined by 20 percentage points (more than one-third of the original rate) in regions affected by adverse weather conditions (Jensen, 2000). The 2011 Thailand flood also induced a decrease in education spending, along with a decline in overall household income (Noy and Patel, 2014). School entry delays and slower progress are also associated with adverse rainfall shocks during pregnancy in the Vietnamese context (Thai and Falaris, 2014).

More worryingly, Caruso and Miller (2015) find that the decline in educational attainment that is associated with catastrophic disasters is observable in the second generation of disaster survivors. Caruso and Miller follow up on mothers who were themselves very young (or even in utero) during a very large earthquake in 1970 in Peru. They find that the children of these affected mothers had lower educational achievement than peers whose mothers were not similarly affected by the 1970 earthquake, even when the general parental education level is controlled for.

Maccini and Yang (2009) report that a 20% increase in rainfall in Indonesia during early childhood led to 0.57cm greater height in adulthood when compared to cohorts who did not experience this rainfall-related bonanza. The high-rainfall cohorts also completed 0.22 additional grades of schooling. Another similar research project, in Nepal, found a 0.15 standard deviation increase in weight-for-age for children aged 0–36 months due to 10% higher rainfall (Tiwari *et al.*, 2013). This has also been evident in Zimbabwe, where Hoddinott *et al.* (2006, 2013) showed lower annual growth in height of 1.5–2 cm among children aged 12–24 months after drought, with the most severe impacts occurring in poor households. However, this finding did not seem to be uniform across regions within countries. In the Mexican case, Skoufias and Vinha (2012) pointed out that positive temperature shocks negatively impacted certain sub populations — namely boys, children between 12 and 23 months at the time of measurement, and children of less educated mothers (in some regions).

Moreover, in the long run, children from wealthier households recovered this lost physical growth while children from poorer homes did not (Hoddinott, 2006). The same study also found a decrease in women's body-mass index by about 3% in the aftermath of a 1994–95 drought. Similarly, in Ethiopia, Yamano *et al.* (2005) found that children 6–24 months old experienced about 0.9 cm less growth if they lived in communities with substantial crop damage after severe droughts. Though they also found that food aid acted as an effective insurance mechanism in reducing child malnutrition. In estimating the long-term impacts of 1984 Ethiopian famine, Porter (2008) reveals that children who were under the age of 36 months during the famine are, years later, still shorter by almost 3 cm, on average, than those who did not experience the famine. An interesting article on the impacts of early childhood nutritional intervention in Guatemala by Hoddinott *et al.* (2008) demonstrates that improving nutritional status before age 3 could substantially increase wage rates for men (though surprisingly not for women). However, positive rainfall shocks can also contribute to adverse changes in early childhood nutrition, with increasing risk of termination of breastfeeding reported in India (Mendiratta, 2012).

Evidence from India suggests that parents and children work less and have lower wages during drought years, and that the reverse happens when households experience positive rainfall shocks (Shah and Steinberg, 2016). This decline in work and wages is most likely associated with a decrease in demand for this labour. In contrast, disasters can lead to an increase in the supply of child labour, as evidenced in Bangladesh, where increases in the magnitudes of adverse shocks in the absence of credit is associated with more child labour (Alvi and Dendir, 2011). The same study further identifies deleterious effects on health, schooling, and, more interestingly, on later-life wages, all due to early life exposure to droughts. A similar argument has also been posed by Banerjee (2007) in an earlier study on agricultural wages in Bangladesh. The author argues that floods have positive impacts on wages in the long-run in flood months, with declines in wages in inundated areas. The study further identifies productivity and labour demand, along with land distribution and bargaining power of workers, as impact factors.

If wages are adversely impacted, it follows that household income will most likely decline as well. The negative effects of a natural disaster on per capita income (per capita expenditure) are estimated to be 6.9% (7.1%), at least in the case of Vietnam (Bui *et al.*, 2014).

Two newer studies on rural Vietnam looked at the impacts of floods, storms and droughts on household resilience and health expenditures (Arouri, Nguyen and Youssef, 2015 and Lohmann and Lechtenfeld, 2015). These studies identified similar negative impacts on household income and expenditures. The more recent investigation by Karim (2018) further justified these negative impacts particularly on agricultural income and expenditure identifying different treatment groups in the advent of recurrent flooding in the Bangladeshi context.

In a study on different types of workers' income, Mueller and Quisumbing (2011) point out that the real wages of casual and salaried agricultural workers declined only in the short-term, with significant but temporary reductions between 34.3% and 45.6% in salaried income. Dercon (2004) finds that a 10% lower rainfall has an impact of one percentage point on consumption growth rates up to 4 or 5 years later. After controlling for heterogeneity, the paper identifies a substantial negative impact of about 16% on growth when comparing groups that suffered significantly with groups that were moderately affected. Also in Ethiopia, Foltz *et al.* (2013) concludes that both food and non-food consumption is directly related to rainfall. Similar evidence has also been identified by Skoufias and Vinha (2013) in the Mexican case, where temperature shocks, along with rainfall, affect both food and non-food consumption. This effect, however, nuanced, as Hou (2010) finds that after a drought-related negative income shock occurs, households tend to buy cheaper calories, resulting in a net increase in total calories consumed.

Asiimwe and Mpuga (2007) point out that the timing of the rainfall shock appears to matter. In their examination of Uganda, positive rainfall shocks experienced during planting or harvest times actually result in lower household consumption expenditure. Analyzing data on Indonesian rice farmers, Skoufias *et al.* (2012) argue that although a delayed monsoon does not have a significant impact on average, farmers located in low rainfall exposure areas following the monsoon are negatively affected. Agricultural year and regional climate are also found to be influential in affecting households' ability to protect consumption, as shown by Skoufias and Vinha (2013) in the Mexican case. A study on Indian agricultural labour markets by Mahajan (2012) reported that low rainfall years affect the male-female wage gap adversely in rain-fed, rice-growing regions. Rainfall, of course, matters much more in rural/agricultural communities than in the urban ones (at least directly).

Variations in rainfall influence the choices made by households in rural Bangladesh as they make crucial occupational decisions. In flood-prone areas, less productive employment diversification choices, at the cost of skill-swap and reduced consumption, has been identified by Bandyopadhyay and Skoufias (2015). Employment diversification has also been identified, in the same paper, as an *ex-ante* adaptation strategy in the presence of stable local rainfall variability. The authors further highlight that with comparison to credit and safety nets, access to markets provides better coping opportunities in protection against costly occupational diversification within households. In a similar case study in rural Nepal, Menon (2009) found that for a 1 per cent increase in the coefficient of variation of rain, there is a 0.61 per cent decrease in the probability of an individual choosing the same occupation as the household head, particularly in agriculture. In this context, the negative effect on occupational choice is reduced in households that have access to credit and relatively high levels of human capital.

Even more nuanced observations about the way different conditions lead to different outcomes in the face of similar shocks have been proposed by Reardon and Taylor (1996). They compare the impact of similarly adverse drought shocks over two regions in Burkina Faso (the semi-arid Sahel, and the wetter Guinean region); they find the impacts of drought appear to be very different, in some cases leading to increases in poverty, and in others the opposite.

5. THE INDIRECT IMPACTS OF SUDDEN-ONSET EVENTS

The direct impacts are only a part of the economic significance of natural disasters. In general, we do not understand the indirect impacts as well as we do the direct ones, though they are potentially more severe. These impacts may result from direct damage to the inputs used in production, to infrastructure, or from the fact that reconstruction and rehabilitation pull resources away from other sectors. Further on, the indirect impacts can manifest themselves in a new equilibrium steady-state in which the economy/society are in a different position to what they were pre-disaster. Anttila-Hughes and Hsiang (2013), for example, find that for Philippine households, the indirect impacts wreaked by typhoons are almost an order of magnitude larger than the direct damages.

It is clear that the poor are more exposed, more vulnerable and less resilient to the direct impact of natural hazards. Baez and Mason (2008) find low levels of income to be the prime limiting factor towards the damage mitigation response of households. In a range of studies, the impact of disasters on income and consumption levels of the poorest households is found to be disproportionately strong (Rentschler, 2013).

In contrast to these adverse consequences, reconstruction spending can provide a boost to the domestic economy and specifically employees and employers in that sector. Both government funding and privately funded reconstruction from insurance payments, accumulated saving, or other sources, is bound to provide some temporary stimulus to the local economy (Cavallo and Noy, 2011). In the longer-run, there is a potential to "build-back-better;" reconstruction can, at least in theory, lead to newer, more advanced and more innovative infrastructure including better housing for the poor.

Post-disaster realignment of interest groups (weakening some and strengthening others) may even facilitate a new political equilibrium that enables better policies (whatever "better" means in practice).[3] Equally plausible is the possibility that the new political equilibrium

---

[3] One can already observe this possibility in the aftermath of what is sometime considered the first international modern natural disaster, the Lisbon earthquake of 1755. Sebastião José de Carvalho e Melo, the prime minister of Portugal, appointed to run the relief operations after the earthquake, wrote: "Politics is not always the cause of revolutions of State. Dreadful phenomena frequently change the face of Empires...We could say that it is necessary that across the land provinces are wasted and cities ruined in order to dispel the blindness of certain nations." (quoted in Shrady, 2008).

will actually be less beneficial to the poor, if the external shock removed what John Kenneth Galbraith called the "countervailing forces" that prevented elites from capturing specific assets.[4]

Most of the recent research suggests that aggregate adverse short-run effects at the national level can be observed in middle- and low-income countries experiencing catastrophic disasters. These countries have difficulty financing reconstruction, as they generally face difficulties conducting counter-cyclical fiscal policy, and their insurance and re-insurance markets are significantly shallower (see Noy, 2009; von Peter *et al.*, 2012 and Strobl, 2012).[5] The same financing constraints that seem to prevent middle- and low-income countries from adequately paying for and implementing successful reconstruction are also the ones that typically inhibit lower-income households.

Analyzing the impacts of several types of natural disasters at the municipal level in Mexico, Rodriguez-Oreggia *et al.* (2013) argue that natural disasters reduce human development and increase measures of poverty (food, capacity and asset). They further conclude that floods and droughts are associated with more significant adverse effects than frost, extreme rainfalls and other types of natural hazards. Similarly, Lal *et al.* (2009) identify evidence from Fiji indicating a negative relationship between disasters and broad human development, and leading, particularly, to higher poverty levels.

Two UNDP projects explore the relationship between natural hazards and poverty in Latin American countries (Baez and Santos, 2008 and Glave *et al.*, 2008). Baez and Santos (2008), on El Salvador, report that the combined effects of two earthquakes in 2001 led to reduction of household income by one-third of the pre shock average. Evidence from Peru, in Glave *et al.* (2008), suggests that the effect of disasters on poverty rates ranges between a 0.16 and 0.23 percentage point increase in poverty. From a distributional point of view, the

---

[4]Some realizations of this possibility are described in Naomi Klein's book-length investigation in *The Shock Doctrine*.
[5]Most of the research on high-income countries fails to find much aggregate impact of even large disasters (e.g., Doyle and Noy, 2015).

authors concluded that an increase in average shocks reduces the median monthly per capita consumption in the bottom 25th and 50th of the distribution by 3.85% and 2.68%, respectively.[6]

Baez and Santos (2007) investigate the impact of hurricane Mitch in Nicaragua, and find a range of distinct adverse medium-term effects; in particular, they focus on topics that are more relevant for the poor, and identify increased probability of undernourishment and a significant increase in labour force participation among children (though this increase did not correspond with a decline in school enrolments). As in Baez and Santos (2007), most research has not attempted to isolate the impact of these sudden shocks on the poor versus other income groups. However, most of the mechanisms and impact this research has identified are likely to be especially relevant to low-income households. Evidence from Vietnam, for example, reveals that riverine floods and hurricanes caused welfare losses of up to 23% and 52%, respectively, inside cities with a population over 500,000 (Thomas *et al.*, 2010); flood-prone urban areas are typically associated with lower-income households.

The importance of credit in facilitating recovery is well documented. Sawada and Shimizutani (2008) report that in the aftermath of the 1995 Kobe earthquake in Japan, households that were credit constrained did not manage to regain their consumption levels, while households that had better access to credit were more successful in their recovery. Credit constraints may also lead households to suboptimally sell productive assets in order to smooth consumption after a major but temporary income shock (Mueller and Osgood, 2009a). Anttila-Hughes and Hsiang (2013) also find similar dynamics for Philippine households. In their case, while both low- and high-income households experience similar level of damages in the initial impact of an exceptionally strong typhoon, it is only the lower-income

---

[6]Comparing impacts of El-Niño shocks to the financial crisis in 1998, Datt and Hoogeveen (2003) show that the largest share of the overall impact on poverty is attributable to the El-Niño shock, ranging between 47% and 57% of the total impact on measures of incidence, depth and severity of poverty relative to the 1998 shock that only accounts for 10–17% of the total poverty impact.

households whose consumption does not recover in the years that follow.

Impacts on the poor in the aftermath of a natural disaster are also being observed through migration and remittances pattern (see Gray and Mueller, 2012b; Boustan *et al.*, 2012; Attzs, 2008; Clarke and Wallsten, 2003; Dillon *et al.*, 2011; Halliday, 2012 and Ebeke and Combes, 2013). A household panel dataset for Jamaica after hurricane Gilbert reveals that remittances increased by only about 25 cents for every dollar of damage (Clarke and Wallsten, 2003). However, this effect disappears for a remittance ratio above 8% of GDP, with worsening effect when it exceeds 17% of GDP (Ebeke and Combes, 2013). Attzs (2008) observes an increase in migration after a hurricane, and an increased inflow of remittances (which constitute 87% of income for the poorest deciles in Jamaica). In addition, hydro-meteorological emergencies significantly increase population in metropolitan areas, with non-metropolitan areas experiencing the opposite in severe cases (Robalino *et al.*, 2015). During the 1984 drought, Ethiopia also experienced an increase in male labour migration.[7] Intriguingly, in El Salvador, Halliday (2012) identifies that the 2001 catastrophic earthquake resulted in a large negative effect on female migration, with absolutely no effect on male migration.[8] In Ethiopia, marriage related migration amongst women decreases with drought, as evident in a case study (Gray and Mueller, 2012a). As we have seen with direct impacts, these studies further emphasize that women and the poor are more exposed and are affected by the aftermath of a disaster more significantly.[9]

Using unique long time-series data on internal migration in Nigeria, Dillon *et al.* (2011) distinguish between genders when examining the impact of weather variation on migration. They find that male migration increases in response to *ex post* variation in particular, but with some evidence also suggesting that households

---

[7]See Gray and Mueller (2012a).

[8]In El Salvador, over 90% of aftermath may explain this pattern (Halliday, 2012).

[9]Boustan *et al.* (2012) adds another layer of complexity by identifying ways in which disaster mitigation efforts may interact with individual migration decisions.

are responding to *ex ante* risk. Women, they argue, are more exposed to *ex post* covariate risks. They highlight differences in expected male and female labour market returns from migration as the rationale for households' preference for male migration. On the issue of migratory income, Mueller and Osgood (2009b) find that, in Brazil, precipitation shocks have long-term adverse impacts on rural emigrants' income once they arrive in urban areas. Their finding that urban poverty may be associated with rural climatic pressures to migrate is indicative of the fact that the absence of worthy alternatives may be a likely reason for migration, a reason that is powerful enough to outweigh the damage from migration itself.

Another group of projects have examined the evidence on the impacts of natural shocks on household assets and on consequent income distribution (see Carter *et al.*, 2007; Mogues, 2011; Anttila-Hughes and Hsiang, 2013; Morris *et al.*, 2002; Jakobsen, 2012 and Masozera *et al.*, 2007). Most of these studies point out that, conditional on the severity of the shock, most households suffer a depletion of assets (wealth) beyond the previously documented reduction in current income. Morris *et al.* (2002) reveals that, after hurricane Mitch, assets of households in the lowest wealth quintile were reduced by 18%, compared to a reduction of 3% for the upper wealth quintile. Lopez-Calva and Ortiz-Juarez (2009) examine distributional impacts in Peru, and find that a one unit increase in the occurrence of shocks leads to a reduction of 2 percent in household per capita consumption in the lowest quartile, compared to only 1.2 percent in the richest quartile.

Another important and policy-relevant question is whether disasters can push households down into poverty traps. Carter *et al.* (2007) examined two different outcomes in two different case studies. In Honduras, in the medium-term, relatively wealthy households were able to partially rebuild their lost assets, unlike the lowest wealth quintiles. However, in Ethiopia, the poorest households (in wealth) tried to hold on to their few assets, despite the fact that their consumption possibilities shrank, during drought periods and periods of severe loss in agricultural production/income. Van den Berg (2010) adds more nuance about the ability of households at various income levels to pursue possible strategies that allow them to maintain their capital. She concludes that, in the case of Hurricane Mitch, there is little evidence of changes in the transitions between various income levels, suggesting permanent poverty traps.

Several studies analyze the impacts of natural disasters on population dynamics and fertility response (e.g. Martine and Guzman, 2002; Lin, 2004 and Finlay, 2009). Martine and Guzman (2002) identify a reduction in population growth in some Honduran provinces by 40%–92%, depending on the province, due to the effects of Hurricane Mitch. Lin (2004) also reaches similar conclusions. However, Finlay (2009) argues that a large scale natural disaster may have a positive effect on fertility under the assumption that a child could be used as an insurance mechanism to compensate for income and asset loss. We can speculate that these dynamic incentives may affect poorer households differently than richer ones; for example that increasing fertility will only be observed for poorer households that do not have access to other ways of financing retirement. The evidence on these possible differences, however, does not yet exist.

6. COPING RESPONSES OF THE POOR

A significant body of research has attempted to shed some light on possible coping mechanisms of dealing with natural disasters, typically focusing on the rural poor in low-income countries. Baez and Mason (2008) argue, for example, that rural households possess limited capacity to fully and efficiently adjust to weather related shocks. This limited capacity is associated with a lack of access to formal financing and other tools that can facilitate optimal coping strategies (such as re-training). A recent study on the Pacific island of Samoa revealed that the poor's lack of access to remittances resulted in a reduced ability to cope with and recover from cyclone Evan (Le de *et al.*, 2015). Intriguingly, one Bangladeshi case study on Cyclone *"Aila"* identifies a greater ability amongst the poor to withstand the shock, compared to their non-poor neighbours, despite negative impacts on the socio-economic and infrastructural determinants (Akter and Mallick, 2013). However, in line with the argument that the poor have less access to coping mechanisms, Bandyopadhyay and Skoufias (2015) provide evidence on effects of occupational choice as an *ex ante* adaptation strategy.

Sawada (2007) provides an earlier survey of some of the potential coping mechanisms in the local, regional, and global contexts, while Ghorpade (2012) provides a more recent version. Helgeson *et al.* (2013) provides a recent example of a careful study identifying the possible coping mechanisms and evaluating their prevalence with a large survey of Ugandan farmers. Patnaik and Narayanan (2010) examine similar questions with data from two districts in rural India. Yet, an evaluation of the differences among income groups in their coping mechanisms is less common.

Khandker (2007) finds that sixty percent of sampled households adopted some form of what appears to be a sub-optimal coping mechanism during a sudden shock. These involved borrowing (often at high interest), skipping meals, selling productive assets or migrating away from affected areas. However, a recent survey study conducted in Southeastern Mexico by Mardero *et al.* (2015) reveals several more productive mechanisms of adaptation, including adjustment of the agricultural calendar, water storage, and livelihood diversification both within and outside of agriculture.

The use of livestock as a buffer stock in terms of reducing the probability of being "always poor" in the aftermath of a natural disaster has also been examined. Fafchamps *et al.* (1998) argue that livestock sales offset at most 30%, and probably closer to 15%, of income loss resulting from village level rainfall shocks in West Africa. In Uganda and India, in contrast, livestock are held as a form of liquid savings, and selling livestock has been used as the most frequent form of coping strategy after a weather disaster (Helgeson *et al.*, 2013, and Patnaik and Narayanan, 2010). Another recent Ugandan household survey finds that larger households are more likely to engage in asset reduction as a coping mechanism than smaller ones. (Lawson and Kasirye, 2015). Interestingly, this particular coping mechanism is more likely to be adopted by households in the case of floods, with a reduction in food consumption being the more popular choice when faced with a drought. Landownership is also found to play a role in

reducing vulnerability to floods (Kurosaki, 2015). Thiede (2014) finds
that reductions in rainfall in Ethiopia sometimes have an equalizing
impact on inequalities in livestock ownership within a community,
though there are regional differences in this finding.

Formal insurance policies are typically unaffordable or unsuited
to conditions in rural, low-income regions/countries. Thus other
insurance products have been developed to deal with weather risks,
with a recent enthusiasm for index insurance. Equally important are
other recent methods and ideas for disaster coping strategies, such
as disaster micro-insurance or contingent repayment in microfinance
loans (see Jensen, 2000; Barnett and Mahul, 2007; Mechler *et al.*,
2006; Shoji, 2010 and Janzen and Carter, 2013). Yet the introduction
of insurance tools for the poor is still in its infancy, and the poor
often rely on accumulated savings, the mortgaging of available
assets, donations, remittances, emergency loans from microcredit
institutions or traditional moneylenders, and if these fail, direct
support from family, neighbours, and friends (Mechler *et al.*, 2006).

Estimating an acceptable and affordable premium for disaster
insurance specifically for the poor seems to be extremely difficult,
not only due to multiple risks on life, health and property, but
also due to the "fat-tailed" nature of catastrophic natural hazards.
However, index- or micro-insurance products could potentially be
effective mechanisms in transferring covariate weather risks for the
rural poor, as has been (provisionally) observed in Mexico and India
(Barnett and Mahul, 2007).

Shoji (2010) employ a unique dataset and examine the impact of
rescheduling of savings and repayment installments in microfinance
(i.e., contingent repayment) on affected members during a natural
disaster. The paper points out that rescheduling decreased the
probability of avoiding meals by 5.1% during negative shocks, with
larger impact on the poor and a particularly large impact on
females. Another study on drought impacts in Kenya by Janzen and
Carter (2013) reveals that insured households are 8–41 percentage
points less likely to reduce meals and 18–50 percentage points less
likely to sell productive assets during the recovery process. Yet,
an identification of whether targeted programs in microfinance and

micro insurance are able to compensate the losses adequately and prevent households from resorting to sub-optimal strategies remains to be found.

The evidence suggests that insurance substantially reduces the probability of selling livestock during a drought, thus improving the chances of advancement in the recovery process (Janzen and Carter, 2013). Drawing a gender distinction on this issue, Hoddinott and Kinsey (2000) suggest that women in poor households are heavily affected by drought shock and *ex ante* private coping strategies. In the region they examine, the accumulation of livestock proves to be more effective in comparison to *ex post* public responses in protecting women against adverse consequences.

Silbert and Pilar Useche (2012) find that although male-headed households are less vulnerable, and therefore reduce their total consumption to a lesser extent, education can still lead female-headed households to better coping decisions. As already noted, *ex ante* income diversification has also been demonstrated to be an important coping mechanism for consumption smoothing (Wong and Brown, 2011). Zheng and Byg (2014) also emphasize the practice of seeking alternative income sources via sideline activities in the case of hailstorms and drought in the Chinese context.

Several projects have looked at vulnerability and coping strategies in selected South and South east Asian countries (see Karim 2018; Hallegatte *et al.*, 2010; Zoleta-Nantes, 2002; Few, 2003; Patnaik and Narayanan, 2010; Takashi *et al.*, 2012 and Israel and Briones, 2014). A recent study by Karim (2018) investigated the impacts of climate disasters (i.e. recurrent flooding) on Bangladeshi households and reveals a paradoxical outcome of a declining total income associated with higher daily wages. This finding indicates coping and/or adaptation strategy i.e. diversifying livelihoods and income source among households particularly located in the North-eastern parts of the country. Zoleta-Nantes (2002) show the differential impacts of flood hazards on three vulnerable groups-street children, the urban poor and residents of wealthy neighborhoods — in metro Manila, the Philippines. She concludes that spatial isolation and lack of participation in decision-making intensified present and future vulnerability at the household and community levels.[10] A study on the Indian State of Mumbai by Hallegatte *et al.* (2010) assesses the risk and benefits of adaptation due to flood exposure, and provides evidence of potential sensitivity and vulnerability to heavy precipitation, signifying that improving drainage as part of disaster risk management and extended insurance could reduce the indirect effects of flooding on marginalized groups. Another study by Takashi *et al.* (2012) on household level recovery after floods in North Pakistan concludes that although households with fewer assets did struggle in the recovery process, the speed of recovery was slower for the richer households later on, leaving an income distribution that was characterized by a mass of households around the income poverty line.

Most researchers have focused on first moment impacts of disasters and on the impact of disasters on average levels (of income, of wealth, of health, etc.), but it is also important to point out that disasters can be an important source of damaging fluctuations (second moments). These generated fluctuations might trigger behavioural and policy responses that can in turn lead to chronic or intergenerational poverty (Sinha *et al.*, 2002).

7. LONG-TERM SCENARIOS IN DISASTERS' AFTERMATH

The determination of the long-term effects of catastrophic disasters on various income groups is perhaps of even greater importance than determining only their direct and indirect short-term impacts. The limited empirical evidence suggests that large natural shocks can have important regional consequences that may persist for decades. The population of New Orleans, for example, is unlikely to recover from the dramatic exodus of people from the region after

---

[10]Another study in Metro Manila, on the impacts of typhoon-related floods by Israel and Briones (2014), found that the occurrence and intensity of aforementioned disasters has a significant negative effect on household income and consequently on household poverty.

Hurricane Katrina — in July 2012, seven years after the hurricane, the population of the city was still 20% lower than the week before the storm hit. Additionally, sudden onset events like the 1995 Kobe earthquake have resulted in significant adverse long-term impacts, with a 12% reduction in GDP per capita in Kobe's case, from which Hyogo prefecture has never fully recovered (DuPont IV and Noy, 2015). Emigration, as in Katrina's case, is one possible long-term consequence, and at least in Katrina's case, it seems that the poor and the disenfranchised were disproportionally more likely to emigrate in the storm's aftermath.[11] This evidence, however, is only anecdotal; we have no direct evidence that disasters' long-term impacts affect the poor any differently than other segments of society, nor do we have substantial evidence on the distributional consequences, in the long-term, of disaster events.

Analyzing the case of Indonesia, Silbert and Pilar Useche (2012) point out that larger households are 16 percent more vulnerable to future poverty in the presence of shocks, and holding all else equal, larger households are likely to be poorer. Moreover, Gaurav (2015) identifies significant heterogeneity in vulnerability to shocks among Indian households due to wealth differences.

The Bangladeshi case reveals negative long-term welfare implications in the event of floods and river erosion, with the poor are more likely to employ coping mechanisms that have negative impacts in the long term (Santos *et al.*, 2011). Similarly, evidence from Brazil suggests that exposure to drought can reduce rural wages by 9% in the longer term (defined as 5–10 years; Mueller and Osgood, 2009a). To shed light on distributional impacts, a recent study by Yamamura (2015) concludes that although natural disasters have

---

[11]Coffman and Noy (2012) describe the impact of a hurricane on a small Hawaiian island, and conclude that the long-term impact of the disaster was a 15% population decline enduring at least two decades after the event. Lynham *et al.* (2012) provide similar evidence for a tsunami in another Hawaiian island. Hornbeck (2012) examines the long-term impact, at the county level, of the American Dust-Bowl during the 1930s. Hornbeck finds that while there was some adjustment in agricultural activities, there were still substantial declines in productivity and land prices that lasted for many decades. The main adjustment mechanism he describes is emigration.

increased income inequality in the short-term, this effect decays over time, and disappears in the medium term.[12]

From the macroeconomic/aggregate literature, we know that certain economic conditions and policies may lead to increased resilience in the aftermath of a disaster, but on the other hand, disasters' negative impact may be exacerbated significantly by other conditions or policies. Relevant factors include the existence or absence of *ex-ante* disaster management plans, the flexibility to re-allocate resources efficiently for disaster relief and reconstruction, the expected access to extra-regional funds from the central government or from other sources (foreign aid, re-insurance payments, etc.), and the ability of the region's dominant economic sectors to rebound. With regards to extra-regional funds, for example, a recent study by Karim and Noy (2015) found significant evidences of government's non-responsiveness to sub-district's risk exposure as a determining factor in the DRR financing mechanism. Institutional, cultural and social factors may also play an important constructive role.[13] Whether these differences also matter in the long-run or at the household level, and whether they differentiate between the poor and others, or have any distributional impacts, are all still open questions.

One issue that may turn out to be the most important in determining post-disaster outcomes is not the degree and level of destruction, or the degree of preparedness, but the adjustment in expectations with regard to future events that catastrophes often prompt. Kobe, for example, was not perceived to be a high-risk area for earthquakes before 1995, an assessment which unsurprisingly changed in the disaster's aftermath. In contrast, the devastation wrought by a war, even a very destructive one, may be perceived as a one-off event and therefore not lead to long-term shifts in economic activity (see Davis and Weinstein, 2002). The perceived increased risk of future catastrophic events, however, may inhibit human and

---

[12]Narayanan and Sahu (2011) investigate climate related disaster in the Indian state of Orissa, and find deteriorating health conditions due to these events that reduce the ability of the poor to participate in income generating economic activities.

[13]For evidence on the importance of social capital, see Aldrich (2012).

capital saving and investment in an affected region for decades (see Aizenman and Noy, 2015).

This may be especially important as these changes in the subjective probabilities assigned to plausible hazards may well matter differently for people from different socio-economic backgrounds, given the additional exposure of the poor to risk and given the possibility of decreased investment leading into poverty traps. Once again, however, this is still an open empirical question, like so many of the other issues highlighted in this paper.

REFERENCES

Aizenman, J and I Noy (2015). Public and private saving and the long shadow of macroeconomic shocks. *Journal of Macroeconomics*, 46, 147–159.

Akter, S and B Mallick (2013). The poverty-vulnerability-resilience nexus: Evidence from Bangladesh. *Ecological Economics*, 96, 114–124.

Aldrich, D (2012). *Building Resilience: Social Capital in Post-Disaster Recovery.* University of Chicago Press.

Alvi, E and S Dendir (2011). Weathering the storms: Credit receipt and child labor in the aftermath of the great floods (1998) in Bangladesh. *World Development*, 39(8), 1398–1409.

Anttila-Hughes, Jesse Keith and Hsiang, Solomon M. (2013). *Destruction, Disinvestment, and Death: Economic and Human Losses Following Environmental Disaster.* Available at SSRN: http://ssrn.com/abstract=2220501 or http://dx.doi.org/10.2139/ssrn.2220501.

Arouri, M, C Nguyen and AB Youssef (2015). Natural Disasters, Household Welfare, and Resilience: Evidence from Rural Vietnam. *World Development*, 70, 59–77.

Asiimwe, JB and P Mpuga (2007). *Implications of rainfall shocks for household income and consumption in Uganda.* AERC Research Paper 168, African Economic Research Consortium.

Attzs, M (2008). *Natural disasters and remittances: Exploring the linkages between poverty, gender and disaster vulnerability in Caribbean.* SIDS No. 2008.61, Research paper/UNU-WIDER.

Auffret, P (2003). *High Consumption Volatility: The Impact of Natural Disasters?* World Bank Policy Research Working Paper 2962, The World Bank.

Baez, J and A Mason (2008). *Dealing with Climate Change: Household Risk Management and Adaptation in Latin America.* SSRN 1320666.

Baez, Javier E and Indhira V. Santos (2008). *On Shaky Ground: The Effects of Earthquakes on Household Income and Poverty.* Background paper of the ISDR/RBLAC-UNDP Project on Disaster Risk and Poverty in Latin America.

Baez, JE and IV Santos (2007). *Children's Vulnerability to Weather Shocks: A Natural Disaster as a Natural Experiment.* Social Science Research Network, New York.

Bandyopadhyay, S and E Skoufias (2015). Rainfall variability, occupational choice, and welfare in rural Bangladesh. *Review of Economics of the Household,* 13(3), 1–46.

Banerjee, L (2007). Effect of flood on agricultural wages in Bangladesh: An empirical analysis. *World Development,* 35(11), 1989–2009.

Barnett, BJ and O Mahul (2007). Weather index insurance for agriculture and rural areas in lower-income countries. *American Journal of Agricultural Economics,* 89(5), 1241–1247.

Boustan, LP, ME Kahn and PW Rhode (2012). Moving to higher ground: migration response to natural disasters in the early twentieth century. *American Economic Review,* 102(3), 238–244.

Bui, AT, M Dungey, CV Nguyen and TP Pham (2014). The impact of natural disasters on household income, expenditure, poverty and inequality: evidence from Vietnam. *Applied Economics,* 46(15), 1751–1766.

Carter, MR, PD Little, T Mogues and W Negatu (2007). Poverty traps and natural disasters in Ethiopia and Honduras. *World Development,* 35(5), 835–856.

Caruso G and SJ Miller (2015). Long run effects and intergenerational transmission of natural disasters: A case study on the 1970 Ancash Earthquake. *Journal of Development Economics,* 117, 134–150.

Cavallo, E and I Noy (2011). The economics of natural disasters — a survey. *International Review of Environmental and Resource Economics,* 5(1), 1–40.

Clarke, G and S Wallsten (2003). *Do remittances act like insurance? Evidence from a natural disaster in Jamaica.* Development Research Group, The World Bank.

Coffman, M and I Noy (2012). Hurricane Iniki: Measuring the Long-Term Economic Impact of a Natural Disaster Using Synthetic Control. *Environment and Development Economics,* 17, 187–205.

Cunguara, B, A Langyintuo and I Darnhofer (2011). The role of nonfarm income in coping with the effects of drought in southern Mozambique. *Agricultural Economics,* 42(6), 701–713.

Datt, G and H Hoogeveen (2003). El Niño or El Peso? Crisis, poverty and income distribution in the Philippines. *World Development,* 31(7), 1103–1124.

Davis, D and D Weinstein (2002). Bones, Bombs, and Break Points: The Geography of Economic Activity. *American Economic Review,* 92(5), 1269–1289.

De la Fuente, A (2010). Natural disaster and poverty in Latin America: Welfare impacts and social protection solutions. *Well-Being and Social Policy,* 6(1), 1–15.

Dercon, S (2004). Growth and shocks: Evidence from rural ethiopia. *Journal of Development Economics,* 74(2), 309–329.

Dillon, A, V Mueller and S Salau (2011). Migratory responses to agricultural risk in northern Nigeria. *American Journal of Agricultural Economics*, 93(4), 1048–1061.

Doyle, L and I Noy (2015). The short-run nationwide macroeconomic effects of the Canterbury earthquakes. *New Zealand Economic Papers*, 49(2), 134–156.

duPont IV, W and I Noy (2015). What happened to Kobe? A reassessment of the impact of the 1995 earthquake in Japan. *Economic Development and Cultural Change*, 63(4), 777–812.

Ebeke, C and JL Combes (2013). Do remittances dampen the effect of natural disasters on output growth volatility in developing countries?. *Applied Economics*, 45(16), 2241–2254.

ECLAC (2003). *Handbook for Estimating the Socio-economic and Environmental Effects of Disasters*. Economic Commission for Latin America and the Caribbean: United Nations.

Escaleras, M, N Anbarci and CA Register (2007). Public sector corruption and major earthquakes: A potentially deadly interaction. *Public Choice*, 132(1/2), 209–230.

Fafchamps, M, C Udry and K Czukas (1998). Drought and saving in West Africa: Are livestock a buffer stock? *Journal of Development Economics*, 55(2), 273–305.

Few, R (2003). Flooding, vulnerability and coping strategies: Local responses to a global threat. *Progress in Development Studies*, 3(1), 43–58.

Finlay, J (2009). *Fertility response to natural disasters: The case of three high mortality earthquakes*. World Bank Policy Research Working Paper Series 4883, The World Bank.

Foltz, J, J Gars, M Özdoğan, B Simane and B Zaitchik (2013). *Weather and Welfare in Ethiopia*. In 2013 Annual Meeting, August 4–6, 2013, Washington DC, No. 150298, Agricultural and Applied Economics Association.

Gaurav, S (2015). Are rainfed agricultural households insured? Evidence from five villages in Vidarbha, India. *World Development*, 66, 719–736.

Giesbert, L and K Schindler (2012). Assets, shocks, and poverty traps in rural Mozambique. *World Development*, 40(8), 1594–1609.

Gignoux, J and M Menéndez (2016). Benefit in the wake of disaster: Long-run effects of earthquakes on welfare in rural Indonesia. *Journal of Development Economics*, 118, 26–44. Available at https://doi.org/10.1016/j.jdeveco.2015.08.004.

Ghorpade, Y (2012). *Coping Strategies in Natural Disasters and under Conflict: A Review of Household Responses and Notes for Public Policy*. Households in Conflict Network, no. 136.

Glave, M, R Fort and C Rosemberg (2008). *Disaster Risk and Poverty in Latin America: The Peruvian Case Study*. Background paper of the ISDR/RBLAC-UNDP Project on Disaster Risk and Poverty in Latin America.

Gray, C and V Mueller (2012a). Drought and population mobility in rural Ethiopia. *World Development*, 40(1), 134–145.

Gray, CL and V Mueller (2012b). Natural disasters and population mobility in Bangladesh. *PNAS*, 109(16), 6000–6005.

Hallegatte, S (2012). *An Exploration of the link between development, economic growth and natural risk.* Policy Research Working Paper Series 6216, The World Bank.

Hallegatte, S, F Henriet, A Patwardhan, K Narayanan, S Ghosh, S Karmakar and N Naville (2010). *Flood Risks, Climate Change Impacts and Adaptation Benefits in Mumbai: An Initial Assessment of Socio-economic Consequences of Present and Climate Change Induced Flood Risks and of Possible Adaptation Options.* OECD Publishing no. 27.

Halliday, TJ (2012). Intra-household labor supply, migration, and subsistence constraints in a risky environment: Evidence from rural El Salvador. *European Economic Review*, 56(6), 1001–1019.

Helgeson, J, S Dietz and S Hochrainer-Stigler (2013). Vulnerability to weather disasters: The choice of coping strategies in rural Uganda. *Ecology and Society*, 18(2), 2.

Hoddinott, J, J Maluccio, JR Behrman, R Martorell, P Melgar, AR Quisumbing and KM Yount (2013). *Adult consequences of growth failure in early childhood.* American Journal of Clinincal Nutrition, 98(5), 1170–1178.

Hoddinott, J, JA Maluccio, JR Behrman, R Flores and R Martorell (2008). Effect of a nutrition intervention during early childhood on economic productivity in Guatemalan adults. *The Lancet*, 371(9610), 411–416.

Hoddinott, J (2006). Shocks and their consequences across and within households in Rural Zimbabwe. *Journal of Development Studies*, 42(2), 301–321.

Hoddinott, J and B Kinsey (2001). Child growth in the time of drought. *Oxford Bulletin of Economics and Statistics*, 63(4), 409–436.

Hoddinott, J and B Kinsey (2000). *Adult Health in the Time of Drought.* Food Consumption and Nutrition Division (FCND) Discussion Paper, no. 79.

Hou, X (2010). Can drought increase total calorie availability? The impact of drought on food consumption and the mitigating effects of a conditional cash transfer program. *Economic Development and Cultural Change*, 58(4), 713–737.

Hornbeck, R (2012). The enduring impact of the American dust bowl: Short- and long-run adjustments to environmental catastrophe. *American Economic Review*, 102(4), 1477–1507.

Huigen, MG and IC Jens (2006). Socio-economic impact of super typhoon Harurot in San Mariano, Isabela, the Philippines. *World Development*, 34(12), 2116–2136.

Intergovernmental Panel on Climate Change (2012). *Managing the Risks of Extreme Events and Disasters to Advance Climate Change Adaptation.* Available at http://www.ipcc.ch/pdf/special-reports/srex/SREX_Full_Report.pdf

Israel, DC and RM Briones (2014). *Disasters, Poverty, and Coping Strategies: The Framework and Empirical Evidence from Micro/Household Data-Philippine Case.* Philippine Institute for Development Studies. Discussion Paper Series No. 2014–06.

Jakobsen, KT (2012). In the Eye of the Storm — The Welfare Impacts of a Hurricane. *World Development,* 40(12), 2578–2589.

Janzen, SA and MR Carter (2013). *The Impact of Microinsurance on Consumption Smoothing and Asset Protection: Evidence from a Drought in Kenya.* Annual Meeting, August 4–6, 2013, Washington DC, no. 151141, Agricultural and Applied Economics Association.

Jensen, R (2000). Agricultural volatility and investments in children. *American Economic Review,* 90(2), 399–404.

Jha, R (2006). *Vulnerability and Natural Disasters in Fiji, Papua New Guinea, Vanuatu and the Kyrgyz Republic.* Available at http://dx.doi.org/10.2139/ ssrn.882203.

Kahn, ME (2005). The death toll from natural disasters: The role of income, geography, and institutions. *Review of Economics and Statistics,* 87(2), 271–284.

Karim, A (2018). The household response to persistent natural disasters: Evidence from Bangladesh. *World Development,* 103(3), 40–59. DOI: https://doi. org/10.1010/j.worlddev.2017.10.026.

Karim, A and I Noy (2015). *The (mis) allocation of public spending in a low income country: Evidence from disaster risk reduction spending in Bangladesh.* School of Economics and Finance. Working Paper no. 4194, Victoria University of Wellington, New Zealand. Available at http:// researcharchive.vuw.ac.nz/handle/10063/4194.

Karim, A and I Noy (2016). *Poverty and natural disasters: A meta-regression analysis.* Review of Economics and Institutions, 7(2). DOI: 10.5202/rei.v7i2. 222. Retrieved from http://www.rei.unipg.it/rei/article/view/222.

Kellenberg, DK and AM Mobarak (2008). Does Rising Income Increase or Decrease Damage Risk from Natural Disasters? *Journal of Urban Economics,* 63(3), 788–802.

Khandker, SR (2007). Coping with flood: role of institutions in Bangladesh. *Agricultural Economics,* 36(2), 169–180.

Kim, N (2012). How much more exposed are the poor to natural disasters? Global and regional measurement. *Disasters,* 36(2), 195–211.

Kishore, A, PK Joshi and D Pandey (2015). Drought, distress, and a conditional cash transfer programme to mitigate the impact of drought in Bihar, India. *Water International,* 40(3), 417–431.

Klein, N (2007). *The Shock Doctrine: The Rise of Disaster Capitalism.* Macmillan.

Kurosaki, T (2015). Vulnerability of household consumption to floods and droughts in developing countries: Evidence from Pakistan. *Environment and Development Economics,* 20, 209–235.

Le De, L, JC Gaillard and W Friesen (2015). Poverty and disasters: Do remittances reproduce vulnerability? *The Journal of Development Studies,* (51)5, 538–553. DOI: 10.1080/00220388.2014.989995.

Lal, PN, R Rita and N Khatri (2009). *Economic Costs of the 2009 Floods in the Fiji Sugar Belt and Policy Implications.* IUCN.

Lal, PN, R Singh and P Holland (2009). *Relationship between Natural Disasters and Poverty: A Fiji Case Study.* SOPAC Miscellaneous Report 678, Global Assessment Report on Disaster Reduction, UNISDR.

Lawson, D and I Kasirye (2013). How The Extreme Poor Cope With Crises: Understanding The Role Of Assets And Consumption. *Journal of International Development,* 25(8), 1129–1143.

Lin, CYC (2004). *The Effects of Natural Disasters and Economic Volatility on Fertility.* Available at SSRN 590421.

Little, PD, MP Stone, T Mogues, AP Castro and W Negatu (2006). 'Moving in place': Drought and poverty dynamics in South Wollo, Ethiopia. *Journal of Development Studies,* 42(2), 200–225.

Lohmann, S and T Lechtenfeld (2015). The effect of drought on health outcomes and health expenditures in rural Vietnam. *World Development,* 72, 432–448.

López-Calva, LF and E Ortiz-Juárez (2009). *Evidence and Policy Lessons on the Links between Disaster Risk and Poverty in Latin America: Methodology and Summary of Country Studies.* Research for Public Policy, MDGs and Poverty, MDG-01-2009, RBLAC-UNDP, New York.

Lynham, J, I Noy and J Page (2012). *The 1960 Tsunami in Hawaii: Long Term Consequences of a Coastal Disaster.* School of Economics and Finance working paper, No. 13, Victoria University of Wellington.

Maccini, SL and D Yang (2009). Under the Weather: Health, Schooling, and Economic Consequences of Early-Life Rainfall. *American Economic Review,* 99(3), 1006–1026.

Mahajan, K (2012). *Rainfall Shocks and Gender Wage Gap: Agricultural Labor in India.* Presented in 8th Annual Conference on Economic Growth and Development, Dec 17–19, 2012, Indian Statistical Institute, New Delhi.

Mardero, S, B Schmook, C Radel, Z Christman, D Lawrence, M Millones and L Schneider (2015). Smallholders' adaptations to droughts and climatic variability in southeastern Mexico. *Environmental Hazards,* 14(4), 271–288.

Martine, G and JM Guzman (2002). Population, poverty, and vulnerability: Mitigating the effects of natural disasters. *Environmental Change and Security Project Report,* 8, 45–64.

Masozera, M, M Bailey and C Kerchner (2007). Distribution of impacts of natural disasters across income groups: A case study of New Orleans. *Ecological Economics,* 63(2), 299–306.

Mechler, R, J Linnerooth-Bayer and D Peppiatt (2006). *Microinsurance for Natural Disaster Risks in Developing Countries.* ProVention Consortium. Available at http://www.climate-insurance.org/upload/pdf/Mechler 2006_MI_for_NatDis.pdf.

Mendiratta, V (2012). *The Impact of Climatic Shocks on Children's Health in India.* Available at http://www.isid.ac.in/~pu/conference/dec_12_conf/ Papers/VibhutiMendiratta.pdf.

Menon, N (2009) Rainfall uncertainty and occupational choice in agricultural households of rural Nepal. *Journal of Development Studies,* 45(6), 864–888.

Milan, A and S Ruano (2014). Rainfall variability, food insecurity and migration in Cabricán, Guatemala. *Climate and Development,* 6(1), 61–68.

Mogues, T (2011). Shocks and asset dynamics in Ethiopia. *Economic Development and Cultural Change*, 60(1), 91–120.

Morris, SS, O Neidecker-Gonzales, C Carletto, M Munguía, JM Medina and Q Wodon (2002). Hurricane Mitch and the livelihoods of the rural poor in Honduras. *World Development*, 30(1), 49–60.

Mueller, V and A Quisumbing (2011). How resilient are labour markets to natural disasters? The case of the 1998 Bangladesh Flood. *Journal of Development Studies*, 47(12), 1954–1971.

Mueller, VA and DE Osgood (2009a). Long-term impacts of droughts on labour markets in developing countries: Evidence from Brazil. *Journal of Development Studies*, 45(10), 1651–1662.

Mueller, VA and DE Osgood (2009b). Long-term consequences of short-term precipitation shocks: evidence from Brazilian migrant households. *Agricultural Economics*, 40(5), 573–586.

Narayanan, K and SK Sahu (2011). *Health, Income Inequality and Climate Related Disasters at Household Level: Reflections from an Orissa District*. Munich Personal RePEc Archive. Available at https://mpra.ub.uni-muenchen.de/35028/1/MPRA_paper_35028.pdf.

Neumayer, E and T Plumper (2007). The gendered nature of natural disasters: The impact of catastrophic events on the gender gap in life expectancy, 1981–2002. *Annals of the Association of American Geographers*, 97(3), 551–566.

Noy, I and P Patel (2014). *Floods and spillovers: Households after the 2011 great flood in Thailand*. School of Economics and Finance Working paper series no. 11/2014, Victoria University of Wellington, New Zealand.

Noy, I (2013). Investing in Disaster Risk Reduction: A Global Fund. In *Global Problems, Smart Solutions: Costs and Benefits*, Lomborg, B (Ed.), pp. 500–509. Cambridge University Press.

Noy, I (2009). The macroeconomic consequences of disasters. *Journal of Development Economics*, 88(2), 221–231.

Patnaik, U and K Narayanan (2010). *Vulnerability and Coping with Disasters: A Study of Household Behaviour in Flood Prone Region of India*. Munich Personal RePEc Archive.

Porter, C (2008). *The Long Run Impact of Severe Shocks in Childhood: Evidence from the Ethiopian Famine of 1984*. Department of Economics, The University of Oxford.

Rabassa, M, E Skoufias and HG Jacoby (2012). *Weather and Child Health in Rural Nigeria*. Policy Research Working Paper No. 6214, The World Bank.

Reardon, T and JE Taylor (1996). Agroclimatic shock, income inequality, and poverty: Evidence from Burkina Faso. *World Development*, 24(5), 901–914.

Rentschler, JE (2013). *Why Resilience Matters — The Poverty Impacts of Disasters*. Policy Research Working Paper No. 6699, The World Bank.

Robalino, J, J Jimenez and A Chacón (2015). The Effect of Hydro-Meteorological Emergencies on Internal Migration. *World Development*, 67, 438–448.

Rodriguez-Oreggia, E, A de la Fuente, R de la Torre, H Moreno and C Rodriguez (2013). The impact of natural disasters on human development and poverty at the municipal level in Mexico. *Journal of Development Studies*, 49(3), 442–455.

Santos, I, I Sharif, HZ Rahman and H Zaman (2011). *How do the Poor Cope with Shocks in Bangladesh? Evidence from Survey Data.* World Bank Policy Research Working Paper No. 5810.

Sawada, Y (2007). The impact of natural and manmade disasters on household welfare. *Agricultural Economics*, 37(s1), 59–73.

Sawada, Y and S Shimizutani (2008). How do people cope with natural disasters? Evidence from the great Hanshin-Awaji (Kobe) Earthquake in 1995. *Journal of Money, Credit and Banking*, 40(2–3), 463–488.

Shah, M and BM Steinberg (2016). Drought of opportunities: Contemporaneous and long-term impacts of rainfall shocks on human capital. *Journal of Political Economy*, forthcoming.

Shoji, M (2010). Does Contingent Repayment in Microfinance Help the Poor During Natural Disasters? *Journal of Development Studies*, 46(2), 191–210.

Shrady, N (2008). *The Last Day: Wrath, Ruin, and Reason in the Great Lisbon Earthquake of 1755.* Viking Press.

Silbert, M and MP Useche (2012). *Repeated Natural Disasters and Poverty in Island Nations: A Decade of Evidence from Indonesia.* University of Florida, Department of Economics, PURC Working Paper.

Sinha, S, M Lipton and S Yaqub (2002). Poverty and damaging fluctuations: How do they relate? *Journal of Asian and African Studies*, 37(2), 186–243.

Skoufias, E, RS Katayama and B Essama-Nssah (2012). Too little too late: Welfare impacts of rainfall shocks in rural Indonesia. *Bulletin of Indonesian Economic Studies*, 48(3), 351–368.

Skoufias, E and K Vinha (2012). Climate variability and child height in rural Mexico. *Economics & Human Biology*, 10(1), 54–73.

Skoufias, E and K Vinha (2013). The impacts of climate variability on household welfare in rural Mexico. *Population and Environment*, 34(3), 370–399.

Strobl, E (2012). The economic growth impact of natural disasters in developing countries: Evidence from hurricane strikes in the Central American and Caribbean regions. *Journal of Development Economics*, 97(1), 131–140.

Takashi, K, K Humayun, S Mir Kalan and T Muhammad (2012). *Household-level Recovery after Floods in a Developing Country: Further Evidence from Khyber Pakhtunkhwa, Pakistan.* Institute of Economic Research, no. 27, Hitotsubashi University.

Tesliuc, ED and K Lindert (2002). *Vulnerability: A Quantitative and Qualitative Assessment.* Guatemala Poverty Assessment Program.

Thai, TQ and EM Falaris (2014). Child schooling, child health, and rainfall shocks: Evidence from rural Vietnam. *The Journal of Development Studies*, 50(7), 1025–1037, DOI:10.1080/00220388.2014.903247.

Thiede, BC (2014). Rainfall shocks and within-community wealth inequality: Evidence from rural Ethiopia. *World Development*, 64, 181–193.

Thomas, T, L Christiaensen, QT Do and LD Trung (2010). *Natural disasters and household welfare: evidence from Vietnam.* World Bank Policy Research Working Paper Series 5491, The World Bank.

Tiwari, S, HG Jacoby and E Skoufias (2013). *Monsoon Babies Rainfall Shocks and Child Nutrition in Nepal.* Policy Research Working Paper 6395, The World Bank.

United Nations International Strategy for Disaster Reduction (2012). *Disaster Risk — Poverty Trends in Jordan, Syria, Yemen: Key Findings and Policy Recommendations.* UNISDR Regional Office for the Arab States, Cairo.

Van den Berg, M (2010). Household income strategies and natural disasters: Dynamic livelihoods in rural Nicaragua. *Ecological Economics,* 69(3), 592–602.

Von Peter, G, S von Dahlen and S Saxena (2012). *Unmitigated disasters? New evidence on the macroeconomic cost of natural catastrophes.* BIS Working Paper No. 394.

Wang, X and Q Zhang (2010). Poverty under drought: an agro-pastoral village in North China. *Journal of Asian Public Policy,* 3(3), 250–262.

Wong, PY and PH Brown (2011). Natural Disasters and Vulnerability: Evidence from the 1997 Forest Fires in Indonesia. *The BE Journal of Economic Analysis & Policy,* 11(1), 1–24. DOI: 10.2202/1935-1682.2658.

World Bank (2011). *Indonesia — Gender equality in disaster management and climate adaptation.* Indonesia gender policy brief, no. 6, World Bank, Washington DC. Available at http://documents.worldbank.org/curated/en/2011/06/17559638/indonesia-gender-equality-disaster-management-climate-adaptation.

World Bank (2010). *Natural Hazards, Unnatural Disasters.* World Bank Publications, Washington, DC.

Yamamura, E (2015). The 1970 impact of natural disasters on income inequality: Analysis using panel data during the period 1965 to 2004. *International Economic Journal,* 29(3), 359–374. DOI: 10.1080/10168737.2015.1020323.

Yamano, T, H Alderman and L Christiaensen (2005). Child growth, shocks, and food aid in rural Ethiopia. *American Journal of Agricultural Economics,* 87(2), 273–288.

Zheng, Y and A Byg (2014). Coping with climate change: households' response strategies to drought and hailstorm in Lijiang, China. *Environmental Hazards,* 13(3), 211–228.

Zoleta-Nantes, DB (2002). Differential impacts of flood hazards among the street children, the urban poor and residents of wealthy neighborhoods in Metro Manila, Philippines. *Mitigation and Adaptation Strategies for Global Change,* 7(3), 239–266.

CHAPTER 3

ECONOMIC LOSSES FROM NATURAL DISASTERS: QUANTIFICATION APPROACHES AND DEVELOPMENTS IN ASIAN COUNTRIES

Jonathan Van der Kamp

European Institute for Energy Research (EIFER), Germany
and
Karlsruhe Institute of Technology (KIT), Germany

Jonathan Neo
London School of Economics and Political Science (LSE),
United Kingdom

Natural disasters, by definition, cause great damage, destruction and human suffering. Estimating the associated economic losses is crucial, as this information supports decision-making in the immediate follow-up period of disaster events, but also for the development of long-term mitigation strategies. To better understand what is meant by *economic losses* from natural disasters and how to quantify them, we propose a classification and present associated economic quantification approaches. In a second, more practical oriented part, we use statistics from an international natural disaster database to analyze disaster events and the underlying losses occurring in Asian countries. Amongst other, we find that huge disaster losses and fatalities are associated with individual major events of particular types. After normalizing losses with GDP and fatalities with population count, the ranking of the most affected countries changed from more developed to less developed countries. We finish by giving some recommendations on how to improve the availability and quality of disaster-related loss estimates.

1. CONTEXT AND OBJECTIVE

Natural disasters, by definition, cause great damage, destruction and human suffering (Bokwa, 2013, IPCC, 2012). Estimating the associated economic losses is crucial, as this information supports decision-making in the immediate follow-up period of disaster events, but also for the development of long-term mitigation strategies.

To better understand what is meant by *economic losses* from natural disasters and how to quantify them, the first part of this chapter sets out to: (1) classify loss components and (2) present associated economic quantification approaches for disaster loss accounting. The objective is to provide an overview of assessment approaches rather than to provide detailed guidance for practitioners.

In the second part, a quantitative analysis of economic losses from natural disasters in East, South and South-East Asia during the time period 1990 to 2015 is presented. The statistics, taken from the EM-DAT international disaster database (Guha-Sapir *et al.*, 2016), are used to illustrate the implications of different types of natural disasters in a range of countries that are among the most affected by natural disasters worldwide (Munich Re, 2016). Moreover, we include data on socio-economic factors such as population density or level of economic development into our analyses in order to allow for better informed comparisons of results.

More specifically, the following items are addressed in this chapter: to set the scope, the terms "natural disaster" and "natural hazard" are defined (2.1) and a classification of different types of disasters is provided (2.2). This is followed by a demarcation between the terms "impacts", "damages", "losses" and "costs" (2.3). Section 3 starts with a classification of natural disaster loss components before associated quantification approaches are described in Section 3.1. To conclude the first part, practical constraints and related solutions are outlined in Section 3.2.

In the second part of this chapter, the focus is on natural disaster databases that feature loss estimates (Section 4.1). A statistical overview on natural disaster-related losses in countries in East, South and South-East Asia regions is given. Developments of losses over time are analyzed and patterns for given regions and countries are identified in Section 4.2, whilst also discussing limitations (Section 4.3) and global influencing factors (Section 4.4). This chapter concludes with a summary of key findings, main recommendations and an outlook on future developments concerning natural disaster loss assessment (Section 5).

2. TERMS AND DEFINITIONS

2.1. *Definitions: Natural Hazard vs. Natural Disaster*

Following the terminology of Bokwa (2013) and consistent with definitions provided by the IPCC (2012), a natural hazard is defined as *"an unexpected and/or uncontrollable natural event of unusual magnitude that might threaten people."*

A disaster is defined as *"the impact of a hazard on a community/society"*, in many cases implying *"significant loss of life and property, often beyond the ability of the local community to recover from, without assistance"* (Bokwa, 2013).

Consequently, a necessary condition for categorizing a hazardous event as a disaster is its adverse effect on society. Disaster databases also set their own criteria, such as monetary thresholds, to be satisfied before they classify an event as a natural disaster (cf. Section 4.1).

2.2. *Classification of Natural Disasters*

Disasters are broadly categorized into natural disasters and technological (also called man-made) disasters. Here, the focus is on natural disasters, which can be further divided based on their causative natural origin and other characteristics.

The classification of natural disasters as presented in Table 1 is commonly used by the most relevant global disaster databases (Integrated Research on Disaster Risk, 2014). Six disaster subgroups are defined, each with its respective main disaster types, e.g. earthquakes as a geophysical event. Although not displayed here, these main types can be further disaggregated into subtypes (e.g. ground shaking as a subtype of an earthquake) or sub-sub types (e.g. snow avalanche as a sub-sub type of avalanche, which in turn is a sub-type of landslide).

Table 1:   Harmonized Classification of Natural Disasters: Subgroups and Disaster Main Types

Disaster Subgroup	Definition	Disaster Main Type
Geophysical	A hazard originating from solid earth. This term is used interchangeably with the term geological hazard.	Earthquake, Volcano activity, Mass Movement (dry)
Meteorological	A hazard caused by short-lived, micro- to meso-scale extreme weather and atmospheric conditions that last from minutes to days.	Extreme Temperature, Fog, Storm
Hydrological	A hazard caused by the occurrence, movement, and distribution of surface and subsurface freshwater and saltwater.	Flood, Landslide, Wave action
Climatological	A hazard caused by long-lived, meso- to macro-scale atmospheric processes ranging from intra-seasonal to multi-decadal climate variability.	Drought, Glacial Lake Outburst, Wildfire
Biological	A hazard caused by the exposure to living organisms and their toxic substances (e.g. venom, mold) or vector-borne diseases that they may carry. Examples are venomous wildlife and insects, poisonous plants, and mosquitoes carrying disease-causing agents such as parasites, bacteria, or viruses (e.g. malaria).	Epidemic, Insect infestation, Animal Accident
Extraterrestrial	A hazard caused by asteroids, meteoroids, and comets as they pass near-earth, enter the Earth's atmosphere, and/or strike the Earth, and by changes in interplanetary conditions that effect the Earth's magnetosphere, ionosphere, and thermosphere.	Impact, Space weather

Source: Based on (Integrated Research on Disaster Risk, 2014).

2.3. *Distinguishing Impacts, Losses, Costs and Damages of Disasters*

Various terms can be used to describe the economic consequences of natural disasters, since a standardized set of definitions does not exist. We present a set of definitions that were issued by the US National Research Council (1999):

- **Impacts** of a disaster is the broadest term, and includes both market-based and nonmarket effects.
- **Losses** of disasters represents market-based negative economic impacts. These consist of direct losses that result from the physical destruction of buildings, crops, and natural resources and indirect losses that represent the consequences of that destruction, such as temporary unemployment and business interruption.
- **Costs** of disasters, as the term is conventionally used, typically refers to cash payouts by insurers and governments to reimburse some (and in certain cases all) of the losses suffered by individuals and businesses.
- **Damages** caused by disasters refers to physical destruction, measured by physical indicators, such as the numbers of deaths and injuries or the number of buildings destroyed. When valued in monetary terms, damages become direct losses.

It should be noted that these definitions may be deemed arbitrary and do not strictly rely on economic or accounting theory (Dore and Etkin, 2000). In an attempt to cover economic impacts more broadly and following the concept of total economic value (Pearce *et al.*, 2006), we also consider quantification approaches for non-market-based losses such as the (monetized) loss of human life (cf. Section 3.1.3).

The lack of common and consistent definitions also creates a methodological difficulty for researchers to compare and evaluate impact estimates from different sources (De Groeve *et al.*, 2013, Guha-Sapir and Hoyois, 2012). Moreover, database providers sometimes use their own terminology which differs from the above definitions. For example, the EM-DAT database (cf. Section 4.1) labels monetary direct losses as "total damage."

3. ASSESSING ECONOMIC LOSSES OF NATURAL DISASTERS: CLASSIFICATION AND QUANTIFICATION APPROACHES

Drawing from the frameworks proposed by the National Research Council (1999) and BTE (2001),[1] we develop a classification of natural disaster impacts that includes the main components of a comprehensive economic loss assessment (Figure 1). Alternative ways of classifying disaster impacts have also been incorporated to support the methodological basis of our classification (Dore and Etkin, 2000, ECLAC, 2003, Howe and Cochrane, 1993).

A primary distinction is made between market-based (or tangible) and nonmarket-based (or intangible) impacts:

- **Market-based impacts** are related to marketable goods or services as indicated by the name. They can be further divided into direct or indirect (also called higher-order) losses. While damages to physical assets or stocks are usually categorized under direct losses, effects on the flow of economic goods or services are

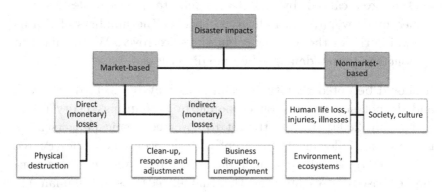

Figure 1: Classification of Natural Disaster Impacts and Main Valuation Components

---

[1]In the classification proposed here, indirect losses include expenses for clean-up, response and adjustment. Although these effects are classified as direct losses by the National Research Council (1999), it seems more appropriate to consider them as intermediate reactions to the disaster event and hence as indirect losses. This view is also supported by the BTE (2001).

counted as indirect losses. Sometimes, macroeconomic effects, such as gross domestic product (GDP) changes, are considered as a third category next to direct and indirect losses (De Groeve *et al.*, 2013, ECLAC, 2003). However, as these effects are directly related to indirect losses, this distinction is not made here.

- **Nonmarket-based impacts** are related to non-marketable or intangible goods, such as human health or ecosystems. Although impacts such as the loss of human life or effects on ecosystems can be increasingly monetized, their quantification is subject to higher uncertainty and data constraints. Societal impacts, e.g. related to the increase in incidence of poverty after a disaster event, are even harder to quantify and more likely to be considered in a qualitative way.

3.1. *Assessment Approaches for Natural Disaster Impacts*

Before monetary losses are estimated, it is useful to first express impacts in physical units. Several references such as (ECLAC, 2003) give guidance on how to collect the necessary information for assessment. The most important data sources are surveys conducted with public bodies and insurance companies, and the press.

For the monetary assessment of market-based impacts, information can be obtained from the market itself. In the case of nonmarket-based impacts, alternative approaches are required.

3.1.1. *Market-based impacts: assessment of direct losses*

Direct losses result from immediate or directly induced physical consequences of natural disasters, principally affecting:

- Structures (building types);
- Infrastructure (e.g. roads, utilities);
- Contents (equipment and inventory/supplies).

Destroyed structures, equipment and infrastructures typically need to be rebuilt, replaced or repaired after a disaster. Restoration and replacement cost approaches are therefore most suitable to approximate the associated losses:

- Restoration (or repair) cost approaches aim to define the expenditures of re-establishing the pre-disaster condition of a damaged asset;
- Replacement cost approaches aim to define the expenditures of replacing a damaged asset with a new one, offering the same functionality. In order not to overestimate losses, the residual value of the lost asset should be accounted for, requiring specific information on lifetime and depreciation principles. In the absence of this information, replacement costs can be regarded as an upper limit of the true losses.

If an asset is not immediately restored or replaced, indirect losses may be incurred, e.g. foregone production (cf. next section).

Destroyed inventory and supplies such as marketable goods are typically valued using recent or expected future market price. For agricultural products, specific principles may apply, as further described in ECLAC (2003). For instance, the assessment will depend on the state of the product at the moment the disaster strikes: whether it is harvested, ready to harvest, or still in growth.

3.1.2. *Market-based impacts: assessment of indirect losses*

Indirect losses are caused by the consequences of natural disasters, occurring in the aftermath of the event. They are generally more difficult to identify and quantify than direct losses for several reasons: they depend on the spatial and temporal scope of the analysis, occur over longer time periods, require assumptions about economic development including resiliency to disaster impacts, and may involve complex economic spillover effects. For these reasons, disaster databases, such as EM-DAT, and insurance companies concentrate on the assessment of direct losses (Guha-Sapir *et al.*, 2013, Hallegatte and Przyluski, 2010).

Indirect losses often have macro-economic implications on a national scale or even across countries. But they can also include benefits, e.g. temporary economic upturns observed in the wake of distinct disaster events (Fomby *et al.*, 2009). Therefore, the net effects after considering both indirect losses and benefits need to be taken into account in a full assessment.

Prominent examples of indirect losses include:

- **Business Disruption**: Business disruption implies losses in produced goods or services in part through direct damages, e.g. destroyed production assets, and through external disruptions, e.g. destroyed transport infrastructure.

- **Unemployment**: From a household perspective, losses may result from temporary or permanent unemployment and in turn have non-tangible effects such as mental stress or illnesses (cf. Section 3.1.3). However, there can be risks of double counting if wage or salary losses are included in the losses of business disruption (cf. Section 3.2).

- **Clean-up, Response and Adjustment**: Clean-up, response and adjustment-related losses not only concern businesses but also public bodies and households, requiring a careful allocation of losses between stakeholders. Physical assets built in line with these activities, e.g. related to prevention, should be counted separately from those assets meant to replace damaged structures, the latter being allocated to direct losses.

For a monetary assessment of indirect losses, the preferred approach is to estimate the loss of value added. Value added can be defined in two ways: (1) *"market value of the product produced, less the value of inputs purchased from other producers"*, or (2) *"accounting profits plus depreciation expenses, wages and salaries and taxes"* (Howe and Cochrane, 1993). The loss of value added is estimated over the period from the occurrence of the disaster to the moment when pre-disaster conditions are re-established. A comparison of the disaster scenario to a control scenario without disaster impacts is therefore required. If resources such as labor or production assets generate earnings from other employments during the disruption period, this should be considered in the estimate of foregone value added (Howe and Cochrane, 1993). Approaches to assess business disruption losses after specific disaster types (i.e. floods, droughts, coastal hazards, alpine hazards) are presented by Bubeck and Kreibich (2011).

Different data sources and techniques can be used to estimate indirect losses:

- **Empirical data collection**: Common data sources are public bodies, firms, households or other concerned stakeholders. Guidelines on data collection for different economic sectors are provided by ECLAC (2003), for instance.
- **Econometric approaches**: Using empirical datasets at different aggregation levels, econometric analysis aims to identify and quantify disaster-related determinants that explain observed developments over time or across space, e.g. changes of GDP. For more details on these approaches, see Rose (2004).
- **Model-based approaches**: Using equations and data that describe the (simplified) functioning of the economy and dependencies between economic actors, models can be used to assess indirect losses of past or future disaster events. Typical examples are input-output (I-O) modelling and computable general equilibrium (CGE) models. The practical applicability of these approaches is often limited by data constraints. For further details, see (Hallegatte and Przyluski, 2010, Rose, 2004).

3.1.3. *Assessment of nonmarket-based impacts*

Nonmarket-based impacts of natural disasters are often reported in physical units, e.g. number of deaths or number of affected people (cf. Section 4.2). A more refined assessment of these and other nonmarket impacts is complex, requires specific approaches, and is often impeded by a lack of standardized methodology.

In practice, monetary valuation of nonmarket-based impacts remains rare, largely due to uncertainties and data gaps. Some scholars have conducted related research on the short-term impacts of climate change, covering disaster impacts (Rose, 2004). In line with Rose (2004), we recognize that monetary valuation of nonmarket-based impacts can facilitate decision-making and lead to a more complete economic assessment of disaster losses. A brief overview of related economic approaches is therefore given.

A distinction between direct and indirect effects is not made for nonmarket-based impacts since most of the quantifiable effects are direct consequences of the disaster. At the same time, non-market-based indirect effects, e.g. societal impacts in terms of poverty or inequality, are complex to assess and the influence of natural disasters in relation to other socio-economic factors cannot be clearly separated (Lindell and Prater, 2003, National Research Council, 2006).

From an economic perspective, the valuation of nonmarket-based disaster impacts should reflect the utility losses of affected individuals. Examples include pain and suffering, illnesses, death, and loss of environmental assets and services. An overview of related valuation approaches is given by Freeman (2003) and, more specifically on natural disaster impacts, by ECLAC (2003).

The utility losses of the affected population can typically be elicited using two types of techniques — revealed preference and stated preference approaches:

- **Revealed preferences approaches**: these use observational data in order to derive a monetary estimate for the value of a nonmarket good, e.g. human life. Direct approaches include observed market data, such as in the human capital approach, where labor productivity during an average worker's lifetime is taken as a proxy for the value of human life. Indirect approaches such as the hedonic wage approach use observed wage premiums for risky activities as the basis for quantification of human life (OECD, 2012, Pearce *et al.*, 2006).
- **Stated preferences approaches**: these address individual's preferences by explicitly asking for their willingness to pay (WTP) or willingness to accept (WTA) with regard to changes in risk, environmental or health quality. The most prominent direct approach is the contingent valuation method (CVM) that elicits people's WTP or WTA using questionnaires. It is regularly used for the valuation of mortality risks and allows assigning a value to human life, although sometimes contested for moral or ethical reasons

(OECD, 2012). Indirect approaches, such as choice modelling (also known as conjoint analysis) derive information on the value of non-market goods from individual's choices in experimental settings.

According to welfare economic principles, stated preferences approaches are preferable over revealed preference approaches, as they allow explicitly addressing individual preferences (Pearce *et al.*, 2002).

3.2. *Practical Constraints*

The approaches presented so far are constrained in their practical applicability due to several factors. We discuss some key constraints and make respective recommendations on how to deal with them.

Coping with limited data availability

A comprehensive disaster loss assessment can only be conducted in the ideal scenario where all necessary data is readily available. But this is often not the case in the wake of a natural disaster which is characterized not only by the destruction of physical assets but often also of information-related infrastructure and inventories. Particularly in developing countries, data availability and data quality are the main barriers to a robust and consistent loss assessment and to model-based assessment approaches.

As a consequence, trade-offs need to be made between what is theoretically desirable and what is practically feasible. Using simplified assumptions and aggregated data may help to produce first loss estimates before more detailed information becomes available. Prioritization plays an important role in such a context. Limitations in data availability may also explain a practitioner's focus on the assessment of direct losses which are more straightforward to estimate (Guha-Sapir and Hoyois, 2012).

Coping with complexity

Complexity increases with the spatial and temporal dimension of the disaster event, particularly for indirect losses. This is due to interactions between economic actors, data needs, and dynamic effects over time. Moreover, complexity may differ based on disaster characteristics. While geophysical events such as earthquakes typically lead to immediate damages at physical infrastructures, climatological events such as droughts induce more indirect losses over a longer period of time. For this reason, disaster databases such as EM-DAT often define explicit rules on the loss assessment of different types of disasters (Guha-Sapir *et al.*, 2013).

Coping with uncertainty

Induced by data limitations and complexity amongst others, uncertainty is an important issue to be addressed when quantifying disaster losses. Potential sources of uncertainty include data uncertainty, model uncertainty, uncertainty resulting from expert choices and uncertainty related to future assumptions. For instance, the data used in loss assessments may be incomplete, approximated, taken from different sources and compiled using different methodologies, making comparisons difficult to be conducted. For reasons discussed above, uncertainties are generally higher for indirect loss estimates as compared to direct loss estimates, and for nonmarket-based impacts as compared to market-based impacts. Uncertainty can be addressed in either a qualitative or quantitative way — describing potential uncertainty factors and accounting for their implications, or using statistical methods for data treatment (Morgan and Small, 1992).

Avoiding double counting

A central question related to the assessment of disaster losses is: Who bears the loss? It is often difficult to define as to whether private entities or the public administration should be responsible for absorbing losses. This aspect should nevertheless be addressed, not least to avoid double counting. In the same line of thought, reimbursed or insured losses should also be separated from unreimbursed or uninsured losses (National Research Council, 1999).

Loss assessments often bear a risk of double counting, especially for indirect losses. For instance, business disruptions may lead to losses that affect both businesses (production-side) and employees (income-side) but the loss of value added should only be counted once. Similarly, transactions between economic agents (household, firm or government) should only be counted once and the perspective from which the transaction is calculated should be clearly defined (BTE, 2001). One way to avoid double counting is therefore to attribute losses of private assets to one economic agent at a time.

Normalization across time and space for better comparability

A detail that is sometimes lacking in published loss estimates is the monetary base year. Specifying the base year enables to normalize the data via inflation adjustments and perform a more accurate comparison across different sources and years. Likewise, when comparing losses across countries, conversion to a common monetary unit, such as the US dollar, can be useful. Another option to normalize data for better comparison is to account for differences in purchasing power between countries, though such an adjustment is rarely ever used in practice (Neumayer and Barthel, 2011). When estimating long-term disaster impacts, future gains and losses also need to be discounted to the present value using an appropriate, context-specific, discount rate (BTE, 2001).

4. ECONOMIC LOSSES DUE TO NATURAL DISASTERS IN ASIAN COUNTRIES

> *"A better understanding of issues such as who bears disaster losses, what are the main types of damages in different disasters, and how those losses differ spatially, are of critical importance in making decisions about allocating resources for mitigation, research, and response."* (National Research Council, 1999)

Having presented the theoretical basis for a comprehensive natural disaster-related loss assessment, this section analyses empirical data on losses from natural disasters in a particular geographic context, i.e. countries in East, South, and South-East Asia. Using disaster statistics from the freely accessible international EM-DAT database (Guha-Sapir *et al.*, 2016), direct economic losses and related statistics due to natural disasters for the period 1990 to 2015 are presented. Finally, key influencing factors on natural disaster-related losses as well as limitations concerning the use of disaster databases are discussed.

4.1. *Disaster Databases Featuring Loss Estimates*

This section draws on existing overviews of international disaster databases and their features (De Groeve *et al.*, 2013, GRIP, 2016, Guha-Sapir and Hoyois, 2012, Integrated Research on Disaster Risk, 2014, Tschoegl *et al.*, 2006).

Reinsurance companies provide comprehensive and accurate global statistics on natural disaster events and related impacts, notably MunichRe (NatCat SERVICE) and SwissRE (Sigma). However, these companies offer only limited free access to their data and underlying methodology. Information from these databases is therefore useful to provide global overviews rather than for a detailed analysis.

As alternatives to commercial databases, freely accessible databases[2] can be used. The two most comprehensive databases for the chosen geographic context, EM-DAT and DesInventar, are compared in Table 2.

The most important differences between the two freely accessible databases are the temporal and geographical coverage, the definition (or lack) of inclusion criteria, the level of details provided and the application (or lack) of a validation process (Table 3). Although DesInventar aims to include more detailed data per event, an analysis for the countries of interested showed that the actual availability of detailed information is quite limited (e.g. statistics on deaths and affected people were only available for respectively about 20% of all events in the dataset considered). An advantage of DesInventar over EM-DAT is the partial indication of data sources.

EM-DAT was assessed to be best suited for the analysis of natural disaster-related losses in Asian countries for two reasons.

---

[2]It should be noted that detailed access to the EM-DAT data requires the submission of a data request form and signing a memorandum of understanding.

Table 2:   Comparison of Two Freely Accessible International Natural Disaster Databases

	EM-DAT (Guha-Sapir *et al.*, 2016)	DesInventar (2016)
Developer, maintenance	Centre for Research on the Epidemiology of Disasters (CRED) since 1988	Network for Social Studies on Disaster Prevention in Latin America (LA RED) since 1994
Temporal and geographic scope	Data record from 1900 onwards; over 18000 disaster events worldwide included; country-level data	Limited data availability before 1990 (from 1986 onwards for the countries covered here); over 44000 single events included; only specific countries covered (for the regions of interest, cf. Table 3) country-level data
Data included	— Unique disaster number — Dates: start, end — Geo: continent, region, country, location — Disaster: group, sub-group, type, subtype, sub-subtype, origin, associated disaster, event name — Statistics: total deaths, total injured, total homeless, total affected, total damage (in US$ current value) Criteria for inclusion of events; at least one of the following: — 10 or more people reported killed — 100 or more people reported affected — declaration of a state of emergency — call for international assistance	— Unique serial and identification number — Start date — Disaster type, type of cause, observations about the cause — Country, place — Statistics: deaths, missing, injured/wounded, affected, evacuated, homes destroyed, homes affected, damage to crops and woods, loss value (in US$, base year of the event) — Data source No criteria for inclusion of events

(Continued)

	EM-DAT (Guha-Sapir *et al.*, 2016)	DesInventar (2016)
Data sources	Governments, UN agencies, NGOs, research institutions, insurance institutions and press agencies	Government agencies, NGOs, research institutes and news media
Data validation	Validation process applied	No validation process applied

Firstly, EM-DAT provides a comprehensive data coverage and has greater availability of direct loss estimates. Second, EM-DAT features inclusion criteria, a standardized framework and a data validation process, none of which are available on DesInventar.

4.2. *Natural Disaster-Related Statistics in Asian Countries for the Period 1990–2015*

In the following section, statistics extracted from the EM-DAT database for the countries of interest in three Asian regions (East, South and South-East Asia) in the time period from 1990 to 2015 are presented. A comprehensive analysis of all available data was carried out, but only selected results are presented here, i.e. time trends, comparisons between countries and between different types of disasters.

Normalization of the data is conducted using statistics on population counts and GDP from the World Bank (2016) and, where lacking, the IMF (2013). Although major disaster events may cause losses and deaths beyond national boundaries, the normalization is conducted at the country level. The following data needed for normalization is lacking and could not be considered: GDP data from 1990 to 2000 for Afghanistan, from 1990 to 1997 for Myanmar, from 1990 to 1999 for Timor-Leste, from 1991 to 1992 for Iran, and from 1990 to 2015 for Democratic People's Republic of Korea.

For reasons previously discussed, the validity of the presented data is constrained in several ways (Section 3.2). We further highlight

Table 3:   Regions and Countries of Interest and their Coverage in the EM-DAT and DesInventar Databases

Region-Country	Database Coverage	
East Asia		
China P Rep	EM-DAT	
Hong Kong (China)	EM-DAT	
Japan	EM-DAT	
Korea Dem P Rep	EM-DAT	
Korea Rep	EM-DAT	
Macau	EM-DAT	
Mongolia	EM-DAT	
Taiwan (China)	EM-DAT	
South Asia		
Afghanistan	EM-DAT	
Bangladesh	EM-DAT	
Bhutan	EM-DAT	
India	EM-DAT	DesInventar
Iran Islam Rep*	EM-DAT	DesInventar
Maldives	EM-DAT	DesInventar
Nepal	EM-DAT	DesInventar
Pakistan	EM-DAT	
Sri Lanka	EM-DAT	DesInventar
South-East Asia		
Brunei Darussalam	EM-DAT	
Cambodia	EM-DAT	
Indonesia	EM-DAT	DesInventar
Lao P Dem Rep	EM-DAT	DesInventar
Malaysia	EM-DAT	
Myanmar	EM-DAT	
Philippines	EM-DAT	
Singapore	EM-DAT	
Thailand	EM-DAT	
Timor-Leste	EM-DAT	DesInventar
Vietnam	EM-DAT	DesInventar

*Included according to United Nations classification

the key constraints of our research in Section 4.3 below. As such, the conclusions drawn from the following analyses need to be interpreted with caution.

4.2.1. *Global developments in the regions of interest*

After aggregation at the regional level (i.e. for the three Asian regions of interest), there is no clear trend in the annual developments of number of natural disaster events, people killed or affected and estimated damage over time (Figure 2).

Substantial differences between single years are observed, and maximum numbers are often driven by single events. We further discuss these differences below. In terms of estimated damage, i.e. monetized direct losses, the largest annual number was reported for the year 2011 (note the logarithmic scale). While this observation applies to the three Asian regions of interest, it also holds true at the global level where 2011 marked the "costliest year for overall losses due to natural catastrophes" (Munich Re, 2016).

A closer look at the annual estimated damages reveals that the most costly types of natural disasters in the regions and period of interest were earthquakes and floods (Figure 3).

Similarly, when comparing the number of people killed per type of natural disaster, earthquakes and its potential consequences, such as tsunamis, appear as the most lethal events, followed by storms (Figure 4).

As seen from comparing Figure 3 with Figure 4, disasters causing high recorded direct losses are not necessarily the most lethal ones. For example, in the year 2011, while estimated damages were the highest, the number of people killed was relatively low compared to other years.

4.2.2. *Regional comparison — estimated damages*

China (649), India (391), Philippines (376) and Indonesia (308) are the countries which suffered from the highest number of recorded natural disaster events in the regions of interest. In terms of estimated damages, some countries recorded particularly high losses in certain years (Figure 5).

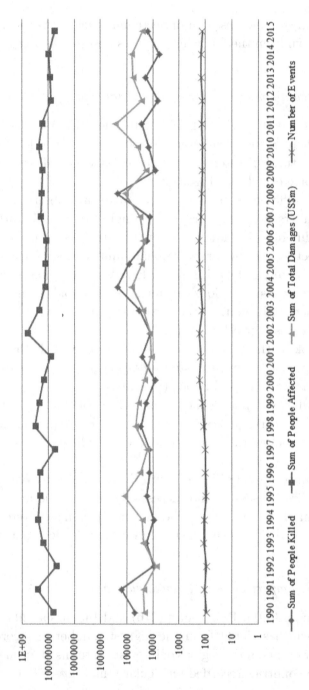

Figure 2: Aggregated Natural-disaster Related Statistics for the Three Regions of Interest

Source: Guha-Sapir *et al.* (2016).

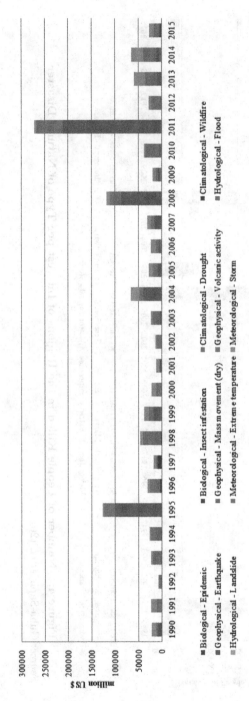

Figure 3: Estimated Damages in the Regions of Interest per Type of Natural Disaster

Source: Guha-Sapir *et al.* (2016).

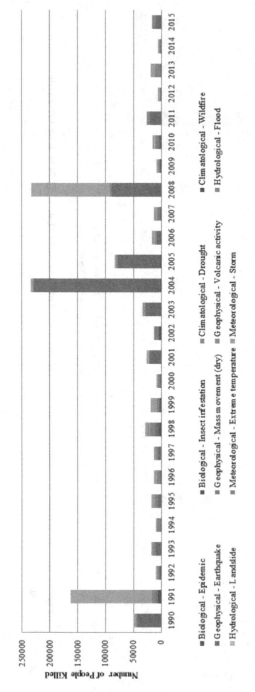

Figure 4: **Number of People Killed in the Regions of Interest per Type of Natural Disaster**

Source: Guha-Sapir *et al.* (2016).

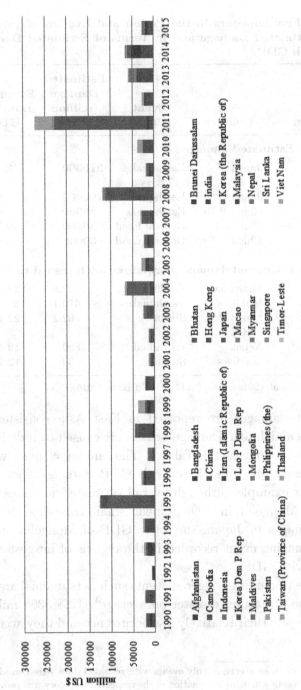

Figure 5: Estimated Damages due to Natural Disasters in the Countries of Interest from 1990 to 2013

Source: Guha-Sapir *et al.* (2016).

**Table 4: Top Five Disasters in the Period and Regions of Interest
in Terms of Estimated Damage and in Terms of Estimated Damage
Normalized with GDP**

Year	Region	Country	Event (Place)	Estimated Damage (million US$)	Estimated Damage/ GDP
Top 5 disasters: Estimated damage					
2011	East Asia	Japan	Earthquake, Tsunami	**210000**	3.56%
1995	East Asia	Japan	Earthquake	**100000**	1.87%
2008	East Asia	China P Rep	Earthquake	**85000**	1.86%
2011	South-East Asia	Thailand	General flood	**40000**	10.79%
1998	East Asia	China P Rep	General flood	**30000**	2.93%
Top 5 disasters: Estimated damage, normalized with regard to GDP					
1996	East Asia	Mongolia	Wildfire	1712.8	**127.28%**
2004	South Asia	Maldives	Earthquake	470.1	**39.10%**
1993	South-East Asia	Lao P Dem Rep	Storm	302.2	**22.76%**
2015	South Asia	Nepal	Earthquake	3860	**19.52%**
1991	South Asia	Maldives	Storm	30	**12.27%**

Sources: Guha-Sapir *et al.* (2016); IMF (2013); World Bank (2016).

The highest damages are reported in East Asia consistently, mainly in China and Japan. Damage peaks were caused by individual major events, as summarized in Table 4. The ranking changes when estimated damages are normalized with GDP data as illustrated by the following example: although overall estimated losses caused by wildfire in Mongolia in 1996 appear small compared to the earthquake damages in Japan, the lower GDP of Mongolia makes it the most damaging event recorded in the regions of interest after normalization with GDP.

Earthquakes (including triggered events such as tsunamis) are the most costly type of natural disaster on average[3] (US$ 3308 million per incident) despite their relatively low occurrence and they account

---

[3]For the calculation of these averages, only events with recorded data were considered, i.e. excluding those events where no information in the respective category was provided.

for 43.34% of all estimated damages incurred. This is compared to floods (US$ 732 million per incident; 32.59% of total) and storms (US$ 383 million per incident; 17.92% of total) that were less costly on the overall despite having higher occurrences in terms of events.

4.2.3. *Regional comparison — number of fatalities*

Similar to the results observed for estimated damages, individual major events in single countries and certain years are responsible for a large number of fatalities caused by natural disasters (Figure 6). Countries in South and South-East Asia were particularly affected in the period of interest and again, single events explain the annual peaks observed (Table 5).

After normalization of fatality numbers with population counts, three of the most deadly events reappear in the normalized ranking. Developing countries (e.g. Indonesia) are observed to be more affected in terms of people killed than more developed countries (e.g. Japan).

On average, earthquakes cause the highest loss of human life per incident (2184 deaths per incident) and account for 50.98% of all recorded deaths, followed by storms (430 deaths per incident; 32.75% of recorded deaths) and droughts (378 deaths per incident; 0.28% of recorded deaths).

4.3. *Limitations of the Data Analysis*

Some specific and general limitations concerning the analysis of disaster-related statistics will be discussed below.

4.3.1. *Data coverage in EM-DAT*

For the regions and period of interest, data availability for all single disaster events in EM-DAT in terms of "total damages" is low (39%) compared to data availability for "total people killed" (82%). There is no clear trend on data availability across the years. In particular, we do not observe any clear increase in data availability despite the spread of information technology or other technological advancements during the time period.

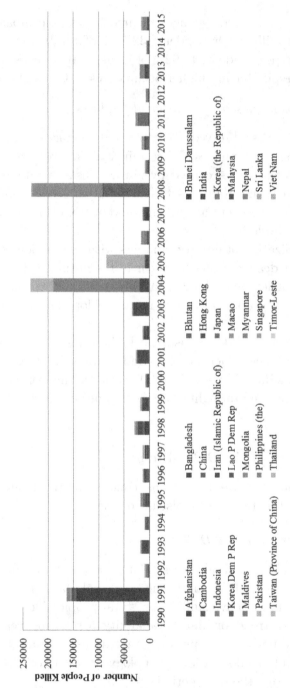

Figure 6: Number of People Killed due to Natural Disasters in the Countries of Interest from 1990 to 2013

Source: Guha-Sapir *et al.* (2016).

Table 5: Top Five Disasters in the Period and Regions of Interest in Terms of People Killed and in Terms of People Killed Normalized with Population

Year	Region	Country	Event	People Killed	People Killed/ Population
Top 5 disasters: Number of people killed					
2004	South-East Asia	Indonesia	Earthquake, Tsunami	**165708**	0.07%
1991	South Asia	Bangladesh	Storm, Tropical cyclone	**138866**	0.13%
2008	South-East Asia	Myanmar	Storm, Tropical cyclone	**138366**	0.27%
2008	East Asia	China P Rep	Earthquake	**87476**	0.01%
2005	South Asia	Pakistan	Earthquake	**73338**	0.05%
Top 5 disasters: Number of people killed, normalized with regard to population count					
2008	South-East Asia	Myanmar	Storm, Tropical cyclone	138366	**0.27%**
2004	South Asia	Sri Lanka	Earthquake, Tsunami	35399	**0.18%**
1991	South Asia	Bangladesh	Storm, Tropical cyclone	138866	**0.13%**
2004	South-East Asia	Indonesia	Earthquake, Tsunami	165708	**0.07%**
1990	South Asia	Iran Islam Rep	Earthquake	40000	**0.07%**

Sources: Guha-Sapir *et al.* (2016); IMF (2013); World Bank (2016).

Among countries with a track record of more than 10 events, Afghanistan (8%) records the lowest data availability for estimated damages, followed by Bangladesh (10%) and Bhutan (11%). Taiwan (77%), China (62%) and Vietnam (62%) have the highest data availability for estimated damages.

4.3.2. *Data quality and completeness of the loss estimates*

The monetary loss data included in EM-DAT is constrained in that it focuses on direct losses. Given that no information is provided on the exact data sources used, the quality of the estimates cannot be verified. Most critically, EM-DAT presents estimated damages per event as aggregate numbers and does not distinguish among different types of impacts, e.g. on structures, contents or infrastructure (cf. Section 3.1.1).

The normalization of loss and mortality data was carried out with respect to the country where the corresponding natural disaster event originated. This approach ignores the fact that losses and deaths can also occur beyond national boundaries. As a result, the comparison of normalized data must be interpreted with caution.

4.3.3. *General limitations and biases concerning loss assessments*

On top of the limitations related to the data provided in EM-DAT, Guha-Sapir and Hoyois (2012) note a number of potential sources of uncertainty and biases related to the assessment of disaster losses in general:

- Lack of standardization and harmonization regarding data sources and quantification approaches;
- The fact that reporting and documentation of disaster statistics generally increases with the level of economic development and over the years;
- Reported losses increase with the level of economic development, thereby reinforcing the discrepancy of reported losses for high-income versus low-income countries;
- Inconsistencies caused by changes over time, e.g. geographical borders, methodologies, etc.;
- Potential political influence on data reporting.

4.4. *What are the Main Influencing Factors Regarding the Economic Losses of Natural Disasters?*

In our data analysis, the two most damaging types of natural disasters in terms of direct losses and number of fatalities were earthquakes and storms. To some extent, the type of natural disaster and its specific characteristics are therefore associated with the amount of direct (and indirect) losses.

Further influencing factors which may influence the magnitude of disaster losses through the exposure and vulnerability faced by a society to disasters include (Bokwa, 2013):

- **Geographic location and size**: areas known to be exposed to seismic activity clearly face a higher risk, just like areas of large river basins and shore lines;
- **Population density**: urban areas with high population densities face a higher risk but at the same time these areas may profit from better mitigation measures and rapid emergency help;
- **Socio-economic context**: availability and quality of infrastructure, warning systems and prevention measures has an important influence on disaster-related losses;
- **Cultural practices**: these can have an influence on people's capabilities to deal with emergency situations, e.g. being able to swim.

Several studies have also looked at the determinants of (macroeconomic) disaster impacts:

- Noy (2009) looked at the determinants for macro-economic outcomes of disasters. Factors that help to limit initial consequences and spillovers into the macro-economy include high literacy rate, better institutions, higher incomes per capita, openness to trade and high levels of government spending. Factors that help to better endure natural disasters consequences include higher foreign exchange reserves, high levels of domestic credit and less-open capital accounts.
- Toya and Skidmore (2007) also analyzed development indicators and their influence on disaster-related losses. They found fewer losses in countries with high-income, high educational standard, greater openness, more complete financial systems and smaller governments.

This type of analysis on macro-economic determinants is difficult to carry out using data from EM-DAT, since it does not include indirect losses from disasters, i.e. macro-economic losses related to natural disasters.

5. SUMMARY AND OUTLOOK

This chapter had three objectives:

(1) To identify and classify those components that enable to assess the full societal impacts of natural disasters;
(2) To present associated economic quantification approaches and their limitations;
(3) To analyze statistics on natural disasters for countries in East, South, and South-East Asia during the period from 1990 to 2015.

A classification was developed to distinguish between market- and nonmarket-based impacts. Market-based impacts were further decomposed into direct and indirect losses.

Quantification of direct losses relies on approaches that incorporate market prices, e.g. restoration or replacement costs. The assessment of indirect losses is typically more complex and depends on the type of disaster. An important indirect effect is business disruption which can be quantified in terms of losses in value added. Econometric and model-based approaches are particularly suitable for the assessment of indirect macro-economic effects, but are constrained by data availability. For nonmarket-based impacts, such as valuation of human health and the environment, specific economic assessment methods such as the stated and revealed preferences approaches have been developed. However, these approaches and their outcomes are subject to higher uncertainty and are rarely implemented in actual assessments of natural disaster impacts.

Two freely accessible international databases on natural disaster events (EM-DAT and DesInventar) were compared. In this paper, we chose EM-DAT for our analyses because of its greater data coverage and higher level of data standardization. Even though EM-DAT remains subjected to uncertainty and methodological limitations, some trends in terms of disaster occurrence and direct losses were discussed.

Earthquakes are found to be the major contributor to reported losses and fatalities. Huge disaster losses and fatalities are associated with individual major events. For example, the earthquakes and tsunamis that struck Japan in 2011 and Indonesia in 2004 caused the highest reported losses (210 billion US$) and deaths (165,708 people) respectively. Other highly damaging events identified were floods and storms. No clear time trends in the absolute number of events, estimated losses or number of fatalities were found over the 15-year period. After normalizing losses with GDP and fatalities with population count, the ranking of the most affected countries changed from more developed to less developed countries. We then presented a number of influencing factors relating to the exposure and vulnerability of society to disasters which may affect the level of losses incurred.

On data availability, serious gaps were observed in particular countries. Data availability in EM-DAT was remarkably higher in East-Asia countries as compared to South-Asia countries. The availability of loss estimates did not increase over the years, despite an assumed improvement in information and communication technologies.

5.1. *Global Recommendations and Outlook*

The biggest constraint related to the compilation and comparative analysis of economic losses from natural disasters is the lack of standardized assessment methods. International initiatives aiming at further harmonization and standardization could help to overcome this problem. As an encouraging example, the harmonization projects initiated by the IRDR working group can be cited (Integrated Research on Disaster Risk 2015, Integrated Research on Disaster Risk 2014). Greater efforts should also be undertaken to improve the representation and transparency of data in repositories such as EM-DAT and DesInventar.

As discussed, a comprehensive quantification of disaster-related losses are often not practicable in emergency situations, especially in poorer countries. For this reason, coordinated global actions should be taken to provide countries, which are most affected but have the least capacities to cope with disaster impacts, with assistance and guidance.

Another area of methodological improvement is to move towards a more comprehensive assessment of societal losses related to natural disasters, especially for nonmarket-based impacts. One way to achieve this is through the monetary valuation of nonmarket-based assets such as human life. This change in methodology could give greater visibility to poorer countries where fatalities tend to matter more than losses in physical assets. However, a key difficulty remains: it is difficult to find an appropriate valuation factor and a consistent way to apply this factor across different countries or regions.

Looking forward, an integral part of this discussion will be on the link between climate change and occurrence of (extreme) natural disasters. The IPCC (2012) has looked into this question. While their findings vary depending on the type of disaster and region, global disaster events are generally expected to increase in number and intensity with the warming climate over the next decade.

A factor that could contribute to the mitigation of detrimental impacts of natural disasters is the rapidly evolving information and communications technology. For example, sensors can be used for the early detection of events and social networks for post-disaster emergency management. However, we need to be aware that an over-reliance on technology may itself increase our vulnerability to disasters and human capacities needed for emergency management cannot be substituted.

ACKNOWLEDGEMENTS

We would like to thank Hanns-Maximilian Schmidt (Karlsruhe Institute of Technology; KIT) for useful comments on this work, which results from research collaboration between KIT, Germany, the London School of Economics and Political Science (LSE), UK, and Nanyang Technological University (NTU), Singapore. The main author gratefully acknowledges a scholarship granted by the Karlsruhe House of Young Scientists (KHYS).

Moreover, we would like to express our gratitude towards the CRED (Centre for Research on the Epidemiology of Disasters) for providing data from the EM-DAT disaster database.

REFERENCES

Bokwa, A (2013). Encyclopedia of Natural Hazards — Chapter "Natural Hazard". In Bobrowsky, PT (Ed.), p. 1135, Springer, Dordrecht. Available at http:// www.springer.com/earth+sciences+and+geography/natural+hazards/book/ 978-90-481-8699-0?detailsPage=authorsAndEditors.

Bokwa (2015). Natural Hazard. In *Encyclopedia of Natural Hazard*, Bobrowsky, PT (Ed.). Dodrecht: Springer.

BTE (2001). Economic costs of natural disasters in Australia. Bureau of Transport Economics, Canberra, Australia. p. 170. Available at http://www. bitre.gov.au/publications/2001/files/report_103.pdf.

Bubeck, P and H Kreibich (2011). Natural Hazards: direct costs and losses due to the disruption of production processes. GFZ, Potsdam, Germany. p. 68. Available at http://conhaz.org/CONHAZ%20REPORT%20WP01_2.pdf.

De Groeve, T, K Poljansek and D Ehrlich (2013). Recording Disaster Losses: Recommendations for a European approach (JRC Scientific and Policy Reports EUR 26111EN). Publications Office of the European Union, Luxembourg. p. 76. Available at http://bookshop.europa.eu/is-bin/INTERSHOP. enfinity/WFS/EU-Bookshop-Site/en_GB/-/EUR/ViewPublication-Start?Pu blicationKey=LBNA26111.

DesInventar (2016). DesInventar.net — Disaster Information Management System. Available at http://www.desinventar.net/. Accessed on 7 April 2016.

Dore, M and D Etkin (2000). The importance of measuring the social costs of natural disasters at a time of climate change. *Australian Journal of Emergency Management*, 15(3), 46–51.

ECLAC (2003). Handbook for Estimating the Socio-economic and Environmental Effects of Disasters. Economic Commission for Latin America and the Caribbean (ECLAC), p. 357. Available at http://www.preventionweb.net/ files/1099_eclachandbook.pdf.

Fomby, T, Y Ikeda and N Loayza (2009). The Growth Aftermath of Natural Disasters. World Bank, Washington, DC. p. 55. Available at http://documen ts.worldbank.org/curated/en/2009/07/10832714/growth-aftermath-natural-disasters.

Freeman, AM (2003). *The Measurement of Environmental and Resource Values: Theory and Methods*. Washington, DC: Resources for the Future. ISBN: 1891853635, 1891853627.

GRIP (2016). Disaster Databases. Available at http://www.gripweb.org/grip web/?q=disaster-database. Accessed on 7 April 2016.

Guha-Sapir, D, R Below and P Hoyoi (2016). EM-DAT: The CRED/OFDA International Disaster Database. Université catholique de Louvain (UCL), Brussels, Belgium. Available at www.emdat.be.

Guha-Sapir, D and P Hoyois (2012). Measuring the Human and Economic Impact of Disasters. CRED, University of Louvain School of Medicine, Commissioned by Foresight, London, UK. p. 48. Available at http://www.bis.gov.uk/assets/foresight/docs/reducing-risk-management/supporting-evidence/12-1295-measuring-human-economic-impact-disasters.pdf.

Guha-Sapir, D, P Hoyois and R Below (2013). Annual Disaster Statistical Review 2012: The numbers and trends. CRED, Brussels, Belgium. p. 42. Available at http://www.cred.be/sites/default/files/ADSR_2012.pdf.

Hallegatte, S and V Przyluski (2010). The economics of natural disasters: concepts and methods. *World Bank Policy Research Working Paper Series* (5507).

Howe, CW and HC Cochrane (1993). Guidelines for the uniform definition, identification, and measurement of economic damages from natural hazard events: With comments on historical assets, human capital, and natural capital. Institute of Behavioral Science, University of Colorado, USA. p. 20. Available at http://scholarcommons.usf.edu/fmhi_pub/64.

IMF (2013). World Economic and Financial Surveys — World Economic Outlook Database 2013. Available at https://www.imf.org/external/pubs/ft/weo/2013/01/weodata/index.aspx. Accessed 10 March 2014.

Integrated Research on Disaster Risk (2015). Guidelines on Measuring Losses from Disasters: Human and Economic Impact Indicators (IRDR DATA Publication No. 2). Integrated Research on Disaster Risk, Beijing, China. p. 23. Available at http://www.irdrinternational.org/wp-content/uploads/2015/03/DATA-Project-Report-No.-2-WEB-7MB.pdf.

Integrated Research on Disaster Risk (2014). Peril Classification and Hazard Glossary (IRDR DATA Publication No. 1). Integrated Research on Disaster Risk (IRDR), Beijing, China. p. 24. Available at http://www.irdrinternational.org/wp-content/uploads/2014/04/IRDR_DATA-Project-Report-No.-1.pdf.

IPCC (2012). Managing the Risks of Extreme Events and Disasters to Advance Climate Change Adaptation. A Special Report of Working Groups I and II of the Intergovernmental Panel on Climate Change. Cambridge University Press, Cambridge, UK, and New York, NY, USA. p. 582. Available at https://www.ipcc.ch/pdf/special-reports/srex/SREX_Full_Report.pdf.

Lindell, M and C Prater (2003). Assessing community impacts of natural disasters. *Natural Hazards Review*, 4(4), 176–185.

Morgan, MG and M Small (1992). *Uncertainty: A Guide to Dealing with Uncertainty in Quantitative Risk and Policy Analysis.* Cambridge University Press. ISBN: 0521427444.

Munich Re (2016). Munich Re — Touch Natural Hazards. Available at https://www.munichre.com/touch/naturalhazards/en/homepage/index.html. Accessed 7 April 2016.

National Research Council (1999). *The Impacts of Natural Disasters: A Framework for Loss Estimation.* The National Academies Press. ISBN: 97803090 75107.

National Research Council (2006). *Facing Hazards and Disasters: Understanding Human Dimensions.* The National Academies Press. ISBN: 9780309101783.

Neumayer, E and F Barthel (2011). Normalizing economic loss from natural disasters: A global analysis. *Global Environmental Change*, 21(1), 13–24.

Noy, I (2009). The macroeconomic consequences of disasters. *Journal of Development Economics*, 88(2), 221–231.

OECD (2012). Mortality Risk Valuation in Environment, Health and Transport Policies. OECD Publishing, p. 139. Available at http://dx.doi.org/10.1787/9789264130807-en.

Pearce, D, G Atkinson and S Mourato (2006). *Cost-Benefit Analysis and the Environment*. OECD, Paris. ISBN: 92-64-01004-1.

Pearce, D, E Özdemiroglu, I Bateman, RT Carson, B Day, M Hanemann, N Hanley, T Hett, M Jones-Lee, G Loomes, S Mourato, R Sugden and J Swanson (2002). Economic Valuation with Stated Preference Techniques — Summary Guide. Department for Transport, Local Government and the Regions (DTLR), London, UK.

Rose, A (2004). Economic Principles, Issues, and Research Priorities in Hazard Loss Estimation. In *Modeling Spatial and Economic Impacts of Disasters*, Okuyama, Y and S Chang (eds.), pp. 13–36. Berlin, Heidelberg: Springer. Available at http://dx.doi.org/10.1007/978-3-540-24787-6_2.

Toya, H and M Skidmore (2007). Economic development and the impacts of natural disasters. *Economics Letters*, 94(1), 20–25.

Tschoegl, L, R Below and D Guha-Sapir (2006). An Analytical Review of Selected Data Sets on Natural Disasters and Impacts. UNDP/CRED Workshop on Improving Compilation of Reliable Data on Disaster Occurrence and Impact. CRED, Brussels, Belgium, Bangkok, Thailand. p. 21. Available at http://www.pacificdisaster.net/pdnadmin/data/original/undp_cred_analytical_review_data_06.pdf.

World Bank (2016). Data — Indicators. Available at http://data.worldbank.org/. Accessed 7 April 2016.

CHAPTER 4

AN ANALYSIS OF EXPOSURE RISK TO EXTREME EVENTS IN NATURE

Lopamudra Banerjee
Bennington College, USA

This chapter studies the common factors that determine people's susceptibility to extreme natural events, and explores how geographic hazards and social conditions determine the chance of disaster exposure. On analyzing datasets from Bangladesh, Indonesia, and Tanzania, the chapter finds that, while a household's chance of experiencing exposure depend on the type of hazard (viz., flood, drought, volcano and tsunami) and its level (viz., low to high), certain common social factors that determine the household's everyday living conditions (viz., occupational mode, household size, and regional poverty), also, determine its susceptibility in exceptional times of disasters.

1. INTRODUCTION

Economic analyses of disasters have traditionally focused either on assessing the exogenous impact of random shock generated by a violent natural event, or on analyzing the efficacies of *ex-ante* mitigation strategies and *ex-post* coping mechanisms in the chance event of a disaster.[1] An alternative approach to disaster analysis may be to examine the latent risk factors that are already always present in the natural physical environment of a population, and the risk factors that are endogenously generated by their everyday living

---

[1]The research on economic analyses of disasters is reviewed extensively in Cavallo and Noy (2010) and Kellenberg and Mobarak (2011).

circumstances. The latter approach is explored in the contemporary
writings of anthropologists, geographers and sociologists, and, of late,
has received the attention of international donor agencies.[2]

The present chapter is motivated by the latter approach. It
analyzes people's susceptibility to a natural extreme in a hazard-
prone region in terms of geographic conditions that exist naturally
in the region, and people's everyday material conditions given
their social, economic and demographic attributes.[3] The chapter
considers as its initial hypothesis the following statement: disaster
risk is "a function of both the physical event and the state of
human society" (Susman *et al.*, 1983, p. 263). It then empirically
examines this hypothesis by considering the disaster experiences of
populations of households located in Bangladesh, Indonesia, and
Tanzania. The three studied populations are rather dissimilar in
terms of their macroeconomic and social structural conditions, but
are similar in that all are located in disaster-prone regions. The
chapter examines this set by focusing on causation of disaster risks
in general, and, in particular, the common and universal influences
that may affect these geographically removed and socially diverse
populations.

The chapter, however, does not aim at a predictive analysis
of risk. Rather, it is a study in retrospect. The chapter analyzes
observational data on exposure levels realizing for households after
a disaster event, to infer about precursory (unobservable) risk borne
by households at the time of the event. In the process, the chapter
seeks the answers to the following two questions: (a) are the patterns
of association between disaster risk, natural hazard conditions,
and socioeconomic vulnerabilities of households generalizable across
different geographic regions (both within and across countries), or

---

[2]See, for example, Varley (1994), Cutter (1996), Tierney (1999), Wisner *et al.* (2004),
UNDP (2004), ODI (2005), UNISDR (2009), and IDB (2011).

[3]Wisner *et al.* (2004, p. 49), for example, notes that disaster risk is a "composite function
of the natural hazard and the number of people, characterized by their varying degrees
of vulnerability to that specific hazard, who occupy the space and time of exposure to
the hazard event." Similar approaches were also employed in Dilley (2005), Thomalla
et al. (2006) and Peduzzi *et al.* (2009).

are these associations specific to a spatial region? And, (b) are the patterns of association similar across different hazard types (e.g., flood, drought, volcanic, and tsunami hazards) and hazard levels (viz., low and high), or do they vary?

The notion of natural hazards employed for this analysis is adopted from earth scientists as "[the dangers that emerge from interactions of natural forces] extraneous to man" (Burton and Kates, 1964). These dangers are already always present at varying degrees in a geographic location (such as, coastlines, earthquake faults, arid zones, volcanic belts, and floodplains), either singly or in combinations (Whittow, 1979). They may lead to disasters of different severity, durations (decade, years, or months), and return periods (decadal cycles, season of the year, or time of day), entailing severe and widespread losses for the exposed population (Wisner *et al.*, 2004).

The notion of vulnerability employed in this chapter refers to the dangers that emanate from social circumstances of population members (Varley, 1994; Wisner *et al.*, 2004). These circumstances determine a household's access to resources (material and non-material), which, in turn, determine the household's capacity to anticipate, cope with, resist and recover from the adverse conditions generated by a disaster event (Hewitt, 1997). Vulnerability conditions are, therefore, recursive. They arise from any deficit in a household's capacities to deal with a crisis situation. These deficits in capacities arise from deficits in the household's resource access. Resource deficits, in turn, are a matter of the household's prevailing socioeconomic attributes, prominent among which are its expenditure capacity and wealth ownership, education and occupation of the household head, and their gender and age (Ravallion, 2000).

In this chapter, the hazard and vulnerability aspects of disaster risk are examined in terms of an empirical model that associates the probability of disaster exposure for a household with its different existing attributes. Geographic and locational attributes are considered to capture the hazard conditions, and socioeconomic and demographic attributes are invoked to capture the vulnerability conditions. The analysis proceeds in the following manner: In

Section 2, a binary response model is considered to capture the relationship between (unobservable) risk, (observable) exposure, and the conditions of hazard and vulnerability existing for households. Section 3 presents the datasets from Bangladesh, Indonesia, and Tanzania. Section 4 describes the estimation techniques. Section 5 presents the estimation results. In Section 6, the main conclusions of the chapter are presented. In Appendix A, the key variables are described, and in Appendix B the details of the empirical model are described.

2. A MODEL OF DISASTER RISK

Recall, the main premise of this chapter is: the potential risk of exposure in the event of a disaster for a member of a population is a function of the prevailing hazard conditions in the natural physical environment, and the vulnerabilities generated by social circumstances. Risk of exposure to a disaster event is obviously higher for those households that are located in a hazardous region, than households that are not. But, not all households in the hazardous region are equally likely to experience exposure if and when a violent natural event occurs. Households with greater access to resources are less vulnerable, and more likely to avoid exposure.

This association between prior material conditions and predisposition to disaster exposure has been well documented in the cases of hurricane Katrina in USA (Masozera *et al.*, 2007; Price, 2008), Asian tsunami in Sri Lanka (Munasinghe, 2007; Ruwanpura, 2008), and hurricane Mitch in Nicaragua (van den Berg, 2010).

Nevertheless, several aspects of this association have remained unexplored. For instance, one may wish to know which of the various influences that generate the disproportionately higher risk are more potent for the poor and the marginalized. Important still, are the influences that are relevant for a particular society and a particular region, also relevant for other societies and other regions?

To explore these issues, the present paper shifts its focus away from the study of any specific disaster event. Instead, it examines the general circumstances of households located in various geographic regions (within and across a country), and encountering an array of hazard and vulnerability conditions.

While the recognition that disaster risk is a composite hazard and vulnerability factors has been with us for some times now, formal estimation of this risk from observational data is challenging, as, precursory risk is not observable. One way to address this problem is to generate the data on subjective perception of risk for respondents. Another way is to infer about *prior* risks from *posterior* knowledge of exposure. The present paper explores the latter approach.

The chapter assumes that precursory risk is a composite of hazard and vulnerability factors, and proposes a structural model of this risk as

$$R_i^* = \alpha' A_i + u_i, \tag{1}$$

where R_i^* is the level of (unobservable) risk borne by each household i; α is a (K × 1) vector of unknown parameters; A_i is a (K × 1) vector of geographic and socioeconomic attributes of i, determining, respectively, its hazard and vulnerability conditions, and $u_i \sim \mathrm{N}(0, \sigma^2)$. The term $\alpha' A_i$ in (1) may be interpreted as a linear composite of various risk-generating factors that are present for household i. Precursory risk of disaster is present for household i if $R_i^* > 0$, i.e., if $u_i > -\alpha' A_i$. Risk is absent for the household if $R_i^* \leq 0$, i.e., if $u_i \leq -\alpha' A_i$. $R_i^* \leq 0$ indicates a condition of "resilience" for the household that enables it to avoid the negative effects (or losses) generated by a violent environmental phenomenon, while $R_i^* > 0$ indicates the household's inability to do so.

Given (1), the level of (unobservable) risk borne by each household i is determinable, if information on its attributes, A_i, are available, and if relative contributions of these attributes can be assessed. With empirical estimation of equation (1), the parameters of the process that generates R_i^* would be known.

Now, while R_i^* may not be observable *prior* to a disaster event, whether or not a household i is exposed to the disaster event can readily be observed *posterior* to the event. Based on the premise that exposure indicates realization of certain latent risk conditions for households, the paper obtains a binary indicator of exposure, X_i, observed for each household i. Let X_i be determined by R_i^*, and let $1(\bullet)$ be an indicator function with $1(b) = 1$ if b is true and 0 otherwise. The paper assumes that

$$X_i = 1(R_i^* > 0). \tag{2}$$

The probability of $X_i = 1$ (i.e., exposure) given the set of attributes A_i of household i can be derived as

$$\Pr(X_i = 1|A_i) = \Pr(\alpha'A_i + u_i > 0|A_i) = \Theta\left(\frac{\alpha'A_i}{\sigma}\right) \tag{3}$$

and the probability of $X_i = 0$ (i.e., non-exposure) as

$$Pr(X_i = 0|A_i) = 1 - \Theta\left(\frac{\alpha'A_i}{\sigma}\right). \tag{3'}$$

In equations (3) and (3'), "Pr" is the probability operator, and Θ is the cumulative standard normal distribution function, $\Theta(\alpha'A_i) \in [0, 1]$. Therefore, the probability on the observed data on disaster exposure is

$$\prod_{i=1}^{r} \Theta\left(\frac{\alpha'A_i}{\sigma}\right) \bullet \prod_{r+1}^{N} \left[1 - \Theta\left(\frac{\alpha'A_i}{\sigma}\right)\right] \tag{3''}$$

when r out of N households experienced exposure, while $(N - r)$ did not.

The expected value of X_i, $E(X_i|A_i)$, indicates the level of disaster exposure that is normally likely for a household given its geographic, socioeconomic, and demographic attributes, which, concomitantly, determine its precursory risk. Accordingly, the coefficients α may have the following two interpretations: On one hand, α capture the change (after normalization) in the level of risk borne by the household as a consequence of a change in a variable included in A_i [invoking equation (1)]; on the other hand, α capture the change (after transformation with Θ) in the probability of exposure brought about by a change in a variable included in A_i [invoking

Equation (3)].[4] We can get an asymptotically efficient estimate of α by using the well-known probit-normalization by σ (van de Ven and van Praag, 1981), and maximizing the likelihood function (3''). The signs of the estimated coefficients indicate the effects of risk factors on response probability $\Pr(X_i = 1|A_i)$ [see equation (3)].

3. DATA

To empirically estimate risk, the chapter draws upon three household datasets from Bangladesh, Indonesia, and Tanzania. According to the World Risk Report (2012), Bangladesh ranks fifth amongst the countries of the world in terms of a national-level disaster risk ranking, and Indonesia and Tanzania respectively ranks thirty-third and fifty-seventh. Of the three countries, Bangladesh ranks highest in terms of the relative hazard proneness at the national-level, followed by Indonesia and Tanzania. Tanzania, in contrast, ranks highest in terms of national-level vulnerability level, followed by Bangladesh and Indonesia.[5]

The present chapter examines the distribution of disaster risk for the nationals of these countries at the micro-level. For Bangladesh, it draws upon the survey dataset that was collected by International Food Policy Research Institute (henceforth, IFPRI, 1998–1999, first round) after the 1998 extreme floods in the country. For Indonesia, the paper draws upon the Family Life Survey (henceforth, IFLS, 2009, fourth round) dataset, and for Tanzania, it draws upon the National Panel Survey (henceforth, TZNPS, 2010–2011, second round) dataset. IFLS (2009) documents household exposure to any flood, volcanic, or tsunami events that occurred in Indonesia in the last five years at the time of survey, and TZNPS (2010–2011) documents exposures to any floods and drought event in Tanzania in the past five years at the time of survey. The number of households

---

[4]However, since the observational data is on X_i, and not on R_i^*, the effects of this change on risk can be estimated only up to a factor of proportionality. The complete bivariate probit model with sample selection is described in Appendix B of the chapter.
[5]In the World Risk Report (2012), disaster vulnerability level of a country is determined in terms of its aggregated macro-level socioeconomic indicators.

surveyed in the IFPRI dataset is 757, IFLS dataset is 13535, and in the TZNPS dataset is 3923.

Together with the information on disaster exposure, each of these three survey datasets presents detailed information on geographic locations, socioeconomic and demographic attributes of the surveyed households. The present chapter exploits these information to examine the hazard and vulnerability factors at the household-level.

Given the datasets, four categories of hazards are examined in this chapter: floods (in Bangladesh, Indonesia and Tanzania), drought (in Tanzania), volcanic activities (in Indonesia), and tsunami (in Indonesia).

To study the hazard level present for each household in each datasets, the chapter merges the survey datasets with regional-level geographic data obtained from other sources. For the region-level geographic data for Bangladesh, the chapter draws upon the district-wise geomorphologic and flood hazard data from Bangladesh Ministry of Irrigation (1986). This data classifies districts of Bangladesh as "more" and "less" flood-prone. For Indonesia, the paper draws upon the region-level geographic data from OCHA (2011) and CHRR (2005a). These datasets classify provinces of Indonesia in terms of their relative "hazard rank." The rank ordering are given separately for each type of hazard (flood, volcanic and tsunami) present in a province. For Tanzania, the paper draws upon region-level geographic data from WHO (2010) and CHRR (2005b). These datasets classifies regions of Tanzania in terms of their relative "hazard rank." The rank ordering are given separately for flood hazards and drought hazards.

The information on a household's location from each household survey dataset is then matched with the information on relative hazard-proneness of that location from the geographic dataset. For Bangladesh, the flood hazard level present for a household is identified in terms of its location in a "more" or a "less" flood-prone district. For Indonesia, tsunami hazard is similarly identified in terms of household's location in a "tsunami-prone" or a "not tsunami-prone" province. For flood and volcanic hazards in Indonesia, and for flood and drought hazards in Tanzania, the relative level of hazard present for a household is identified on the basis of "hazard rank" of the region, the ranking being in a scale of 0 to 3, with "0" indicating the hazard is "absent" and 3 indicating the hazard level is "extremely high." Additionally, an indicator variable is included in the analysis to identify of whether or not the region actually experienced exposure to a disaster event.

To identify the vulnerability-generating attributes of households, the chapter invokes antecedents in literature. In particular, it follows the analysis presented in Ravallion (2000) in context of Bangladesh and Indonesia, and in Atkinson and Lugo (2010) in context of Tanzania, and considers the following set of household attributes: age, gender, education and occupation of household head; size, consumption expenditure quintile and wealth quintile of household; and household location in rural (vis-à-vis urban) area, and household location in a "poor" (vis-à-vis "non poor") area.[6]

While the household-specific variables indicate a household's command over resources that enable them to avoid and/or cope with any fluctuations in their living conditions during crises, the region-specific variables indicate the conditions that a household shares with other households in the neighborhood. The latter aspect of disaster risk would be present for all members of a population in the region, irrespective of their individual socioeconomic status.

The count data on exposed and non-exposed households in each datasets are presented in Table A.1 in Appendix A. Summary statistics of vulnerability indicators for the exposed and non-exposed households are presented in Table A.2; and the information on hazards and regional chronic poverty is presented in Table A.3 in Appendix A.

4. ESTIMATION

In assessing unobservable risk from observational data on exposure, the chapter, however, encounters an annoying problem. In each

---

[6] "Male", "no education" and "unpaid family workers" are held as control variables, respectively, for gender, education and occupation categories.

dataset, values of X_i are missing for some of the respondents. The missing data poses the following problem for the present analysis: the outcome model of exposure [in Equation (3)] is linked to the structural model of risk [in Equation (1)], on the assumption that if risk is present, then exposure is observed. However, if no exposure is recorded (either because exposure was not observed, or because the respondents were not tracked), then it cannot be automatically assumed that no risk is present.

In particular, a household may not be exposed to disaster conditions if the neighborhood was, fortuitously, relatively unaffected during a particular episode of a natural extreme. Accordingly, the survey data collected in aftermath of the event would record "not exposed" for the household. Yet, risk may exist for the household if hazard and vulnerability conditions are present. In this case, the observational data on disaster exposure may under-represent the risk bearing households, and coefficient estimates of the analytical model derived from the censored data may be biased.

To address this issue, we assess probability of exposure for households in a region exposed to a disaster event. At the same time, to ensure that the conclusions derived are valid for the entire population, and not just the subpopulation for whom exposure is recorded in the survey datasets, the paper incorporates a sample selection criterion in the model. Towards this, it employs the well-known methodology suggested in Maddala (1983) and later adapted in Greene (1998) in the following manner:

We consider separately the following two exposure variables,

$X_i = 1$ if household i experiences disaster exposure, 0 otherwise,

$\xi_i = 1$ if the region (where i inhabits) experiences disaster exposure, 0 otherwise, and estimates the bivariate probit model with sample selection

$$\Pr(X_i = 1, \xi_i = 1 | A_i, B_i) = \tilde{\Theta}(\alpha' A_i, \beta' B_i, \rho), \qquad (4)$$

where, "Pr" is the probability operator and $\tilde{\Theta}$ is the bivariate cumulative standard normal distribution function. Equation (4) models probability of household disaster exposure in a region exposed to a disaster event given the vectors of household-level risk factors A_i, and regional-level risk factors B_i. α_i and β_i are vectors of unknown parameters, and ρ captures the correlation between the unexplained aspects of household exposure (that are not account for by A_i) and the unexplained aspects of regional exposure (that are not account for by B_i). The complete model is described in Appendix B.

Elements of A_i are hazard and vulnerability variables for a household (described earlier in Section 3 of the paper). Elements of B_i are the following region-level variables: category and level of hazard present in the region; regional poverty and population density; and a binary indicator of whether or not the region experienced repeated occurrences of natural extremes in the recent past.[7]

The aforementioned regional variables are considered for the following reasons: A region may not be exposed to disaster conditions if certain "buffering" factors exist (Varley, 1994). These buffering factors include adequate infrastructural barriers and adequate emergency preparedness to anticipate and cope with impending threat of a disaster.[8] The buffering factors act as public goods or as "collective" resources shared by all households inhabiting the region. Earlier studies have shown that deficits in these resources are more likely in regions of endemic poverty and regions of high population density. "Poor" regions typically have poor disaster infrastructures, while "populous" regions often have insufficient emergency preparedness and inadequate information dissemination systems to cover for all households (Oliver-Smith, 1996). Moreover, in regions where disaster infrastructures and emergency preparedness were initially adequate, repeated occurrences of natural extremes may overwhelm the structures and arrangements, thereby increasing the chance of a breach during a next round of events (UNISDR, 2009).

---

[7]The household-level and regional-level variables are chosen after tests of multiple exclusion restrictions that are run to rule out any model specification errors.

[8]The infrastructural barriers may include dams and embankments to protect against floods; water reservoirs and irrigation canals to protect against droughts; and land use planning and zoning designs to protect against flooding, volcanic activities and tsunami (UNDP, 2004; IDB, 2011). The emergency preparedness plans may include disaster forecast and early warning systems (ibid).

By controlling for region-level variables, the chapter controls for the common factors that determine disaster exposure for all households in a region. In so doing, it aims to ensure that (a) any differences detected between the exposed and non-exposed households in a region are due to substantive reasons, and not due to data censoring, and (b) any effects on exposure can be attributed to the underlying household-level risk factors, and not to the household-selection factors. In this manner, the paper attempts to associate observed exposure to (unobservable) risks.

Information on the region-level variables are collected from various sources. The data on regional poverty (before disaster) for Bangladesh is obtained from the original IFPRI dataset, for Indonesia is obtained from Pradhan (2000), and for Tanzania is obtained from Mkenda *et al.* (2004) and PHDR (2005). The data on regional population density and regional frequency of disaster events for Bangladesh are obtained from DRR (1999). For Indonesia, the data on regional population density is from CDES (2010), and that on regional frequency of disaster events is from BNPB (various years). For Tanzania, the data on regional population density is from NBS (2013), and that on regional frequency of disaster events is from the TRCNS (2009).

The chapter obtains maximum likelihood estimates (MLE, with sample selection correction) of the coefficients in the probit model [in Equation (4)]. It considers a battery of other test statistics, to examine the goodness of fit of the model. The test results are presented in Table A.4 in Appendix A. The marginal effects of hazard types (viz., flood, drought, volcanic, and tsunami hazards) and levels (viz., low to high) on probability of exposure for a household are examined by holding the vulnerability factors at their expected (mean) levels (the so-called Marginal Effects at the Means (MEMS) derived from the model with selection). Further, the expected marginal effects of each type of hazard and their levels on chance of exposure at the regional-level are examined by averaging the effects across all households inhabiting in the region (the so-called Average Marginal Effects (AMES) derived from the selection model). The derivation methods of the marginal effects are described in Appendix B.

5. RESULTS

Table 1 presents the coefficient estimates of the binary response model [Equation (4)] on household risk conditions in Bangladesh, Indonesia, and Tanzania.

From Table 1, certain common themes emerge regarding the vulnerability aspect of disaster risk. First, risk is significantly lower for a household if the household head is a service holder (either in the public sector or in the private sector), if the household size is smaller, and if the household is located in a non-poor region. These results are valid for all three datasets, irrespective of a household's geographic location. Second, risk is lower for households belonging to higher expenditure or wealth strata. In particular, for Bangladesh, access to wealth (captured in terms of landownership) has a statistically significant negative influence on risk. Third, risk is lower for households headed by a male member, and when the household head has some formal education rather than being uneducated. Coefficient estimates of gender and education of household head are, however, not statistically significant in any of the three datasets studied.

From Table 1, certain differences are also observed in the effects of vulnerability factors on risk. While it has been found elsewhere in the literature that households located in rural areas are more susceptible to disaster exposure (see, for example, Oliver-Smith, 1996), the evidences from the present analyses are mixed. For Bangladesh, risk is higher for a rural household than an urban household; for Indonesia and Tanzania, risk is higher for an urban household than a rural household.

Mixed evidences are also found regarding certain other variables. For example, when the household is headed by relatively an older member, risk is lowered for households in Bangladesh and Indonesia, but raised for households in Tanzania. Also, if the household headed by an agricultural worker, risk is lowered for households in Bangladesh and Indonesia; but raised for households in Tanzania; and, if it is headed by a non-agricultural (casual) worker, risk is lowered for households in Indonesia, but raised for households

Table 1:   Probit Estimates of Hazard and Vulnerability Indicators of Disaster Risk[1,2]

Explanatory Variables	Bangladesh	Indonesia	Tanzania
Household-level exposure			
Probability of household exposure is explained in terms of household-level risk factors (A_i).[†]			
Attributes of household head: Age	−0.0012	−0.0529	0.0051
	(0.0083)	(0.0068)	(0.0037)
Gender (female)	0.6191	0.7090	0.2084
	(0.4699)	(0.2155)	(0.1307)
Education: Primary	−0.1557	−0.2599	−0.0894
	(0.2236)	(0.2357)	(0.1289)
Secondary	−0.1725	−0.3508	−0.1266
	(0.2773)	(0.2944)	(0.2742)
Post Secondary	−0.3556	−0.3989	−0.1720
	(0.6755)	(0.3108)	(0.3591)
Occupation: Self-employed, without employee	0.1885	0.1143	0.1155
	(0.4907)	(0.2961)	(0.3217)
Self-employed, with household members as employees	0.2743	0.3678	n.a.
	(0.5375)	(0.2468)	
Self-employed, with hired employee	−0.8008	−0.2912	−0.3929
	(0.7142)	(0.2276)	(0.5586)
Service in (public or private sector)	**−0.5102**	**−0.5619**	**−1.4798**
	(0.1478)	**(0.6895)**	**(0.3916)**
Agricultural (casual) worker	−0.5474	−0.5618	0.2771
	(0.7281)	(0.6895)	(0.2332)
Non-agricultural (casual) worker	0.1549	−0.0699	n.a.
	(0.4646)	(0.3402)	
Attributes of household: Size	**0.1492**	**0.0529**	**0.0518**
	(0.0521)	**(0.0267)**	**(0.0190)**
Expenditure quintile	−0.0179	−0.0769	−0.0295
	(0.0362)	(0.0880)	(0.1131)
Wealth quintile	**−0.8965**	−0.4253	−0.0635
	(0.1803)	(0.1767)	(0.0572)
Household location: Rural region	0.1198	−0.4729	−0.0928
	(0.3323)	(0.1750)	(0.1521)
Poor region	**0.6307**	**(0.0537)**	**0.0788**
	(0.2265)	**(0.0173)**	**(0.0102)**
Hazard categories: Flood	**0.5308**	**0.4564**	**0.5140**
	(0.2107)	**(0.1173)**	**(0.0727)**

(Continued)

Table 1: *(Continued)*

Explanatory Variables	Bangladesh	Indonesia	Tanzania
Drought	n.a.	n.a.	0.0826
			(0.0613)
Volcano	n.a.	0.1993	n.a.
		(0.1149)	
Tsunami	n.a.	0.3368	n.a.
		(0.0739)	
Region-level exposure	**0.5144**	**0.3094**	**(0.2499)**
	(0.0641)	**(0.1416)**	**(0.1218)**
Constant of regression	(−0.0243)	**(−7.2025)**	−0.3311
	(0.6214)	**(1.0435)**	(0.4607)

Region-level exposure equation
Probability of regional exposure is explained in terms of region-level
risk factors (B_i).[†]

Hazards: Flood	**0.5471**	**0.7936**	**0.5140**
	(0.2022)	**(0.1381)**	**(0.0727)**
Drought	n.a.	n.a.	0.0730
			(0.0667)
Volcano	n.a.	0.3031	n.a.
		(0.2491)	
Tsunami	n.a.	**0.6060**	n.a.
		(0.1739)	
Rural region	0.0142	−0.8333	−0.0728
	(0.1033)	(0.3041)	(0.1021)
Poor region	**0.5007**	**(0.0737)**	**0.0611**
	(0.1267)	**(0.0190)**	**(0.0100)**
Population density of region	0.1885	0.2482	0.1758
	(0.4907)	(0.6154)	(0.5465)
Region frequently experienced	0.1492	0.1974	0.0860
extreme events in past five years	(0.0521)	(0.0675)	(0.0041)
Pseudo R-squared	0.2857	0.5326	0.3085
Log-likelihood value	−363.65	−603.061	−978.58
ρ	0.114	0.211	0.070

Notes: [1]Standard errors are in parenthesis. Coefficient estimates are in bold if $P > |z|$.
[2]"No education" and "unpaid family workers" are held as the control dummies for the
education and occupation categories of the household head.
[†]See Appendix B for details of the model.
n.a.: The data is not sufficient to estimate the effect of this variable.

in Bangladesh.[9] None of these coefficient estimates are, however, statistically significant.

Several results on the hazard aspect of disaster risk that are common across the three datasets are also observed from Table 1. Once the effects of vulnerability factors are controlled for, risks, unsurprisingly, increase with the increase in the level of hazard present in a region. Not all types of hazards, however, have equal effects on disaster risk. Flood and tsunami hazards, apparently, are more potent than volcanic or drought hazards. In particular, households inhabiting in a flood-prone region invariably bear higher risks than households that do not, irrespective of the country of its location.

As a final point, Table 1 shows that a primary determinant of probable disaster exposure for a household is the region's exposure to a disaster event. Probability of exposure for a region, in turn, is significantly higher if the region is poor. This result is obtained after controlling for the hazard conditions in the region. Evidently, disaster-buffer mechanisms are weaker in resource-deprived locations, and there exists an overlap between asymmetries in resource distribution generated by social structural conditions and that of regional distribution of disaster risks.

To analyze the role of hazard factors more closely, marginal effects of different categories and levels of hazard on disaster risk are examined in Table 2 and Table 3 (after controlling for the vulnerability factors). Panel I of the tables presents Marginal Effects at the Means (MEMS) at the household-level, while Panel II presents Average Marginal Effects (AMES) at the regional-level.

The key results in Table 2 are the following: Of the different hazard types, presence of flood hazard wields the greatest effect (at the margin) on disaster risk borne by a household. This result is observed no matter the household's country of location. MEMS of flood hazard indicate that when all other hazard and vulnerability factors are held at their expected levels, the predicted chance

---

[9]The data for Tanzania is not sufficient to estimate the effect of this variable.

Table 2: **Marginal Effects of Hazard Types on Disaster Risk**[1,2,3]

Type of Hazard	Bangladesh	Indonesia	Tanzania
Panel I: Marginal Effects at the Means (MEMS) of Hazard Types at the Household-level			
Flood	0.3461	0.1422	0.1965
	(0.0321)	(0.0865)	(0.0451)
Drought	n.a.	n.a.	0.0321
			(0.0590)
Volcano	n.a.	0.0154	n.a.
		(0.0744)	
Tsunami	n.a.	0.1021	n.a.
		(0.0041)	
Panel II: Average Marginal Effects (AMEs) of Hazard Types at the Regional-level			
Flood	0.3316	0.1254	0.1700
	(0.0116)	(0.0632)	(0.0321)
Drought	n.a.	n.a.	0.0229
			(0.0432)
Volcano	n.a.	0.0201	n.a.
		(0.0533)	
Tsunami	n.a.	0.0823	n.a.
		(0.0067)	

Notes: [1] Standard errors are in parenthesis.
[2] The Marginal Effects at the Means (MEMS) of hazard types at the household-level are computed from the bivariate probit model with selection [given by Equation (4)], by setting the vulnerability indicators with continuous values at their mean levels, and vulnerability indicators with discrete values at their given levels. The Average Marginal Effects (AMEs) of hazard types at the regional-level are computed from the selection model [see Appendix C]. For each type of hazard, the marginal effects are calculated for all households experiencing that type of hazard (irrespective of hazard level).
[3] The marginal effects are derived after controlling for the household-level risk factors (A_i), and region-level risk factors (B_i).

of exposure for a household in Bangladesh increases by almost 35 percent if it is located in a "more" flood-prone region rather than a "less" flood-prone region. This predicted chance increases by almost 15 percent for a household in Indonesia, and by almost 20 percent for a household in Tanzania, if the household is located in a "flood-prone" region rather than a "not flood-prone" region. Presence of tsunami hazard also wields a substantial, though lesser in magnitude, effect on probability of exposure. Presences of drought and volcanic hazards have comparatively smaller, though positive, marginal effects, with volcanic hazards wielding the lowest marginal effect amongst all hazard types.

Table 3:   **Marginal Effects of Hazard Levels on Disaster Risk**[1,2,3,4]

Level of Hazard	Bangladesh	Indonesia	Tanzania
Panel I: Marginal Effects at the Means (MEMS) of Hazard Levels at the Household-level			
Level 1	0.3461	0.1967	0.2111
	(0.0321)	(0.0416)	(0.0175)
Level 2	n.a.	0.3438	0.2987
		(0.0097)	(0.0654)
Level 3	n.a.	0.5921	0.4462
		(0.0052)	(0.0491)
Panel II: Average Marginal Effects (AMEs) of Hazard Levels at the Regional-level			
Level 1	0.3316	0.1833	0.2031
	(0.0116)	(0.0666)	(0.0185)
Level 2	n.a.	0.3145	0.2791
		(0.0127)	(0.0711)
Level 3	n.a.	0.5600	0.4358
		(0.0102)	(0.0601)

Notes: [1]Standard errors are in parenthesis.
[2]The Marginal Effects at the Means (MEMS) of hazard levels are computed at household-level from the bivariate probit model with selection [given by Equation (4)] by setting the vulnerability indicators with continuous values at their mean levels, and vulnerability indicators with discrete values at their given levels. The Average Marginal Effects (AMEs) of hazard levels are computed at the regional-level from the selection model [see Appendix C]. At each level of hazard, the marginal effects are calculated for all households experiencing that level of hazard (irrespective of hazard type).
[3]The marginal effects are derived after controlling for the household-level risk factors (A_i), and region-level risk factors (B_i).
[4]Flood hazard level dummy in Bangladesh = 0 if hazard level is "less", = 1 if hazard level is "more"; tsunami hazard level dummy in Indonesia = 0 if hazard is "absent", = 1 if hazard is "present"; indicator variable for flood hazard level in Indonesia and Tanzania, volcanic hazard level in Indonesia, and drought hazard level in Tanzania = 0 if hazard is "absent", = 1 if hazard is "moderate", = 2 if hazard is "high", = 3 if hazard is "extremely high."

The results on AMES of hazards at the regional-level reconfirm the general pattern of results on MEMS of hazards at the household-level. The average level of risk is significantly higher in a region prone to flooding than a region that is not. If multiple hazards are present in a region, the risk generated on account of flood hazards are greater than that generated on account of other hazards.

The results from Table 3 indicate that increases in hazard levels monotonically increase the risk levels for households and for regions. The result is valid for all categories of hazards, and across all the studied countries. The results on MEMS of hazard levels can be interpreted in the following manner: For two hypothetical households in Indonesia, both being average in terms of the values of all other risk factors, but one located in a region of "extremely high" hazard (i.e., Level 3) and the other in a region where hazard is least or absent (i.e., Level 0), the predicated chance of exposure for the former household is higher by almost 60 percent than the latter. In Tanzania, this chance is higher by almost 45 percent for the household located in a region of "extremely high" hazard (i.e., Level 3) than the household located in a region of least or no hazard (i.e., Level 0). The results on marginal effects of hazard levels at the household-level (i.e., MEMS) are reinforced by the results on marginal effects of hazard levels at the regional-levels (i.e., AMES).

6. CONCLUSIONS

The analyses in this chapter focused on hazard and vulnerability conditions of households across various geographic regions to examine the latent factors that generate disaster risks. Two findings are particularly noteworthy in this regard. First, while disaster risks are higher when higher levels of hazards are present in a household's habitat, certain categories of hazards (viz., flood and tsunami hazards) entail greater risks than others (viz., drought or volcanic hazards). Second, while the chance of experiencing disaster conditions is obviously greater for households if the region is afflicted by a natural extreme, probability of exposure is lower for households that have relatively secured prior access to resources under normal conditions (i.e., in absence of disasters).

One implication of the first result is that, apparently, it is easier to lower the probability of exposure when droughts or volcanic eruptions occur, than when floods and tsunamis occur. There can be multiple explanations for this result. Anecdotal evidences suggest that investment of private resources and public resources may generate more effective buffers for droughts and volcanic hazards, than for flood or tsunami hazards.[10] Thus, regional risks may higher in flood-prone and tsunami-prone areas, than in drought-prone or volcanic activity-prone areas. Also, population concentrations tend to be higher in floodplains and coastal areas (including the areas where tsunami hazards are present), thus making relocation to safer grounds harder in the case of flooding and tsunami occurrences (Wisner *et al.*, 2004).

Regardless of the level and type of hazard present, the second result indicates that certain attributes of households, which ordinarily determine their access to resources under normal conditions, play an important role in determining their resilience under exceptional conditions of disasters. Occupation of the household head is significant in this regard. Presumably, households that have relatively stable livelihood conditions and relatively steady flow of income have greater material ability to cope with the adverse situations generated by a disaster event. Thus, these households have greater chances of avoiding losses and bear lower risks. Risks are also lower for households with smaller members. Smaller household sizes entail, on one hand, lower consumption expenditures and greater access to ready savings to tide over a period of crisis, and, on

---

[10]Investment of public resources to deploy buffers may entail construction and maintenance of irrigational canals to mitigate the effects of drought and floods, that of embankments and dams to control floods, and that of roads public transport systems to facilitate evacuations in the case of volcanic eruptions and tsunami. Investment of private resources may entail installation of pump and well irrigation systems to cope with drought, access to vehicles to assist evacuation in the case of volcanic eruptions, and so forth. For extensive discussions on the role of "buffering" factors, see UNDP (2004) and Thomalla *et al.* (2006).

the other, greater mobility for the family when the crisis situation arises.[11] Thus, these households have greater ability to remove themselves from a potentially dangerous situation. Furthermore, risks are lower for households located in relatively prosperous regions. These households have greater access to private resources, and may also have greater collective access to public resources, and benefit from better provisioning of public goods (e.g., disaster prevention, warning and rescue systems), which they share with other households in the neighborhood.

In a divided society, where resource entitlements are conditional upon social and economic statuses of households, any deficits in the social and economic determinants of a household's material conditions under ordinary circumstances additionally constrains the household's ability to obtain private goods, and weaken its claim over public goods, in a emergency situation.[12] These deficits generate the latent vulnerability conditions for the households, which are brought into surface when a violent environmental event occurs. The results in this chapter, obtained in context of three rather (socially and economically) dissimilar countries of Bangladesh, Indonesia and Tanzania, universally, highlight this phenomenon. They indicate that risk of disaster is neither exogenous nor indiscriminate. Rather, disaster risk can be associated with prior deterministic conditions that are already always generated through the functionings and organization of a social system, long before a violent event occurs in nature.

---

[11]The relationship between household size and resource access is explored in detail in Lanjouw and Ravallion (1995).

[12]Of particular relevance in this regard is the seminal work of Sen (1981), and that of later commentators (especially, Osmani (2000) and Devereux (2001)), that established how the effects of crises (in particular, famines) realize in presence of entitlement failures.

APPENDIX A

DESCRIPTION OF KEY HAZARD AND VULNERABILITY VARIABLES

Table A.1:   Count Data on Exposed and Non-exposed Households, Bangladesh, Indonesia, Tanzania

	Exposed		Non-exposed		Total
	Freq.	%	Freq.	%	(100%)
Bangladesh	363	49.66	368	50.34	731
Indonesia	337	94.09	5,361	5.91	5,698
Tanzania	674	21.36	2,481	78.64	3,155

Table A.2:   Summary Statistics: Selected Vulnerability Indicators, Exposed and Non-exposed Households, Bangladesh, Indonesia, Tanzania

	Vulnerability Indicators	Min	Max	Mean	Std. Dev.
Panel I: Exposed Households					
Bangladesh	Household head, age (in years)	18	90	45.16	12.07
	Education (in years)	0	13	2.52	3.74
	Household, expenditure (in Taka)	874	28,955	4,527	3,162
Indonesia	Household head, age (in years)	28	87	54.79	13.49
	Education (in years)	0	7	4.64	2.77
	Household, expenditure (in Indonesian rupiah)	17,000	414,000,000	5,409,826	32,800,000
Tanzania	Household head, age (in years)	21	105	49.80	15.83

(Continued)

106

Table A.2: *(Continued)*

Vulnerability Indicators	Min	Max	Mean	Std. Dev.
Education (in years)	1	5	1.80	0.63
Household, expenditure (in Tanzanian shilling)	2,800	2,153,100	215,613	252,943

Panel II: Non-exposed Households

Bangladesh	Household head, age (in years)	0	90	44.90	13.07
	Education (in years)	0	13	2.64	3.65
	Household, expenditure (in Taka)	387	31,320	4,385	3,685
Indonesia	Household head, age (in years)	18	100	53.30	12.43
	Education (in years)	0	7	4.38	2.88
	Household, expenditure (in Indonesian rupiah)	3,000	1,110,000,000	4,095,200	31,400,000
Tanzania	Household head, age (in years)	16	99	45.62	15.54
	Education (in years)	1	5	2.05	0.78
	Household, expenditure (in Tanzanian shilling)	1,200	83,900,000	406,645.9	1,855,487

Table A.3: Hazard Type and Levels, and Chronic Poverty, by Regions, Bangladesh, Indonesia, and Tanzania[1,2,3]

Thana	District	Region	Relative Poverty of *Thana*	Relative Flood-Proneness of Region
Panel I. Flood Hazards and Chronic Poverty, by Regions (*Thana*, district, region), Bangladesh				
Derai	Sunamganj	Sylhet	Poor	More
Madaripur	Madaripur	Dhaka	Poor	More
Mohammadpur	Magura	Khulna	Poor	Less
Muladi	Barisal	Barisal	Not poor	Less
Shahrasti	Chandpur	Chittagong	Not poor	Less
Saturia	Manikganj	Dhaka	Poor	More
Shibpur	Narsingdi	Dhaka	Not poor	More

(Continued)

Table A.3:   *(Continued)*

Province	Poverty Headcount (1999)	"Hazard Rank", Flood Hazard	"Hazard Rank", Volcanic Hazard	"Hazard Rank", Tsunami Hazard
Panel II. "Hazard Rank" (Flood, Volcanic and Tsunami Hazards) and Chronic Poverty (Head Count Ratio), by Regions (Province), Indonesia				
N. Aceh	12.89	1	1	1
North Sumatera	15.27	0	2	1
West Sumatera	9.47	2	1	1
Riau	9.21	0	3	0
South Sumatera	23.81	2	2	0
Lampung	36.8	1	2	1
Bangka Belitung	23.81	0	1	0
Jakarta	2.82	0	3	0
West Java	26.6	3	3	1
Central Java	32.78	3	3	1
DI Yogyakarta	26.95	3	3	1
East Java	33.31	3	3	1
Banten	26.6	3	3	1
Bali	13.62	3	1	1
West Nusa Tenggara	41.78	2	1	1
West Kalimantan	30.76	0	1	0
Central Kalimantan	11.15	0	0	1
South Kalimantan	20.64	0	0	1
East Kalimantan	21.67	0	0	1
North Sulawesi	22.47	1	1	1
South Sulawesi	22.63	0	1	1

Region	Poverty Headcount (2004)	Level of Hazard Present, Drought Hazard	Level of Hazard Present, Flood Hazard
Panel III. "Hazard Rank" (Drought and Flood Hazards) and Chronic Poverty (Head Count Ratio), by regions (Region), Tanzania			
Dodoma	35.3	3	2
Arusha	32.5	1	3
Kilimanjaro	26.5	1	2
Tanga	17.6	1	3
Morogoro	23.3	3	1
Pwani	20.8	1	1

(Continued)

Table A.3: (*Continued*)

Region	Poverty Headcount (2004)	Level of Hazard Present, Drought Hazard	Level of Hazard Present, Flood Hazard

Panel III. "Hazard Rank" (Drought and Flood Hazards) and Chronic Poverty (Head Count Ratio), by regions (Region), Tanzania

Region	Poverty Headcount (2004)	Drought	Flood
Dar es Salaam	17.5	1	2
Lindi	27.1	0	0
Mtwara	19.6	2	1
Ruvuma	30.2	2	0
Iringa	31.7	2	1
Mbeya	16.4	1	1
Singida	33.8	1	1
Tabora	12.1	1	1
Rukwa	22.1	1	0
Kigoma	24.7	2	1
Shinyanga	30	1	1
Kagera	24.6	0	1
Mwanza	22.5	0	2
Mara	26.7	0	2

Notes: [1] For Bangladesh, information on regional poverty is from IFPRI (first round, 1998–1999), and regional flood-proneness is from Bangladesh Ministry of Irrigation (1986).
[2] For Indonesia, information on regional poverty is from Pradhan (2000), and regional hazard-proneness is from OCHA (2011) and CHRR (2005). Hazard level of "0" indicate absence of hazard, and those of "1", "2", "3" indicate progressively higher levels, with "3" indicating the highest level.
[3] For Tanzania, information on regional poverty is from Mkenda *et al.*, (2004) and PHDR (2005), and regional hazard-proneness is from WHO (2010) and CHRR (2005). Hazard level of "0" indicate absence of hazard, and those of "1", "2", "3" indicate progressively higher levels, with "3" indicating the highest level.

Table A.4: Test Results on Goodness of Fit of the Bivariate Probit Model

	Bangladesh	Indonesia	Tanzania
Log-Likelihood Intercept Only	−397.741	−1254.378	−998.061
Log-Likelihood Full Model	−363.058	−603.061	−978.582
McFadden's R2	0.087	0.519	0.058
McFadden's Adj R2	0.022	0.497	0.039
AIC:	1.356	0.229	1.191
BIC:	−2755.125	−46007.970	−11254.234

APPENDIX B

COMPLETE BIVARIATE PROBIT MODEL WITH SAMPLE SELECTION

The main concern here is with the analysis of unobservable risk based on the observed data on disaster exposure. The analysis assumes that exposure observed *after* an event indicates presence of risk *prior* to the event. How compelling is this assumption? Can there be situations when risk is present, but exposure is not observed? The disconnection between risk and exposure is likely to occur if the set of explanatory factors for risk do not include all the explanatory factors for exposure. To rule this out, the paper adopts the methods prescribed in Maddala (1983) and Greene (1998) to probit analysis. The model explicitly formalizes the risk borne by households, and implicitly considers a model of region-level disaster risk. It then considers correlated disturbances between these two risks for a household to ensure an overlap between the risk factors and exposure factors.

There are four key variables in the complete model:

R_i^* = disaster risk present for i,
S_i^* = disaster risk present for the region where i inhabits,
X_i = binary indicator of disaster exposure for household i,
ξ_i = binary indicator of disaster exposure for the region where i inhabits.

X_i and ξ_i are the two variables that we can observe, and are determined by the unobserved risks R_i^* and S_i^*.

The complete model is formalized in terms of the following set of equations:

$$R_i^* = \alpha' A_i + u_i = \alpha'_H H_i + \alpha'_V V_i + u_i$$

[structural model of household risk]

If $R_i^* > 0$ then $X_i = 1$, if $R_i^* \leq 0$ then $X_i = 0$;

[outcome model of household exposure]

$$S_i^* = \beta' B_i + v_i;$$ [structural model of regional risk]

If $S_i^* > 0$ then $\xi_i = 1$, if $S_i^* \leq 0$ then $\xi_i = 0$;

[outcome model of regional exposure]

$$E(u_i|A_i, B_i) = E(v_i|A_i, B_i) = 0;$$
$$Var(u_i|A_i, B_i) = Var(v_i|A_i, B_i) = 1;$$
$$Cov(u_i, v_i|A_i, B_i) = \rho. \tag{I}$$

In (I), α_H, α_V and β are vectors of unknown parameters; A_i is a vector of all observed regressor variables for R_i^*, and includes hazard factors, H_i, and vulnerability factors, V_i, for household i; B_i in turn, is a vector of all observed regressor variables for S_i^*. u_i in (I) captures other determinates of R_i^* not included in A_i, and v_i captures all other determinates of S_i^* not included in B_i. Let the correlation coefficient between u_i and v_i be $Corr(u_i,v_i)$. If $Corr(u_i,v_i) = 0$ (i.e., $\rho = 0$), the terms do not contain any common omitted variables; if $Corr(u_i, v_i) \neq 0$ (i.e., $\rho \neq 0$) they do. Note, the structural model of household risk and outcome model of household exposure in (I) were, respectively, presented as Equations (1) and (3) in Section 2 of the paper.

Let the bivariate normal cumulative distribution function of disaster exposure be

$$\Pr(X < x, \xi < \xi) = \int_{-\infty}^{x} \int_{-\infty}^{\xi} \tilde{\Theta}(x', \xi', \rho) dx' d\xi' = \tilde{\Theta}(x, \xi, \rho).$$

Now, the data on exposure variables are generated by the following rule:

$X_i = 1$ if household i experiences disaster exposure, 0 otherwise;

$\xi_i = 1$ if the region where household i inhabits experiences disaster exposure, 0 otherwise.

On examining the survey datasets, the paper finds three types of observation on exposure: $\xi_i = 0$, $X_i = 0$; $\xi_i = 1$, $X_i = 0$; and $\xi_i = 1$, $X_i = 1$.

The unconditional probabilities associated with each type of observation are

$$\xi_i = 0 \qquad \Pr(\xi_i = 0 | A_i, B_i) = 1 - \tilde{\Theta}(\beta' B_i)$$

$$X_i = 0, \ \xi_i = 1 \quad \Pr(X_i = 0, \xi_i = 1 | A_i, B_i) = \tilde{\Theta}(-\alpha' A_i, \beta' B_i, -\rho)$$

$$X_i = 1, \ \xi_i = 1 \quad \Pr(X_i = 1, \xi_i = 1 | A_i, B_i) = \tilde{\Theta}(\alpha' A_i, \beta' B_i, \rho).$$

Thus, there are two situations in which no exposure is recorded for a household i: (i) when the region (where household i inhabits) was, fortuitously, not exposed to any disaster event in the period covered by the survey (i.e., $\xi_i = 0$, $X_i = 0$), and (ii) when the region was exposed to one or multiple disaster events, but household i experienced no exposure (i.e., $\xi_i = 1$, $X_i = 0$).

In situation (i), risk may be present for the household (i.e., R_i^*) if hazard and vulnerability conditions are present, even though exposure is not observed. In this case, is a disconnection between precursory risk and observed exposure. In situation (ii), there is no such disconnection.

To separate out the observations for which (i) is valid from those for which (ii) is valid, and to ensure that the empirical estimation of the analytical model [given by (I)] is not afflicted by sampling bias, the paper incorporates a sample selection criterion to assess disaster risk from exposure data. Accordingly, it focuses on households experiencing disaster exposure in regions exposed to disaster conditions, and examines the role of risk-generating factors in determining the likelihood of exposure for these households, in terms of the following bivariate probit with sample selection:

$$\Pr(X_i = 1, \xi_i = 1 | A_i, B_i)$$

$$= \Pr(X_i = 1 | \xi_i = 1, A_i, B_i) \Pr(\xi_i = 1 | A_i, B_i)$$

$$= \Pr(X_i = 1 | \xi_i = 1, A_i) \Pr(\xi_i = 1 | B_i) = \tilde{\Theta}(\alpha' A_i, \beta' B_i, \rho)$$

$$= \tilde{\Theta}(\alpha'_H H_i + \alpha'_V V_i + \gamma \xi_i, \beta' B_i, \rho).$$

Note, the above probit was formalized in Equation (4) in Section 4 of the paper. Here γ is a unknown scalar parameter that captures the effects of sample selection criterion on the outcome equation of household exposure, given the structural equation on household risk. The explanatory variables in the probit are listed below:

Household-level risk factors (A_i):

Hazard variables (H_i): flood hazard (relevant for Bangladesh, Indonesia and Tanzania), drought hazard (relevant for Tanzania), volcanic hazard (relevant for Indonesia), and tsunami hazard (relevant for Indonesia).

> For Bangladesh, flood hazard dummy = 0 if hazard level is "less", = 1 if hazard level is "more"; for Indonesia, tsunami hazard dummy = 0 if hazard is "absent", = 1 if hazard is "present"; for Indonesia, flood hazard categorical variable = 0 if hazard is "absent", = 1 if hazard is "moderate", = 2 if hazard is "high", = 3 if hazard is "extremely high"; for Indonesia, volcano hazard categorical variable = 0 if hazard is "absent", = 1 if hazard is "moderate", = 2 if hazard is "high", = 3 if hazard is "extremely high"; for Tanzania, drought hazard categorical variable = 0 if hazard is "absent", = 1 if hazard is "moderate", = 2 if hazard is "high", = 3 if hazard is "extremely high"; for Tanzania, flood hazard categorical variable = 0 if hazard is "absent", = 1 if hazard is "moderate", = 2 if hazard is "high", = 3 if hazard is "extremely high."

Vulnerability variables (V_i):

Attributes of household head: age, gender of household head (= 0 if male, = 1 if female); education (indicated by a categorical variable with value = 0 if no education, = 1 if completed primary education, = 2 if completed secondary education, = 3 if undertaking/completed post secondary education); occupation of household head (indicated by six dummy variables, each for one occupational categories: Self-employed without employee, self-employed with household members as employees, self-employed with hired employee, service in (public or private sector), agricultural (casual) worker, non-agricultural (casual) worker, with "unpaid family workers" held as the control); Attributes of household: Size; consumption expenditure quintile; wealth quintile; rural location dummy (= 0 if located in urban area, = 1 if located in rural area); regional poverty dummy (= 0 if located in "non poor" region, = 1 if located in "poor" region.

Region-level risk factors (B_i):

> Categories and levels of hazard present in the region; regional poverty dummy; regional population density; dummy indicating region frequently affected by natural extremes in recent past ($= 0$ if no; $= 1$ if yes).

DERIVATION OF MARGINAL EFFECTS OF HAZARD CATEGORIES AND LEVELS ON DISASTER RISK

The marginal effects of a hazard on a household's risk and chance of exposure realize through two channels: First, there is a direct effect produced by its presence in the structural model of household risk; second, there is an indirect effect produced by its presence in the structural model of regional risk (see I).

Now, the conditional expectation of household exposure is

$$E(X_i|A_i, B_i) = E(X_i|\xi_i = 1, A_i, B_i)\text{Pr}(\xi_i = 1)$$
$$+ E(X_i|\xi_i = 0, A_i, B_i)\text{Pr}(\xi_i = 0)$$
$$\times \tilde{\Theta}(\alpha'_H H_i + \alpha'_V V_i + \gamma\xi_i, \beta' B_i, \rho) + [1 - \tilde{\Theta}(\beta' B_i)].$$

For hazard category dummies (viz., flood, drought, volcano and tsunami) and hazard level dummies (viz., flood hazard level in Bangladesh, and tsunami hazard level in Indonesia), the conditional mean function is computed by setting the explanatory variable to one and then to zero, with all other explanatory variables held at their mean value. The marginal effects are then obtained by taking the difference. For hazard level categorical variables (viz., drought hazard level in Tanzania, flood hazard levels in Indonesia and Tanzania, volcano hazard level in Indonesia), the marginal effects are obtained by taking the differentials of conditional expectation function. In all cases, standard errors of the estimated marginal effects are computed by using the delta method.

To compute the average marginal effects of a hazard on regional risk and chance of exposure, a marginal effect is computed at the household-level, and then all the computed effects are averaged for each region.

ACKNOWLEDGEMENTS

This chapter has extensively drawn upon the information on disaster profile for Bangladesh, Tanzania, and Indonesia generated by the Center For Hazards & Risk Research at Columbia University, and on the following household survey datasets — the Bangladesh household dataset (November 1998–December 1999) collected by the International Food Policy Research Institute (IFPRI), the Tanzania National Panel Survey dataset (2010–2011, Wave 2) collected by the National Bureau of Statistics (of the Ministry of Finance) of Tanzania, and the Indonesia Family Life Survey dataset (2007, fourth wave) collected by the RAND institute. I thank these institutions. I also thank the Bangladesh Institute of Development Studies (BIDS) for allowing me the use of the longitudinal data on hydro-meteorological conditions across various regions of Bangladesh and the cross-sectional data on 1998 flood severity in the country. I thank Joshua Greenstein for his support at various stages of research on this paper, and Duncan Foley for his numerous comments and suggestions that benefitted my study. I am indebted to Snehashish Bhattacharya for his comments and insights.

REFERENCES

Atkinson, AB and Lugo, MA (2010). Growth, poverty and distribution in Tanzania. Working Paper 10/0831, International Growth Centre (IGC), London School of Economics and Political Science.

Bangladesh Ministry of Irrigation, (1986). National Water Plan (Vol. I), Sector analysis (Vol. II), Resources (Vol. III), Alternative Plans; and Summary Reports, Government of Bangladesh, Dhaka.

BNPB (various years). National Agency for Disaster Management (BNPB), Indonesia. Available at http://www.bnpb.go.id/

Burton, I and RW Kates (1964). The perception of natural hazards in resource management. *Natural Resources Journal*, III(3), 412–441.

Cavallo, E and I Noy (2010). The economics of natural disasters: A Survey, IDB Working Paper Series, IDP-WP-124. Inter-American Development Bank (IDB).

CDES (2010). Indonesia Country Profile 2010 Center for Data and Epidemiological Surveillance (CDES). Ministry of Health, Indonesia.

CHRR (2005b). Tanzania Natural Disaster Profile, Center For Hazards and Risk Research (CHRR) at Columbia University. Available at http://www.ldeo.columbia.edu/chrr/research/profiles/pdfs/tanzania_profile.pdf.

CHRR (2005a). Indonesia Natural Disaster Profile, Center For Hazards and Risk Research (CHRR) at Columbia University. URL: http://www.ldgo.columbia.edu/chrr/research/profiles/indonesia.html

Cutter, SL (1996). Vulnerability to environmental hazards. Progress in Human Geography, 20, 529–539.

Devereux, SN (2001). Sen's entitlement approach: Critiques and counter-critiques, *Oxford Development Studies*, 29(3), 245–263.

Dilley, M, Chen, RS, Deichmann, U, Lerner-Lam, AL, Arnold, M, Agwe, J, Buys, P, Kjekstad, O, Lyon, B and Yetman, G (2005). Natural disaster hotspots: A global risk analysis. Washington DC: International Bank for Reconstruction and Development/The World Bank and Columbia University.

DRR (1999). Department of Relief and Rehabilitation (DRR). Ministry of Food and Disaster Management (MoFDM) of Bangladesh. Available at http://www.drr.gov.bd/index.php.

Greene, WH (1998). Gender economics courses in liberal arts colleges: Further results. The *Journal of Economic Education*, 29(4), 291–300.

IDB (2011). Indicators for Disaster Risk and Risk Management: Programme for Latin-America and The Caribbean: Belize. Technical Notes No. IDB-TN-276, Inter-American Development Bank (IDB). Available at http://www.iadb.org.

IFLS (2009). The Indonesian Family Life Survey (IFLS-4), RAND. The Center for Population and Policy Studies (CPPS) of the University of Gadjah Mada and Survey METRE.

IFPRI (1998–1999). Study on Household Coping Strategies after 1998 Flood in Bangladesh (1998–1999), International Food Policy Research Institute (IFPRI), Dhaka Office.

Kellenberg, D and AM Mobarak (2011). The economics of natural disasters. *Annual Review of Resource Economics*, 3(1), 297–312.

Lanjouw, P and M Ravallion (1995). Poverty and household size. *The Economic Journal*, 1415–1434.

Maddala, GS (1983). *Limited-dependent and Qualitative variables in econometrics* (No. 3). New York: Cambridge University Press.

Masozera, M, M Bailey and C Kerchner (2007). Distribution of impacts of natural disasters across income groups: A case study of New Orleans. *Ecological Economics*, 63(2), 299–306.

Mkenda, AF, EG Luvanda, L Rutasitara and A Naho (2004). Poverty in Tanzania: Comparisons across Administrative Regions. Interim Report for the Government of Tanzania. Poverty and Economic Policy Network, Dakar.

Munasinghe, M (2007). The importance of social capital: Comparing the impacts of the 2004 Asian Tsunami on Sri Lanka, and Hurricane Katrina 2005 on New Orleans. *Ecological Economics*, 64(1), 9–11.

NBS (2013). 2012 Population and Housing Census. Population Distribution by Administrative Areas. National Bureau of Statistics and Office of Chief Government Statistician, Dar es Salaam and Zanzibar.

OCHA (2011). Indonesia: Natural Hazard Risks, Map document OCHA_ROAP_Hazards_v4_110606 (Issued: 01 March 2011), Office for the Coordination of Humanitarian Affairs (OCHA), Regional Office for Asia-Pacific, United Nations.

ODI (2005). Aftershocks: Natural disaster risk and economic development policy. ODI Briefing Paper (November 2005), Overseas Development Institute (ODI), London.

Oliver-Smith, A (1996). Anthropological research on hazards and disasters. *Annual Review of Anthropology*, 25, 303–328.

Osmani, SR (2000). The Entitlement Approach to Famine: An Assessment. In K. Basu, P. K. Pattanaik and K. Suzumura (eds), Choice, Welfare and Development: Festschrift in Honor of Amartya Sen, Oxford University Press, New Delhi, 253–294.

Peduzzi, P, H Dao, C Herold and F Mouton (2009). Assessing global exposure and vulnerability towards natural hazards: The Disaster Risk Index. Natural Hazards and Earth System Science, 9(4), 1149–1159.

PHDR (2005). Poverty at the district level in mainland Tanzania, The Poverty and Human Development Report (PHDR) 2005, The Poverty Eradication Division, Ministry of Planning, Economy and Empowerment, Dar es Salaam.

Pradhan, M, A Suryahadi, S Sumarto and L Pritchett (2000). Measurements of Poverty in Indonesia: 1996, 1999, and Beyond. SMERU Working Paper, Social Monitoring and Early Response unit (SMERU), World Bank, East Asia and Pacific Region, Environment and Social Development Sector Unit, 2000.

Price, GN (2008). Hurricane Katrina: Was there a political economy of death? *Review of Black Political Economy*, 35, 163–180.

Ravallion, M (2000). Household vulnerability to aggregate shocks: Differing fortunes of the poor in Bangladesh and Indonesia. In *Choice, Welfare and Development: Festschrift in Honor of Amartya Sen*, Basu, K, PK Pattanaik and K Suzumura (Eds.), 295–312. New Delhi: Oxford University Press.

Ruwanpura, KN (2008). Temporality of disasters: The politics of women's livelihoods 'after' the 2004 tsunami in Sri Lanka. *Singapore Journal of Tropical Geography*, 29(3), 325–340.

Sen, A (1981). *Poverty and Famines: An Essay on Entitlement and Deprivation.* Oxford University Press.

Susman, P, O'Keefe, P and Wisner, B (1983). Global disasters, a radical interpretation. In K. Hewitt (ed), Interpretations of Calamity: From the Viewpoint of Human Ecology, George Allen and Unwin (Publishers) Ltd., 263–383.

Thomalla, F, T Downing, E Spanger-Siegfried, G Han and J Rockström (2006). Reducing hazard vulnerability: Towards a common approach between disaster risk reduction and climate adaptation. *Disasters*, 30(1), 39–48.

Tierney, KJ (2007). From the margins to the mainstream? Disaster research at the crossroads. *Annual Review of Sociology*, 33, 503–525.

TRCNS (2009). Executive Summary, Disaster preparedness and response plan 2009–2010. Tanzania, The Tanzania Red Cross National Society (TRCNS).

TZNPS (2010–2011). The Tanzania National Panel Survey (TZNPS-2), Tanzania National Bureau of Statistics (NBS). Ministry of Finance, Dar es Salaam.

UNDP (2004). Reducing disaster risk a challenge for development, UNDP Global Report, Bureau for Crisis Prevention and Recovery, United Nations Development Programme (UNDP), New York.

UNISDR (2009). UNISDR Terminology on disaster risk reduction (May 2009). United Nations International Strategy for Disaster Reduction (UNISDR), Geneva.

Van de Ven, WP and B Van Praag (1981). The demand for deductibles in private health insurance: A probit model with sample selection. *Journal of Econometrics*, 17(2), 229–252.

Van den Berg, M (2010). Household income strategies and natural disasters: Dynamic livelihoods in rural Nicaragua. *Ecological Economics*, 69(3), 592–602.

Varley, A (1994). The exceptional and the everyday: Vulnerability analysis in the international decade for natural disaster reduction. In *Disasters, Development and Environment*, New York. John Wiley. Varley, A (ed.), 1–11.

Whittow, J (1979). *Disasters: The Anatomy of Environmental Hazards*. Athens: University of Georgia Press.

WHO (2010). United Republic of Tanzania: Flood Hazard Distribution Map, Emergency & Humanitarian Action in the African Region, World Health Organization (WHO). Available at http://www.who-eatlas.org/africa/ images/map/united-republic-of-tanzania/tza-flood.pdf

Wisner, B, P Blaikie, T Cannon and I Davis (2004). *At Risk: Natural Hazards, People's Vulnerability and Disasters*, Routledge.

World Risk Report (2012). Alliance Development Works (Bündnis Entwicklung Hilft) in collaboration with the UN University Institute for Environment and Human Security (UNU-EHS) and The Nature Conservancy. Available at www.worldriskreport.com/uploads/media/WRR_2012_en_online.pdf.

CHAPTER 5

AFTER THE THRILL IS GONE: IMPACT ANALYSIS OF THE 1995 KOBE EARTHQUAKE AND ITS RECONSTRUCTION

Yasuhide Okuyama
University of Kitakyushu, Japan

In January 1995, the Kobe earthquake occurred in the second largest economic region of Japan, and its economic damages were estimated around 10 trillion yen. This chapter investigates the economic effects from the event, based on the empirical data using the econometric technique and structural analysis method. The results indicate that the event had created statistically significant deviations from the pre-earthquake growth path of Kobe. In addition, the damages from the earthquake and subsequent reconstruction activities led to significant structural changes in the regional economy, which further affected Kobe's long-run growth trend. These results are elucidated with the reconstruction plans implemented by the City of Kobe and the Hyogo Prefecture.

1. INTRODUCTION

Natural hazards, such as earthquakes, severe storms, flooding, and so forth, and their consequences, namely disasters, have had significant and intense effects not only on the areas hit by such events, but also the surrounding and/or economically connected regions. The recent catastrophic events, such as the 2004 Indian Ocean Earthquake and Tsunami, the 2005 Hurricane Katrina in the United States, the 2011 Tohoku Earthquake and Tsunami in Japan, and the 2011 Great

Flooding in Thailand, remind us how serious and devastating the impact of a severe natural hazard can be to the modern society and/or country (or even countries).

While significant progress has been made in recent years in economic analysis of disasters, especially in the field of economic modeling for disaster impact (for example, Okuyama, 2007 and Okuyama and Santos, 2014; and an excellent compilation of related papers by Kunreuther and Rose, 2004), recent advancements have been more toward short-run impact analysis to estimate the cost of a particular event with strategies for modeling extensions and modifications to fit them to disaster situations, rather than toward evaluation of long-run effect of such events. This tendency of emphasis on short-run impact analysis is mainly due to the increased demand in such estimate for recovery and reconstruction strategies, finance and also improved data availability of disaster damages and losses (Okuyama and Santos, 2014). At the same time, the uniqueness of each natural hazard and the intensity and distribution of its damages and losses present enormous challenges to economic analysis of disaster impact and effect. In particular, while some research suggests that the impact of a catastrophic natural hazard may spread over not only to the surrounding regions but also to the distant regions via tightened interdependency of economic activities (for example, Okuyama *et al.*, 1999 and Okuyama, 2010), some other researchers claimed that the impact of even a large disaster ends up having "insignificant total impacts" (Albala-Bertrand, 1993).

Empirical ex-post investigations of long-run impact and effect of disasters have been limited. Most of those ex-post studies estimated, not measured, the short-run impacts of a particular disaster based on the available damage data and some economic models, like input-output models and so on (see Okuyama, 2007 for other modeling frameworks). The dearth of research on the long-run effect of a disaster may be due to the fact that it is cumbersome to extract disaster impact and effect from empirically available macroeconomic data. This is because in macroeconomic indicators, such as gross domestic products (GDPs) or gross regional products (GRPs), economic impacts of a particular disaster can be potentially hidden within macroeconomic fluctuations and are more likely cancelled out between negative impacts from damages and positive impacts of recovery and reconstruction activities. Also, disaster statistics are not standardized even among developed countries (Okuyama and Chang, 2012) and come with "somewhat crude measures" (Skidmore and Toya, 2002). Of all these difficulties, empirical measurement of long-run effects of disasters is crucial not only to investigate how intensely a natural hazard and rapid reconstruction activities can affect economies, but also to understand how this type of event influences the growth path of a region.

In this chapter, impacts of the 1995 the Great Hanshin-Awaji Earthquake (also known as the Kobe earthquake) are investigated empirically, based on time-series data with the econometric technique and input-output tables with the structural decomposition method. Section 2 briefly summarizes previous studies and findings related to the economic impact and effect of disasters. Section 3 presents the econometric analysis of the disaster effects on the Kobe economy. Structural analyses of the Kobe economy after the event are analyzed and discussed in Section 4. Section 5 concludes the findings along with Kobe's reconstruction plans.

2. ECONOMIC IMPACTS OF DISASTERS

The economic impact and effect of disasters has been studied in various contexts over a range of time periods. Ex-ante analysis of a hypothetical or potential hazard occurrence is often carried out for the decision-making of preparedness and mitigation strategies; and ex-post analysis of actual hazards and disasters is usually carried out to investigate how the event affected the economy and to examine to what extent the relief efforts by various levels of public sector and by other institutions are needed (Okuyama and Santos, 2014). Economic analysis of disasters can be divided into two categories: analyses of short-run impact and that of long-run effect. Short-run impact analysis of disaster intends to estimate the total (flow) impacts of a hazard for the duration of a few years, and typically employs an economic model, for example, the input-output model, social accounting matrix, or computable general equilibrium model of a particular region, regions, or a nation. By its nature, short-run impact analysis estimates only changes in flows (production levels) and is able to distinguish between the negative impacts of losses and the positive impacts of recovery and reconstruction activities, which serve as concentrated demand injections to the region, as well as between (first-order) losses and higher-order effects. On the other hand, long-run analysis of disaster effects aims to measure the effects of damages on stock, which may affect the long-run growth path of the damaged region that, resulted from the changes in the levels of physical and human capital accumulation and technology replacement (Okuyama, 2003). The long-run analysis of disasters usually employs econometric models with time series data; and because of this, it is not possible to distinguish between negative and positive impacts of a disaster and can derive only net effects. Compared to short-run impact analyses, long-run analyses of disasters have been limited, mainly due to the uniqueness of each disaster and also due to the difference in details and extent of damage data gathered over time (Okuyama and Santos, 2014). Notable examples of studies that used cross-country data to analyze the tendency among various indices of economic growth and disaster occurrences include Skidmore and Toya (2002), Rasmussen (2004), Cuaresma *et al.* (2008), and Cavallo *et al.* (2010). Interestingly, some of these studies provide conflicting or inconclusive results in terms of the relationship between economic growth and disasters. In particular, Cavallo *et al.* (2010) found that natural disasters focusing only on the largest events do not have any significant effect on subsequent economic growth. Meanwhile, empirical evaluation of a particular disaster's long-run effect has been also limited, for instance Odell and Weidenmier (2002) for the 1906 San Francisco earthquake, Hornbeck (2009) for the 1930's American Dust Bowl, and Baade *et al.* (2007) for the 1992 LA Riot and 1992 Hurricane Andrew among others. Few recent examples in this line of research include Coffman and Noy (2011) for the Hurricane Iniki in Hawaii, and Chang (2010), DuPont and Noy (2015), and Okuyama (2014) for the 1995 Kobe earthquake. In particular, DuPont and Noy (2015) analyzed the long-run trend of the Hyogo Prefecture, instead of the City of Kobe, using econometric models with the synthetic control methodology to extract the earthquake's effect from the macroeconomic indicators, such as GRP and local government expenditures. They found a persistent and continuing adverse impact of the event even after 15 years.

The conclusions of these studies support Albala-Bertrand's (2007) claim that a disaster causes localized damages and losses but may not affect the macro-economy negatively or positively, such as a national economy, either in short-run or longer-run. At the same time, this claim implies that localized damages and losses may cause localized economic impacts, which may be significant to the local economy hit by the disaster. This chapter investigates how the Kobe earthquake affected the regional economy in the long-run and the factors that gave rise to long-run effects.

3. ECONOMETRIC ANALYSIS OF THE KOBE EARTHQUAKE'S IMPACT[1]

The 1995 Kobe earthquake is employed as the case study for empirically evaluating its impact over time. In doing so, we construct a set of time-series models for the City of Kobe and the Hyogo Prefecture that includes Kobe.

3.1. *The 1995 Kobe Earthquake*

On January 17, 1995, a large earthquake (Hyogo-ken Nanbu Earthquake) struck the second largest region of Japan — the Kinki region. The City of Kobe and surrounding municipalities experienced a massive destruction of houses, buildings, roads, rails, and the overall infrastructure. The magnitude of this event can be shown with the following facts: according to the Hyogo Prefecture Government (2010), the number of casualties was 6,434; the number of injuries

---

[1]This section draws on Okuyama (2016).

was 43,792; the number of evacuees was 316,678 (at its peak); and the number of damaged houses was about 640,000. The direct damages from the Kobe earthquake were estimated at about 10 trillion yen (US$ 100 billion, as $1 = 100$ yen), equivalent to about 2.1% of Japan's GDP and 11% of Kinki's GRP (Gross Regional Product) at that time. These direct damages were concentrated around the destruction of buildings (including houses and production facilities), transportation facilities, and utilities. Although the damaged area amounted to only 4% of the geographical area of Kinki, it included 15% of the Kinki's population. The damages to capital stocks were estimated at about 0.8% of Japan's total stock (Okuyama *et al.*, 1999).

3.2. *Time-Series Econometric Analysis*

In order to gauge the total impact of the Kobe earthquake using the time-series data, a set of time-series models is constructed. The functional form of these models employs an autoregressive-distributed lag model (Hendry, 1995). This is because we are interested in the total impact of an exogenous shock (earthquake) on gross regional product (GRP), and also because we plan to determine the total impact as a deviation from the long-run growth path of an economy. The general form of the linear autoregressive-distributed lag model can be written as follows:

$$y_t = \beta_1 z_t + \beta_2 y_{t-1} + \beta_3 z_{t-1} + \varepsilon_t$$

where y_t is the dependent variable, z_t is the independent variable. In this formulation, z_t can be used to control exogenous and/or macroeconomic factors influencing the growth path of y_t. Any other miscellaneous influences to y_t will be captured by ε_t, as the residuals.

Based on this formulation, three models are constructed to gauge the total impact of the Kobe earthquake. The first model is for the City of Kobe where the earthquake struck and damaged most severely:

$$KOBE_t = \beta_0 + \beta_1 JPN_t + \beta_2 JPN_{t-1} + \beta_3 KOBE_{t-1} + \varepsilon_t \qquad (1)$$

where $KOBE_t$ is the logarithm of GRP per capita for the City of Kobe at t, JPN_t is the logarithm of GDP for Japan at t. JPN_t and its lagged variable intend to control the macroeconomic influences, such as the changes in inflation, interest rate, currency exchange rate, economic booms (bubble economy of mid and late 80's) and slumps (since early 90's), etc., of Japan. The second model is for the Hyogo Prefecture, which includes the City of Kobe and other cities and municipalities hit by the earthquake:

$$HYOGO_t = \beta_0 + \beta_1 JPN_t + \beta_2 JPN_{t-1} + \beta_3 HYOGO_{t-1} + \varepsilon_t \quad (2)$$

where $HYOGO_t$ is the logarithm of GRP per capita for the Hyogo Prefecture at t. As seen above, the basic structure of Equation (2) is exactly the same as the one in Equation (1). One of the assumptions here to use JPN_t and its lagged variable in the right hand side of Equations (1) and (2) is that the earthquake did not have an impact on the Japan's GDP per capita. If it did, the inclusion of JPN_t in the right hand side could lead to the violation of residual distribution assumptions, and the models require some countermeasures, like instrumental variable or others, for estimation. In order to test whether or not the earthquake impacted Japan's GDP, the third model is constructed:

$$JPN_t = \beta_0 + \beta_1 JPN_{t-1} + \varepsilon_t \quad (3)$$

This formulation constitutes a univariate time-series model, a variant of the above linear auto- regressive lag model.

In order to test the hypothesis that the earthquake has some impact on the respective long-run growth path, dummy variables for the year when the earthquake occurred and for the subsequent years are added to each model.

3.3. Data

The data used for this analysis was extracted from the Cabinet Office of Japan's web site.[2] The data used are "National Accounts"

---

[2]http://www.esri.cao.go.jp/jp/sna/toukei.html#kenmin (in Japanese).

for GDP, and "Prefectural Accounts" for GRPs. Since the Japanese government started collecting and releasing these statistics using the Systems of National Accounts (SNA) from 1975, the consistent time series data are also from 1975. Thus, the period of analysis is from 1975 to 2006. Note that all the data that the Japanese government publishes are the fiscal year base, and the Japanese fiscal year starts from April and ends in March of the next year. This implies that while the Kobe earthquake occurred in January 1995, it is within the fiscal year 1994.

All the data are converted to the 2000 constant price. Trends of three variables, *JPN*, *HYOGO*, and *KOBE*, are shown in Figure 1. Japan's GDP per capita had steadily increased throughout the period, while the rate of growth had slowed down a bit after 1990, when the bubble economy collapsed. It showed an increasing trend after 2002. Hyogo's GRP per capita is mostly lower than that of Japan's, and the rate of growth appears to be parallel to that of Japan's till 1993. The rate of GDP per capita growth in fiscal year 1994, when the Kobe earthquake occurred, shows a small dent, whereas in years 1995 and 1996 it shows sharp increases. At the

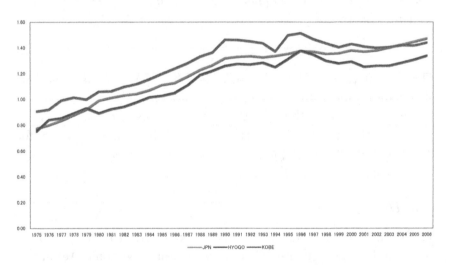

Figure 1:   Trends of Per Capita Gross Productions in Logarithm

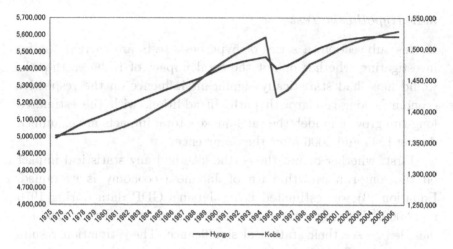

Figure 2: Population Trends of the Hyogo Prefecture and the City of Kobe (Right Vertical Axis for Kobe and Left Vertical Axis for Hyogo)

same time, after 1997, the GDP per capita downward trend Hyogo showed, until it showed an upward trend after 2004. Kobe's growth path mirrors that of Hyogo's, but the values are generally larger than that of Hyogo's and Japan's. The decline in the GDP per capita in 1994 for Kobe is much larger than that of Hyogo's, and the increase in 1995 is also higher. Unlike Hyogo's, Kobe's appears not to show an upward trend until 2006. This may have resulted partly from population changes in the City of Kobe after the earthquake. As displayed in Figure 2, after the sharp decline of its population in 1994, Kobe struggled to regain its population to the pre-earthquake level until 2002, and there has been increase in population since. On the other hand, the Hyogo Prefecture, including the City of Kobe, saw a decrease in population in 1994, but it was not as severe as Kobe's decline in terms of the rate of change. Hyogo regained its previous population level in 1998. However, after 2003, the population trend has shown a flat trend. In the following sub-sections, these trends are investigated in order to determine whether or not these observations are statistically significant.

3.4. Hypothesis Tests

In this sub-section, a series of hypothesis tests are carried out for investigating whether or not the total impact of Kobe earthquake would have had statistically significant influence on the respective economy's long-run growth path. In addition, with the estimated long-run growth model, the earthquake's total impacts are examined during 1995 and 2006 after the occurrence.

First, whether or not the earthquake had any statistical impact on the long-run growth path of Japanese economy is examined. Equation (3) was estimated using Japan's GDP data during 1976 and 2006.[3] Dummy variables for each year after fiscal year 1994 are included to see their statistical significance. The estimation results are shown in Table 1.

Table 1: Significance of the Earthquake Impact on GDP (JPN as Dependent Variable)

	Model 3-1 JPN	Model 3-2 JPN	Model 3-3 JPN	Model 3-4 JPN	Model 3-5 JPN
Constant	1.073*		1.165*	1.194*	1.307**
	(0.566)		(0.582)	(0.585)	(0.602)
JPN (t-1)	0.897***	1.002***	0.888***	0.885***	0.873***
	(0.056)	(0.002)	(0.057)	(0.058)	(0.059)
D94			0.095		0.105
			(0.120)		(0.121)
D95				0.106	0.116
				(0.121)	(0.122)
Number of observations	31	31	31	31	31
R-squared	0.90	0.90	0.90	0.90	0.90
BIC	−20.70	−20.61	−19.32	−19.40	−18.11

Standard error in parentheses.
* Significant at the 10% level.
** Significant at the 5% level.
*** Significant at the 1% level.

---

[3] 1975 data was lost due to the lag structure of the model. Thus, the number of sample for this and subsequent models becomes 31.

Models 3-1 and 3-2 do not include any time dummy variables. Model 3-1 includes the constant term, β_0 in Equation (3), and it is barely significant at 10% revel. While the values of R-squared for both models are nearly identical, the value of BIC for Model 3-1 is slightly better than that of 3-2's. Models with time dummy variables include the constant, indicating a moving average process. Models 3-3, 3-4, and 3-5 include time dummy variables in different ways.[4] Time dummy variables for the fiscal year 1994, when the earthquake occurred, and 1995, when the reconstruction activities were in full swing, are not statistically significant in any of three models. Also, the inclusion of these dummy variables does not improve either the value of R-squared or that of BIC. This is an indication that Kobe earthquake did not influence the long-run growth path of Japan. This also implies that the use of Japan's GDP as an independent variable to control macroeconomic influences in Equations (1) and (2) can be rationalized.

Secondly, we estimate the Equation (2) to test the statistical significance of the earthquake impact on the Hyogo's economy. The results are shown in Table 2.

The results of Models 2-1 and 2-2 illustrate no statistical significance of constant term; thus the following estimations with time variables do not include the constant term in their models. Estimations with time dummy variables display mixed results. The dummy variables for the fiscal year 1994 (when the earthquake occurred) and the following fiscal year, 1995, are not statistically significant with large margins, while the dummy variable for the fiscal year, almost two years after the earthquake is statistically significant at 10% level with a small and positive coefficient value. The value of BIC for the model with the 1996 dummy variable is marginally better than the one without time dummy variables.

---

[4] Time dummy variables after the fiscal year 1996 were also implemented and estimated, but they appeared not statistically significant at all, either included separately or any combined ways. Thus, the results for these cases are not included in this table. This tendency also found in the HYOGO and KOBE cases; therefore, the tables below do not include those results, either.

Table 2: **Significance of the Earthquake Impact on GRP (HYOGO as Dependent Variable)**

·	Model 2-1 HYOGO	Model 2-2 HYOGO	Model 2-3 HYOGO	Model 2-4 HYOGO	Model 2-5 HYOGO
Constant	0.065				
	(0.044)				
JPN	0.602*	0.894***	0.856***	0.911***	0.907***
	(0.316)	(0.250)	(0.250)	(0.244)	(0.239)
JPN (t-1)	−0.354	−0.668**	−0.651**	−0.698**	−0.650**
	(0.335)	(0.263)	(0.261)	(0.256)	(0.251)
HYOGO (t-1)	0.686***	0.760***	0.783***	0.772***	0.725***
	(0.140)	(0.133)	(0.133)	(0.130)	(0.128)
D94			−0.037		
			(0.031)		
D95				0.048	
				(0.030)	
D96					0.057*
					(0.030)
Number of observations	31	31	31	31	31
R-squared	0.97	0.97	0.97	0.98	0.98
BIC	−60.59	−61.13	−60.21	−60.80	−61.40

Standard error in parentheses.
* Significant at the 10% level.
** Significant at the 5% level.
*** Significant at the 1% level.

The interpretation of these results requires some caution. This anomaly of the fiscal year 1996 may or may not be caused by the earthquake, since we cannot distinguish between the impact of the earthquake and related activities, such as recovery and reconstruction activities, and other miscellaneous influences specific to the Hyogo Prefecture in the current model structure. The coefficient for the 1996 dummy variable is positive and relatively small. This suggests a slight increase in Hyogo's GRP, thus departing from the long-run growth path. If it resulted from the earthquake related activities, it implicates that the influence and/or impact of such activities would have required some time, in this case around two years, to materialize in a larger region — the Hyogo Prefecture. The total impact of the earthquake would have been absorbed by a larger economy, balancing the negative impact of the damages and the positive impact of the demand injections through recovery and reconstruction activities for the fiscal years 1994 and 1995. Again, it is difficult to conclude how this positive deviation in the fiscal year 1996 for HYOGO emerged.

Finally, the results of Kobe's model (1) are summarized in Table 3. Based on the Models 1-1 and 1-2, the constant term is not included in the analysis, since the constant term in Model 1-1 is not significant and the model without constant term, Model 1-2, has the better BIC value. Models 1-3 and 1-4 reveal that the fiscal years 1994 and 1995 are statistically different from the long-run

Table 3: Significance of the Earthquake Impact on GRP (KOBE as Dependent Variable)

	Model 1-1 KOBE	Model 1-2 KOBE	Model 1-3 KOBE	Model 1-4 KOBE	Model 1-5 KOBE
Constant	0.030 (0.056)				
JPN	1.175*** (0.352)	1.291*** (0.272)	1.221*** (0.258)	1.298*** (0.203)	1.231*** (0.181)
JPN (t-1)	−1.002** (0.379)	−1.143** (0.268)	−1.096*** (0.254)	−1.225*** (0.201)	−1.179*** (0.179)
KOBE (t-1)	0.808*** (0.138)	0.852*** (0.110)	0.877*** (0.104)	0.919*** (0.083)	0.942*** (0.074)
D94			−0.066** (0.031)		−0.062*** (0.022)
D95				0.119*** (0.025)	0.117*** (0.022)
Number of observations	31	31	31	31	31
R-squared	0.97	0.97	0.98	0.98	0.98
BIC	−57.76	−59.32	−60.00	−67.27	−69.83

Standard error in parentheses.
* Significant at the 10% level.
** Significant at the 5% level.
*** Significant at the 1% level.

growth model.[5] The coefficients are negative for FY1994, when the earthquake occurred, and positive for FY1995. These signs are consistent with the trend observed in the previous sub-section and with disaster theory that destructions by a natural hazard lead to negative impacts on the economy, while the demand injection of recovery and reconstruction activities can create some positive impacts later on.

Model 1-5 is additionally tested, which includes both the dummy variables of 1994 and 1995. The result indicates a better BIC value and the largest R-squared among the models we estimated. All the coefficients become statistically significant at 1% level, and the sign and size of them are consistent with the previous models. Unlike Hyogo's case, it is less ambiguous as to why years 1994 and 1995 are dissociated with Kobe's long-run growth path; these negative and positive deviations are considered to be arisen as the result of Kobe earthquake. However, if this is the case, we may encounter two potential problems: 1) the size of negative impact in 1994 is about a half of that of 1995's positive impact, implying that the earthquake created net positive impact, i.e. net gain, in Kobe; and 2) the impact of the earthquake and recovery and reconstruction activities appeared to have lasted only two years. These issues are investigated in the next section.

3.5. *Measuring the Effects of the Kobe Earthquake*

The total impact of the Kobe earthquake is evaluated based on the model estimated in the previous section. In general, the impact of a shock can be appraised as the difference between the observed values after the shock and the projected values based on the prior trend without the shock. In order to do so, the prior trend before the Kobe earthquake was estimated, using the data from years 1976 and 1993. The estimation results are summarized in Table 4. Since the constant term in Model 1-6 is not statistically significant, the pre-earthquake trend was projected in the later year with Model

---

[5]Dummy variables for all other years after 1996 are not statistically significant.

Table 4:   Comparison Among KOBE Models with Different Periods

Variables Dependent Variable Estimation Period	Model 1-5 KOBE 1976–2006	Model 1-6 KOBE 1976–1993	Model 1-7 KOBE 1976–1993
Constant		0.005 (0.044)	
JPN	1.231*** (0.181)	1.091*** (0.298)	1.110*** (0.248)
JPN (t-1)	−1.179*** (0.179)	−0.741** (0.343)	−0.765** (0.267)
KOBE (t-1)	0.942*** (0.074)	0.672*** (0.184)	0.682*** (0.160)
D94	−0.062*** (0.022)		
D95	0.117*** (0.022)		
Number of observations	31	18	18
R-squared	0.99	0.99	0.99
BIC	−69.83	−39.05	−40.48

Standard error in parentheses.
* Significant at the 10% level.
** Significant at the 5% level.
*** Significant at the 1% level.

1-7, without the constant term. The signs of three coefficients in Model 1-7 are consistent with the ones in 1-5, while the size of them is smaller in Model 1-7 than the ones in 1-5, indicating a relatively smooth trend. In fact, as seen in Figure 1, the trends of Kobe's GRP per capita during 1975 and 1993 seem to have narrower fluctuations except the ones after 1990, when the bubble economy in Japan collapsed.

Based on the above Model 1-7, the projection of Kobe's per capita GRP after 1994 was performed as follows:

$$\left.\begin{array}{l} \widehat{KOBE}_t^{pre} = \hat{\beta}_1^{pre} JPN_t + \hat{\beta}_2^{pre} JPN_{t-1} + \hat{\beta}_3^{pre} KOBE_{t-1} \quad until \ 1994 \\ \widehat{KOBE}_t^{pre} = \hat{\beta}_1^{pre} JPN_t + \hat{\beta}_2^{pre} JPN_{t-1} + \hat{\beta}_3^{pre} \widehat{KOBE}_{t-1}^{pre} \quad after \ 1995 \end{array}\right\}$$

$$(4)$$

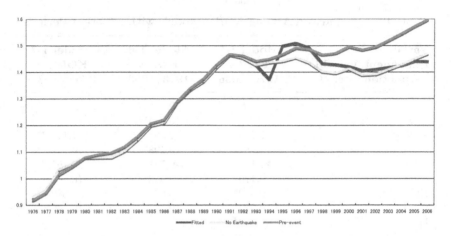

Figure 3: Comparison Among Trends with and Without the Kobe Earthquake (Logarithm of Per Capita GRP; in 2000 Constant Price)

A dotted line in Figure 3 indicates the projection result. The differences between the projected trend and the fitted one (black) based on Model 1-5 after 1994 illustrate quite large and increasing gaps. The initial impact (difference) is a negative one in 1994, followed by positive ones for a few years after 1995. However, these positive impacts are short-lived and the difference becomes negative and increasingly larger after 1998. The projected trend line based on the pre-earthquake trend goes upward after 2002, reflecting the uprising trend of Japan's GDP per capita, as shown in Figure 1. This implies that the total effect of Kobe earthquake appears long lasting with increasing negative values.

In order to further investigate the long-run effect, we calculated another projected trend after 1994, based on Model 1-5 derived in the previous section. The structure of Model 1-5 is as follows:

$$\widehat{KOBE}_t = \hat{\beta}_1 JPN_t + \hat{\beta}_2 JPN_{t-1} + \hat{\beta}_3 KOBE_{t-1} + \hat{\beta}_4 D_{94} + \hat{\beta}_5 D_{95}$$

$$(5)$$

This model is estimated using the data during the years 1976 and 2006, including Kobe earthquake and its effect on Kobe economy after 1994. Two dummy variables in the right hand side of Equation (5) can capture the short-run (yearly) impact of the event for 1994 and 1995, respectively. In other words, the short-run impact of the event can be separated by excluding dummy variables from Equation (5). The trend of Model 1-5 without having two dummy variables can be as follows:

$$\widehat{KOBE}_t = \hat{\beta}_1 JPN_t + \hat{\beta}_2 JPN_{t-1} + \hat{\beta}_3 KOBE_{t-1} \qquad (6)$$

However, Equation (6) includes a lagged variable, $KOBE_{t-1}$, which represents the observed Kobe's GRP values containing the earthquake's influences after its occurrence. This may create a causality problem — for example, the projected 1995 value is derived based on Equation (6) using the actual 1994 value, $KOBE_{94}$, including the earthquake's negative impact, while the aim of Equation (6) is to exclude only the short-run impacts of the earthquake. Therefore, in this case, the projected 1995 value without the short-run impact of the earthquake should not adopt the observed 1994 value in the right hand side; rather, it should employ the estimated 1994 value, $\widehat{KOBE}_{94}$, as the lagged variable. This modifies the Equation (6) as follows after 1995:

$$\left.\begin{array}{l} \widehat{KOBE}_t = \hat{\beta}_1 JPN_t + \hat{\beta}_2 JPN_{t-1} + \hat{\beta}_3 KOBE_{t-1} \quad until\ 1994 \\ \widehat{KOBE}_t = \hat{\beta}_1 JPN_t + \hat{\beta}_2 JPN_{t-1} + \hat{\beta}_3 KOBE_{t-1} \quad after\ 1995 \end{array}\right\} \quad (7)$$

In this way, the short-run impacts of earthquake are excluded in the projected values after 1994. The trends of the fitted case (in black), the projected "no-earthquake" dummy case (in gray) based on the above Equation (7), and the pre-event projection (in dotted line) are shown together in Figure 3. While the total effects of the earthquake can be defined as the difference between with (fitted[6]) and without (pre-event trend projection), this can be decomposed to the short-run impact — the difference between fitted and no-earthquake dummy — and the long-run effects — the difference between no-earthquake dummy and pre-event projection.

---

[6]The reason for using the fitted values instead of the observed values here is to factor out the miscellaneous disturbances, which did not result from the macroeconomic fluctuations controlled by Japan's GDP variables or from the earthquake controlled by the dummy variables above.

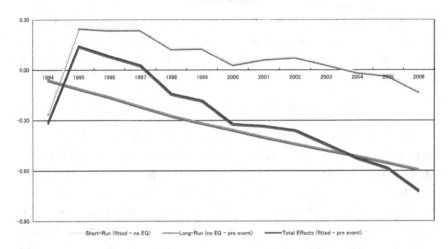

Figure 4: Comparison Among Estimated Effects (Values are Per Capita GRP; Million Yen in 2000 Constant Price)

Figure 4 shows the trends of short-run impact (difference between fitted and no-earthquake dummy cases), the long-run effect (difference between no-earthquake dummy and pre-event projection cases), and total impacts (sum of short-run and long-run effects, equal to the difference between fitted and pre-event cases). The trend of short-run impact supports the results of the previous impact analysis studies (such as Okuyama *et al.*, 1999), indicating an initial negative shock followed by a positive impact from demand injections for several years, and gradually returning to the original trend with a small difference in the fitted values. However, the trend of long-run effect has a distinctive appearance from that of the short-run impact, showing a steady downward decline, while the trend looks a bit flatter after 2000.

Why is there a clear distinction between short-run and long-run effects? One explanation is that the no-earthquake dummy model (Equation (7)) is estimated using data including post-earthquake data of Kobe (1994–2006), while the pre-event model does not, employing only the 1976–1993 data. This implies if any structural change specific to the Kobe economy arose after the earthquake, the "pre-event" model cannot take into account such changes, yielding the projection based only on the past trend, whereas the no-earthquake dummy model implicitly includes such changes. It has been reported that the earthquake's catastrophic destructions resulted in some companies going bankrupt, some other companies moving away from the Kobe area, or some new companies replacing the old and damaged ones, etc. These alterations in the Kobe economy have surely resulted in changes in the economic structure and interindustry relationships of the area. In addition, when companies restore their old and damaged equipment and facilities, they might have replaced the damaged ones with newer and more sophisticated ones, thus embracing new technologies. (Okuyama, 2003). While the trend of short-run impact looks more plausible and appears consistent with the empirical observations and previous studies, the long-run effects, emanating from the resulted structural changes, need to be taken into account for capturing the full range of the effects. If the trend of total effects in Figure 4 is the case, the effects of the Kobe earthquake should become much larger and severe than what we derived previously from the short-run impact analysis with some macroeconomic models, like input-output model and so on.

Through converting the above results in logarithm of per capita GRP to monetary value, Okuyama (2016) found that the effect from the earthquake ended up the GRP decline of about 1.2 to 1.8 trillion yen in 2006, which are about 19–28% of the pre-event GRP level. The Kobe area may have been reconstructed, but the regional production level has never been close to the pre-event trends and the effects of the event have been continuously increasing. Other studies assessing the long-run effects of the Kobe earthquake found a similar tendency. Chang (2010) employed simple indicators to measure the recovery process of the City of Kobe after the earthquake; the results indicate a three- to four-year temporary gain from the reconstruction activities, followed by the downturns at about 10% below the pre-earthquake level. In contrast to a simple method of Chang's, DuPont and Noy (2015) analyzed the long-run economic trend of the Hyogo Prefecture, instead of the City of Kobe, after the 1995 earthquake using econometric models with the synthetic control methodology to extract the earthquake's effect from the macroeconomic indicators, such as GRP and local government expenditures. They found that a persistent and continuing adverse impact of the event after 15 years with the similar level of long-run decline to Chang's study where the GRP per capita in 2007 was 13% less than the projected economic trend without the earthquake. While these studies analyzed similar macroeconomic indicators and derived similar results among them, Chang (2010) extended to indicate that Kobe economy's declining trend after the 1995 earthquake can be attributed to the acceleration of the pre-earthquake trend with some structural change of Kobe's economy. On the other hand, Fujiki and Hsiao (2013) did not find such a persistent declining trend in the Hyogo prefecture in the long-run using macroeconomic data during 1955 and 2009 and the Hsiao, Ching, and Wan (HCW) method (2012). Their results indicate that the stimulation effects from the recovery and reconstruction activities occurred during 1995 and 1998, while smaller negative impacts from the end of the intense demand injections were found during 1999 and 2000. They concluded that the long-run decline of the Hyogo prefecture resulted from the underlying structural change of the economy rather than from the earthquake and the related activities. In order to investigate the gap between the former three studies and Fujiki and Hsiao (2013), it is essential to connect time-series analysis with structural analysis to understand how the effects of the event and the influence of structural change have interacted.

4. STRUCTURAL ANALYSIS OF THE KOBE ECONOMY

As discussed above, Fujiki and Hsiao (2013) found that the steady decline in the growth rate of the Hyogo (or Kobe) economy resulted from the underlying structural change of the regional economy rather than from the effects of the event and related activities. At the same time, they did not further investigate how the underlying structural change occurred or which factor caused such structural change. In order to investigate this structural change of the regional economy and the relationship to the 1995 Kobe earthquake, structural decomposition analysis was employed in a series of studies (Okuyama, 2014 and 2015b). The general description of structural decomposition analysis based on input-output tables can be found in Miller and Blair (2009). The key feature of the structural decomposition analysis is to identify the factors of regional structural change, such as changes in technology, intra-regional linkages, and final demand. At the same time, the outcomes of structural decomposition analysis include all the influences that resulted from the structural change — from macroeconomic fluctuations to region specific causes, such as the Kobe earthquake. Okuyama (2014 and 2015b) utilized the shift-share analysis, another decomposition technique, and combined with the standard structural decomposition analysis to devise the multiplicative decomposition framework as below:

$$RS_i = x_i^0 \cdot (\Delta D_i^N \cdot \Delta A_i^N \cdot \Delta F_i^N) \times \left(\frac{\Delta D_i^r}{\Delta D_i^N} \cdot \frac{\Delta D_i^r}{\Delta A_i^N} \cdot \frac{\Delta F_i^r}{\Delta F_i^N} - 1 \right)$$

(8)

where RS_i is the regional shift (region specific change) for industry i, x_i^0 is the output level of industry i in the initial period, ΔD_i^N represents the changes in intra-regional linkage of industry i for the benchmark region, ΔD_i^r is for the region in question, ΔA_i^N represents the changes in input-structure of industry i for the benchmark region, ΔA_i^r is for the region in question, ΔF_i^N represents changes in final demand of industry i for the benchmark region, ΔF_i^r is for the region in question.

Okuyama (2015b) used the input-output tables for the damaged region, including 10 cities and 10 towns, constructed by Ashiya and Jinushi (2001) for 1990 and 1995,[7] while Okuyama (2014) employed the Kobe input-output table, published by the City of Kobe for years 1985, 1990, 2000, and 2005.[8] The shift-share analysis of total output changes between 1990 and 1995 (Okuyama, 2015b)

---

[7]These input-output tables were constructed for the calendar year.
[8]The 1995 Kobe input-output table was not released due to the Kobe earthquake.

revealed that the values of regional shift, region specific change, for most manufacturing sectors appear negative but small in volume, except for some sectors with diminutive positive regional shift. The pattern of regional shift in manufacturing sectors for 1990–2000 (Okuyama, 2014) mimics these tendencies, as most manufacturing sectors have negative value for regional shift, except few sectors. Meanwhile, it appears that for manufacturing sectors, the tendency of changes caused by the initial shock in 1995 continued until 2000, while some minor differences, especially in terms of the volume of changes, can be seen between 1990–1995 and 1990–2000.

Significant changes in regional shift between these two periods are found among service sectors. Right after the event in 1995, the commerce sector and the transportation services sector decreased their output due to large negative regional shifts. These two sectors show negative regional shifts in the 1990–2000 results — however, these shifts are not very significant for both the sectors. This may illustrate recovery by 2000 from the initial and immediate decline due to the destruction of the facilities for these sectors, such as damaged department stores, highways, and commuter railroads in 1995. The finance and insurance sector, in particular, has a complete turn-around pattern, in which it has a small negative regional shift in the 1990–1995 result but a positive regional shift in the 1990–2000 result. This also leads to the observation that the initial shock in 1995 created a negative impact and the following reconstruction activities resulted in some demand and increased output for this particular sector by 2000. Another evident difference is personal services, which has a negligible positive value in the 1990–1995 result, but a significant positive value in the 1990–2000 result, showing the recovery of this sector's activities.

The comparison of multiplicative decomposition analysis between 1990–1995 and 1990–2000 reveals a clear distinction, and the notable findings are as follows. The 1990–1995 result exhibits a negative and mostly good-sized contribution of final demand to regional shift throughout manufacturing sectors with generally positive and noticeable contribution of intra-regional linkages. On the other hand, the 1990–2000 results indicate several negative contributions as well as a couple of positive contributions (heavy electrical equipment and shipbuilding sectors) of final demand, and other factors are largely insignificant with different signs. Among the service sectors, the differences between 1990–1995 and 1990–2000 appear more prevalent. A large negative value seen in the commerce sector during 1990–1995 is attributed mostly to final demand change, followed by changes in input structure and in intra-regional linkages. A much smaller negative regional shift in the 1990–2000 result for commerce sector is decomposed to a small positive final demand change and negative contribution of intra-regional linkage changes, partly due to the weakened connection with local inter-industry relationships of this particular sector. The finance and insurance sector shows a small negative regional shift, caused mainly by the decline of final demand in 1990–1995, while a positive regional shift in 1990–2000 is factored mostly to change in the input-structure, i.e. changes in production function, rather than through change in final demand, which is actually negative for this sector.

If the difference between the results of 1990–1995 and of 1990–2000 implies the recovery process from the event, the manufacturing sectors overcome the initial decline of production due to the decrease in final demand through an increase in intra-regional linkages. In 1990–2000, on the other hand, the regional final demand for these sectors regained (still negative values for several manufacturing sectors), while the role of intra-regional linkages diminished or even became negative. The service sectors' recovery process is quite diverse: shrunken negative or even positive contribution of final demand change is common to most of service sectors, while the contributions of changes in the input structure and intra-regional linkage can be positive or negative with a noticeable shift for some sectors, such as commerce, finance and insurance, transportation services.

These analyses and results indicate that the structural change occurred in the Kobe economy appears to be significant and broad, and apparently resulted mainly from decline in the final demand. As Chang (2010) noted, the declining trend of the Kobe economy after the 1995 earthquake can be attributed to the acceleration of the pre-earthquake trend with some structural change in the

Kobe economy. And, this seems consistent with the conclusion of Fujiki and Hsiao (2013). If the underlying structural change is more of the hollowing-out process, it can be attributed to the changes in the input structure and/or decrease in intra-regional linkage. The results here include such changes in addition to the large final demand declines in the majority of sectors, which can be an acceleration factor for the structural change. At the same time, there is much more to this interpretation. Based on the above analyses, immediately after the earthquake in 1995, with the damaged transportation network, manufacturing sectors might have intensified their intra-regional inter-industry relationships during the recovery period, because it might have been difficult to reach their outside suppliers or customers. Since service sectors are usually labor-intensive, they needed to seek and reach out to outside labor or to receive support from outside companies, since the labor within the damaged region might not have been available in the aftermath of the event. Successively, as the reconstruction activities progressed after several years, manufacturing sectors were able to extend their supply chain to other regions, hence the hollowing-out process, progressed in this region. In this way, the acceleration of underlying structural change occurred due to the event and subsequent reconstruction activities.

5. POLICY IMPLICATIONS

This chapter investigated the total effects of the Kobe earthquake using econometric models and structural analysis. The economic recovery from the 1995 Kobe earthquake initially surged for a few years, but declined subsequently thereafter. The decline was quite severe and persistent for the City of Kobe, and it appears that the substantial efforts made and budget allotted for recovery and reconstruction were still insufficient to bring about full recovery from the event. It is found that both the Hyogo Prefecture's and Kobe's reconstruction plans were not intended to revert the regional economy to the pre-event state. Rather, they aimed to pursue the pre-existing long-range development plans proposed before the event and lead to a sustained growth path with the promotion of high value-added industries and through economic structural changes to service industries. As found in Okuyama (2014 and 2015b), the production levels of these high value-added and service industries fluctuated widely after the event and did not result in a consistent growth pattern, whereas most of manufacturing industries decreased the production level mostly due to the underlying hollowing-out process. Perhaps, the local goverments of the Hyogo prefecture and the City of Kobe believed that this event could have accelerated this transformation to a sustained economic growth through enormous reconstruction activities. From a planning perspective, sustaining the long-range plans, even after a catastrophic event, seems legitimate, but utilizing the reconstruction from the event as a springboard to accelerate the development process is rather questionable. In the mean time, the underlying long-range development plan of Kobe assumes the target year of 2025. The City of Kobe may soon return to the original development path and reach its planned and desired targets by 2025 through continued and persistent reconstruction process, while the Kobe earthquake hampered the local economy's long- range development plan.

The long-run analysis of disaster effects provides us an important lesson — solely analyzing that short-run impact and recovery would lead to inaccurate conclusions about reconstruction process. After the Kobe earthquake, underlying structural changes have been somewhat accelerated by reconstruction activities. The resultant structural changes were significant and extensive as seen in this chapter. Therefore, when the long-run effects of a disaster are investigated, the study should include the effects from and the process of the reconstruction activities, since reconstruction activities are the consequences of the disaster process and considerably influence the long-run trends of the regional economy. As a policy implication, in order to hinder the acceleration of or to slow down the pace of underlying structural changes during the reconstruction period, it is important to promote and support regional inter-industry linkages so that the ripple effect of injected reconstruction demand can be predominantly retained within the region.

As seen above, population changes have had a marked influence on the decline of regional economies. The decreased population leads to decreased consumption demand 'and, in turn, to a lower level of economic activities. While the population was restored to the pre-event level in 1999 for Hyogo and in 2004 for Kobe, the per capita income recovered in 2001 for both Hyogo and Kobe still lagged noticeably behind the national average trend. Even though Kobe attempted to promote high value-added industries, this approach appears to be insufficient to generate a noticeable increase in per capita income. A potential explanation for this lack of increase is that out-migration occurred after the event and the in-migration offset the population decline during the reconstruction process might have been composed of different income groups and varying sizes. In addition, uneven population recovery in Kobe, partly resulted from an uneven reconstruction progress over space, would become a deep-rooted problem over time. Hence, it is important and interesting to analyze the rapid changes in population compositions (age and income distributions) after the event and during the reconstruction period over time and space in order to reveal the demographic-economic interactions and their impact on regional economies after a disaster.

REFERENCES

Albala-Bertrand, JM (1993). *The Political Economy of Large Natural Disasters: With Special Reference to Developing Countries.* Oxford, UK: Clarendon Press.

Albala-Bertrand, JM (2007). Globalization and Localization: An Economic Approach. in *Handbook of Disaster Research.* Rodriguez, H, Quarantelli, EL and RR Dynes (Eds.), pp. 147–67. New York: Springer.

Ashiya, T and T Jinushi (2001). Shinsai to Hisaichi Sangyoukouzou no Henka: Hisaichi Chiiki Sangyourennkanhyo no Suitei to Ouyou. *Kokumin Keizai Zasshi,* 183(1), 79–97 (in Japanese).

Baade, RA, Baumann, R and V Matheson (2007). Estimating the Economic Impact of Natural and Social Disasters, with an Application to Hurricane. *Urban Studies,* 44(11), 2061–2076.

Cavallo, E, S Galiani, I Noy and J Pantano (2010). Catastrophic Natural Disasters and Economic Growth. Inter-American Development Bank Working Paper Series: No. IDB-WP-183.

Chang, SE (2010). Urban disaster recovery: A measurement framework and its application to the 1995 Kobe earthquake. *Disasters*, 34(2), 303–327.

Coffman, M and I Noy (2011). Hurricane Iniki: Measuring the long-term economic impact of a natural disaster using synthetic control. *Environment and Development Economics*, 17, 187–205.

Cuaresma, JC, J Hlouskova and M Obersteiner (2008). Natural disasters as creative destruction? Evidence from developing countries. *Economic Inquiry*, 46(2), 214–226.

DuPont, W and I Noy (2015). What happened to Kobe? A reassessment of the impact of the 1995 earthquake. *Economic Development and Cultural Change*, 63(4), 777–812.

Fujiki, H and C Hsiao (2013). Disentangling the Effects of Multiple Treatments — Measuring the Net Economic Impact of the 1995 Great Hanshin-Awaji Earthquake. IMES Discussion Paper 2013-E-3, Institute for Monetary and Economic Studies, the Bank of Japan.

Hendry, DF (1995). *Dynamic Econometrics.* New York, NY: Oxford University Press.

Hornbeck, R (2009). The Enduring Impact of the American Dust Bowl: Short and Long Run Adjustments to Environmental Catastrophe. NBER Working Paper Series: W15605.

Hsiao, C, S Ching and SK Wan (2012). A Panel Data Approach for Program Evaluation: Measuring the Benefits of Political and Economic Integration of Hong Kong with Mainland China. *Journal of Applied Economics*, 27, 705–740.

Hyogo Prefecture Government (2010). *Status of Recovery and Reconstruction after the Hanshin-Awaji Great Earthquake.* (in Japanese).

Kunreuther, H and A Rose (Eds.) (2004). *The Economics of Natural Hazards, Volume I & II.* Northampton, MA: Edward Elgar.

Miller, RE and PD Blair (2009). *Input-Output Analysis: Foundations and Extensions Second Edition.* New York, NY: Cambridge University Press.

Odell, KA and MD Weidenmier (2002). Real Shock, Monetary Aftershock: The San Francisco Earthquake and the Panic of 1907. NBER Working Paper Series: W9176.

Okuyama, Y (2003). Economics of Natural Disasters: a Critical Review, Research Paper 2003–12, Regional Research Institute, West Virginia University.

Okuyama, Y (2007). Economic Modeling for Disaster Impact Analysis: Past, Present, and Future. *Economic Systems Research*, 19(2), 115–124.

Okuyama, Y (2010). "Globalization and Localization of Disaster Impacts: An Empirical Examination." *CEFifo Forum*, 11(2), 56–66.

Okuyama, Y (2014). Disaster and Economic Structural Change: Case Study on the 1995 Kobe Earthquake. *Economic Systems Research*, 26(1), 98–117.

Okuyama, Y (2015a). How shaky was the regional economy after the 1995 Kobe earthquake? A multiplicative decomposition analysis of disaster impact. *Annals of Regional Science*, 55(2), 289–312.

Okuyama, Y (2015b). The Rise and Fall of the Kobe Economy from the 1995 Earthquake. *Journal of Disaster Research*, 10(4), 635–640.

Okuyama, Y (2016). Long-run effect of a disaster: Case study on the Kobe earthquake. *The Singapore Economic Review*, 16(1), 1640009-1–18.

Okuyama, Y and SE Chang (2012). Economic and Planning Approaches to Natural Disasters. In *The Oxford Handbook of Urban Economics and Planning*, Brooks, N, Donaghy, K and GJ Knaap (Eds.), 395–418. New York, NY: Oxford University Press.

Okuyama, Y and JR Santos (2014). Disaster Impact and Input-Output Analysis. *Economic Systems Research*, 26(1), 1–12.

Okuyama, Y, GJD Hewings and M Sonis (1999). Economic Impacts of an Unscheduled, Disruptive Event: A Miyazawa Multiplier Analysis. In *Understanding and Interpreting Economic Structure*, Hewings, GJD, M Sonis, M Madden and Y Kimura (Eds.), 113–144. Springer-Verlag.

Rasmussen, TN (2004). Macroeconomic Implications of Natural Disasters in the Caribbean. IMF Working Paper WP/04/224, International Monetary Fund.

Skidmore, M and H Toya (2002). Do Natural Disasters Promote Long-run Growth? *Economic Inquiry*, 40(4), 664–687.

CHAPTER 6

IMPACT OF NATURAL DISASTERS ON RESIDENTIAL PROPERTY VALUES: EVIDENCE FROM AUSTRALIA*

Wasantha Athukorala
University of Peredeniya, Sri Lanka

Wade Martin
California State University, USA

Prasad Neelawala
APIIT City Campus, Sri Lanka

Darshana Rajapaksa, Jeremy Webb and Clevo Wilson
Queensland University of Technology, Australia

One of the most prominent casualties of a natural disaster is the property market. The private and social costs from such events typically run into millions of dollars. In this chapter, we use a dataset to examine the impact of natural disasters on residential house prices using a hedonic property (HP) values approach. Data before and after both a wildfire and floods, which affected Rockhampton in central coastal part of the state of Queensland, Australia are used. The data is unique because one of Rockhampton's suburb was affected by wildfires and another by floods. For the analysis, three suburbs namely Frenchville, Park Avenue and Norman Gardens are used. Frenchville was significantly affected by wildfires in the latter part of 2009 and to a lesser extent in 2012, while Park Avenue was affected by floods at the end of 2010, January 2011,

*The chapter is an extended version of a paper published in the *Singapore Economic Review* in 2016, entitled "Impact of Wildfires and Floods on Property Values: A Before and After Analysis".

2012 and 2013. Norman Gardens, which was relatively unaffected, is used as a control site. This enables us to examine the before and after effects on residential property values in the three suburbs. The results confirm that in the aftermath of a natural disaster property prices in affected areas decrease even though the large majority of individual houses remain unaffected. Furthermore, the results indicate that while prices in largely unaffected suburbs may gain immediately after a natural disaster, this gain may disappear if natural disasters continue to occur in the area/region due to a flood prone stigma being created. The results have several important policy decision and welfare implications which are briefly discussed in the chapter.

1. INTRODUCTION

In recent years, several major natural disasters have occurred in Australia. They include wildfires (e.g. Victoria, 2009), floods (e.g. South East Queensland, 2011) and cyclones (e.g. Far North Queensland, 2006, 2011). As can be expected, these natural disasters cause major damage to infrastructure, industrial and agricultural production and to the services sector. In such cases the private and social costs runs into millions of dollars. Although precise figures are hard to obtain, recent studies on wildfires show the costs to be in the billions of dollars. For example, the now well documented, black Saturday wildfires of 2009 in Victoria (the worst in the history of Australia) which led to the death of 173 people, destroyed several townships and 4030 houses, and affected more than 450,000 hectares, the total costs were estimated at more than AUD $4 billion (Teague *et al.*, 2010). Depending on the severity of the flood, damage costs can be considerably greater. The economic loss to Queensland from the Brisbane floods of 2011 — one of the worst natural disasters in Australia's recent past — was put at AUD $30 billion (Queensland Government, 2011). Another casualty of natural disasters is the residential property (housing) market. Although the costs to residents are obvious and documented, little work has been undertaken to examine the impact of natural disasters on house prices in affected suburbs after such an event. The issue here is that those areas or suburbs that are badly affected by a natural disaster are likely to witness lower house values in the next several years until stability and confidence returns to the market. On the other hand, it could be expected that areas or suburbs that are unaffected or less affected are likely to witness an increase in house prices, at least in the short term. However, if natural disasters continue to occur in the region or nearby suburbs, then house prices may remain the same or even show a decrease. This chapter investigates this issue using the hedonic property (HP) price approach.

This under researched issue is examined by selecting three suburbs from the Rockhampton Regional Council, located in close proximity to the city of Rockhampton, which is located approximately 600 kilometers north of Queensland's capital, Brisbane. This region is selected because it was affected by wildfires in the latter part of 2009 (October) and to a lesser extent in 2012[1] and by floods at the end of December, 2010/January 2011 and in 2012 and 2013. Interestingly, the suburbs were affected separately — first wildfires affected the suburb of Frenchville, followed by floods affecting the suburb of Park Avenue. Hence, we have two suburbs being affected by two natural disasters, almost a year apart and then the same natural disasters being repeated in 2011, 2012 and 2013 directly affecting the suburbs and/or nearby areas of Rockhampton. This provides us with a unique opportunity to examine the before and after effects of natural disasters on the residential property market in these suburbs. A control site is used in the analysis in which a large area of the selected suburb was unaffected by wildfires. The selected sites are shown in Figure 1.

In this chapter we examine the following. Are residential property prices in the suburb affected after a natural disaster (wildfires and floods) even though the individual property itself is unaffected? Which natural disaster creates the larger stigma in the affected suburb — wildfires or floods? What impact do natural disasters have on the residential property values of unaffected (or largely unaffected) suburbs? Do property values in these suburbs appreciate in value? If so, for how long and under what circumstances? If the natural disasters in the region continue, what will the impact of such

---

[1]Wildfires have also occurred in other parts of the Rockhampton region in 2011.

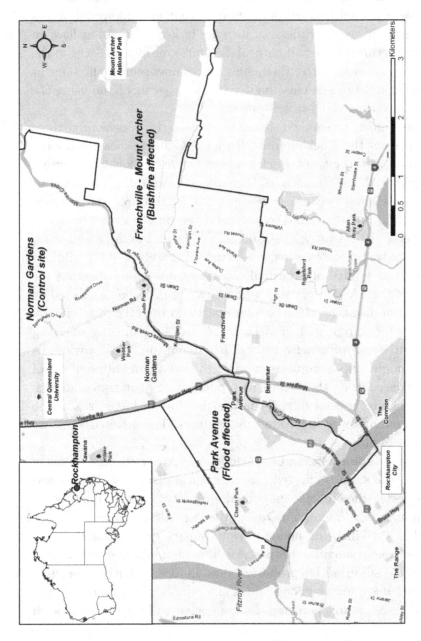

Figure 1: The Three Suburbs Chosen for the Study

Source: Google and Google Earth Maps (2012).

disasters be on unaffected (or largely unaffected) suburbs such as Norman Gardens? As mentioned, we use two suburbs from the same locality, one of which is affected only by wildfires and the other only by floods to test the above first two research questions. This gives us an opportunity to examine the *before* and *after* impact of natural disasters. The results are then compared with a control site from an adjoining suburb (Norman Gardens) which was largely unaffected by the two natural disasters to test the latter three research questions. This enables us to make a comparison with the affected sites as well as the impact of the global financial crisis (GFC) on house prices since 2009. We hypothesize that house prices in the natural disaster affected suburbs are likely to fall after such an event, a fall which will be exacerbated by the GFC.[2] On the other hand, suburbs that are largely unaffected are likely to see an increase in property prices (at least in the short term), although the increase in prices is moderated to some extent by the effects of the GFC. However, an increase in property values may cease to continue (or even show a decrease) if natural disasters in the adjoining areas become more frequent. This would be attributed to the stigma attached to such disasters.

We test the above hypotheses using an HP values model which includes a vector of structural and neighbourhood characteristics and a vector of environmental attributes as explanatory variables. For this purpose, data were collected for years, 2006–2013 from various sources and were merged to create a unique and comprehensive data set. The final data set contains 1573 observations, 593 from Frenchville, 473 from Park Avenue and 507 from Norman Gardens. Dummy variables for year of sale, 2006, 2007, 2008 (before natural disaster) and 2010, 2011, 2012, 2013 (after natural disaster) are designed to capture price changes of the residential property market due to wildfires. Year 2009 is set as the base year. This is because the major wildfire in Rockhampton occurred in 2009. Floods affected Park Avenue at the end of December, 2010/January, 2011, 2012 and 2013.

---

[2]In Australia, the 2009 GFC impacts on property prices lasted for around two years or less.

The regression results show that house prices were positive *before* the two natural disasters (2007 and 2008) in all the three suburbs. However, only in 2007 is the value significant. On the other hand, the results clearly show that *after* the natural disasters (2010 to 2013), house prices record a decline in the affected areas. The coefficients are negative and significant for Frenchville and Park Avenue (disaster affected suburbs). It must be noted here that the fall in prices could also have been exacerbated by the GFC of 2009/2010 which impacted on house prices in Australia during this period. Interestingly, the control site (Norman Gardens) records positive house prices after the natural disasters in 2010 and 2011. However, they, too, show a decline in 2012 and 2013, presumably due to the stigma attached from frequent disasters in the area. For instance, wildfires occurred in areas around Rockhampton in 2011 and in Frenchville in 2012 and after the major fire in 2009. In addition to the 2010/2011 floods, Parkville was affected by floods again in 2012 and 2013. The results indicate that although buyers are willing to pay more to live in natural disaster secure areas than in non-secure areas, this is reversed if natural disasters in the nearby suburbs become more frequent. However, the results also show that the impact on the property market in suburbs not affected by natural disasters is smaller than in disaster prone areas.

The remainder of the chapter is set out as follows. Section 2 provides an introduction to the background of the study areas and Section 3 undertakes a literature review of the existing work related to HP values studies conducted in relation to wildfires and floods. Section 4 presents a brief overview of the underlying theory of the HP model and the data collected. Section 5 summarizes the results of the regression models (ordinary least squares and spatial models) and the final Section summarizes and concludes.

2. BACKGROUND TO THE STUDY AREAS

For this study, we select three suburbs from the Rockhampton Regional Council, in central, coastal part of the state of Queensland

Australia. The city of Rockhampton is approximately 600 kilometers north of the state capital, Brisbane and in 2011 the region's population was estimated to be approximately 117,315 residents (Rockhampton Regional Council, 2012). The Rockhampton region experiences a humid subtropical climate and some areas are prone to wildfires, floods and cyclones. The region is prone to wildfires due to the lower than average rainfall and hot, dry weather combined with large expanses of forested and bushland some of which are declared large national parks and state reserves. Although there have been wildfires in the past, the most recent major wildfire was recorded in October 2009 affecting mostly the suburb of Frenchville. Since then, wildfires have occurred in 2011 in the Rockhampton region and in Frenchville in 2012 (to a lesser extent). As much as some areas are prone to wildfires, there are other areas along the Fitzroy River and its environs that are subject to floods. The Fitzroy River flooding of Rockhampton and adjacent areas is well documented with flood records dating back to 1859. The highest recorded floods occurring in January 1918, and the most recent major flood occurring at the end of December 2010/January 2011 mostly affecting the suburb of Park Avenue. Floods also occurred in 2012 and 2013.

Wildfires and floods have occurred in adjacent suburbs, but no suburb was affected by both events. This situation provides us with a unique opportunity to examine the impact of these two events on property values. As mentioned earlier, the first casualty of natural disasters is the property market. Two suburbs affected by these natural disasters are Frenchville (wildfires) and Park Avenue (floods) which are adjacent to each other. In addition, we select a control site — the suburb of Norman Gardens — that is mostly unaffected by the recent wildfires and floods. The selected three suburbs are shown in Figure 1.

As can be seen from Figure 1, the three suburbs selected for this study are adjacent to each other. Interestingly, the suburb of Frenchville with a population of 5,684 in 2011 bordering the Mount Archer National Park was one of the suburbs most affected by major wildfires in October, 2009 (the worst in 20 years) and (to a lesser extent) during another wildfire in 2012.[3] This suburb has a sizeable area of residential properties bordering Mount Archer National Park, with a few residential areas forming an enclave within the park. Frenchville and two other suburbs (Koongal and Lakes Creek) are frequently mentioned in the media as having suffered the most threat and damage. In addition, houses in approximately seven streets that back onto the bushland facing Mount Archer National Park in the suburb of Norman Gardens (with a population of 9,484 in 2011) were also threatened and some damaged during the wildfires in 2009. We select the suburb of Norman Gardens as the control site because it is adjacent to the two suburbs mostly affected by the two natural disasters and has a section backing into bushland and Mount Archer National Park.

The suburb selected to examine the impact of floods on residential property prices is the suburb of Park Avenue — whose population was 5,684 in 2011 — which is located along the Fitzroy River and is two kilometres from the centre of the city of Rockhampton. A major flood affected this suburb at the end of 2010 and beginning of January, 2011 when parts were submerged by 9 meters of water and many residents had to be evacuated. Since then, the Rockhampton Regional Council has published flood maps for the area (see Rockhampton Regional Council, 2012). The area was also flooded in 2012 and 2013.

3. LITERATURE REVIEW

It is evident from the HP literature that a number of studies have considered various aspects of environmental issues on property values (see, for example, Freeman, 1993; Tyrvainen, 1997; Tyrvainen and Miettinen, 2000; Lutzenhiser and Netusil, 2001; Crompton, 2001; Kim and Johnson, 2002; Hui *et al.*, 2007). However, what is evident from the HP literature is that few studies have analysed the impacts of natural disasters on property values. Two papers are of

---

[3]Note that wildfires have affected the Rockhampton area in 2011 as well.

particular interest in relation to wildfires. In the first, Athukorala *et al.* (2012) show that buyers in the study areas were paying higher prices to live close to green spaces despite these areas being also well known high wildfire prone areas. Their results clearly indicate that residents either discount or are unaware of the risks of wildfires. In the second paper Donovan *et al.* (2007) examine the impact of information available to residents on wildfire risks on housing prices in Colorado Spring's wildland-urban interface website. They showed that in the pre-website era, overall wildfire risk ratings were positively related to house prices. This suggested that the positive amenity values of the house and neighbourhood characteristics that affect a house's wildfire risks outweighed the perceived loss in house utility from increased wildfire risks. However, this relationship between overall wildfire risk rating and housing price was not observed after the web site became available. This shows that the availability of wildfire ratings contributed to an increased awareness of wildfire risks. However, Donovan *et al.* (2007, p. 231) state that they "found evidence that this effect diminished with time."

A review of sales transactions by Eves (2004a) for streets in specific suburbs of Sydney, Australia states that "*the advantages of living close to a national park or bushland setting counteract potential risk associated with these locations.*"

Apart from the above studies, there are other studies that examine wildfire risks in relation to perceptions. Beringer (2000) observed significant differences in wildfire risk perceptions between newcomers and long-term residents in his study. He explained that new residents were unable to identify their level of exposure to risk until they assess the hazards to which they are exposed. Beringer (2000) and Gilbert (2004) found differences in wildfire knowledge between genders. Men tended to have a better understanding of wildfires, and this was statistically significant. According to Beringer (2000) a lack of knowledge may lead to females perceiving the wildfire to be a greater threat. Anderson-Berry (2003) linked level of education with risk perceptions. Accordingly, people with a higher education are likely to have a more accurate perception of risk because they more readily understand the scientific complexities of hazards, and they are likely to be better skilled at searching for and acquiring information. McGee and Russell (2003) show that the high level of risk perception of many of the respondents, and a good knowledge of wildfires, can be attributed to past wildfire experience and a close association with the local fire management institutions.

Fothergill and Peek (2004) reviewed the literature concerning the effect of socioeconomic status on risk perceptions. They showed that people of lower socioeconomic status may perceive higher levels of risk possibly because poorer people have little control over their lives and hold little power in the world. However occupation may affect risk perceptions — people of lower socioeconomic status tend to work in more hazardous occupations which can moderate risk perceptions (Fothergill and Peek, 2004). Fisek *et al.* (2002) alternatively suggested that socioeconomic status does not affect risk perceptions. For example, income had no effect on overall risk perceptions. These studies strongly suggest that while demographics and socioeconomic factors can influence risk perceptions, the resultant effect is largely unpredictable. McCaffrey (2004) also indicates that the lack of action in undertaking wildfire protection activities is additionally due to the fact that people live busy and complicated lives, which often means that natural hazards have low salience compared to other concerns.

The Bureau of Transport Economics (BTE, 2001) has examined the economic cost of disaster level wildfire events in Australia. The study presents a methodological approach to estimating the economic cost of disasters and has applied it to wildfire events. This report firstly identifies the difference between a financial and economic analysis. Secondly it attempts to separate the direct and indirect costs, as well as tangible and intangible costs of disasters.

In relation to floods, only a few HP studies assess the impact of floods on property markets. A recent study has attempted to estimate the likely impact of the release of flood maps on property values within Brisbane City (Rambaldi *et al.*, 2011). The study was carried out after the release of flood maps by the Brisbane City Council in 2008. The paper does not, however, capture the actual impact of floods on affected properties and those that are not affected. Rajapaksa *et al.* (2016) found that the release of flood maps as well as the actual flood (2011 Brisbane flood) negatively impacted on residential property values.

While here are other studies examining the impact of floods on residential property values their results are contradictory. Some argue that flooding negatively impacts on residential properties while others have concluded that there is no real effect. The study conducted by Zhai and Fukuzono (2003) have tried to estimate the actual impact of floods on land values based on the Tokai flood in Japan in 2000. The results revealed a negative effect on land prices.

According to Lamon (2008), flood related estimates are area specific. Moreover, empirical studies have shown that the impact of floods on housing prices is a temporal effect and "fades-of" within a short period (see, for example, Eves, 2004b, Lamond *et al.*, 2010, Lamond and Proverbs, 200; Rajapaksa *et al.*, 2016). According to UK evidence, the negative impact of floods on property values are removed within three years.

Other empirical evidence have shown that floods or floodplain related variables have a negative and a significant effect on property values (see, for example, missing, Zhai and Fukuzono, 2003). According to Donnelly (1989), prices for houses within a floodplain are reduced by 12%. Most of these studies have been conducted to evaluate the impact of floods on properties in the years immediately following a major incident, whereas some studies have simply considered the flood risk. Importantly, these studies considered only properties in flooded areas or floodplain locations but not those in adjacent areas.

Finally, Sirmans *et al.* (2005) who reviewed approximately 125 studies which have estimated HP models in relation to residential property values in the past decade, show that factors which are consistently significant in determining property values are the number of bedrooms, the number of bathrooms, lot size, house size, age of the house, number of garage spaces, the presence of a swimming pool, time on the market as well as the distance to schools, shopping centres and the central bus station. Reviews of these studies show that many hedonic studies attempt to quantify for policy makers and communities, the economic benefits which can be achieved from having some environmental amenities.

Certainly, previous studies show that buyers are willing to pay more to be closer to green space, including forests (see, for example, Athukorala *et al.*, 2012) and near rivers (see, for example, Rajapakse *et al.*, 2016) reservoirs and lakes. This is attributed to the recreational and therapeutic values they generate. In addition, such places are quieter, provide a cleaner environment with premium amenity values and afford an opportunity to live close to nature. However, to date no studies have carried out a *before* and *after* analysis to investigate the impact on the price of such properties which are prone to wildfires and floods. This chapter based on results of Athukorala *et al.* (2016) is designed to fill this void in the literature.

4. METHOD AND DATA

The theoretical developments and extensions of HP are documented by Rosen (1974), Halvorsen and Pollakowski (1981), Anselin (1988), Cropper *et al.* (1988), Freeman (1993), Bockstael (1997), Huh and Kwak (1997) and Griffith *et al.* (2003). Freeman (1993) defined the HP function using three vectors for location-specific environmental amenities, structural characteristics of the house and characteristics of the neighbourhood. Accordingly, the model used to analyse the determinants of house prices can be written as follows:

$$HP = f(H_i, L_i, E_i) \tag{1}$$

where H_i is a vector of the property characteristics (structural characteristic) such as size of the property, number of bathrooms and bedrooms, availability of carport and swimming pool. L_i is a vector of the locality or neighbourhood attributes such as accessibility to schools and shops. E_i is a vector of the environmental characteristics including pollution levels and distance to the environmental risk area. The general form of the model can be expressed as:

$$HP = \beta_i X_i + \epsilon \tag{2}$$

where X_i is a vector of explanatory variables, β_i is a vector of coefficients which describe the implicit prices of the corresponding explanatory variables and ϵ is a normally distributed random error term. The dependent variable HP is generally defined as the recent selling price, which acts as a proxy for the true value of the property. As widely discussed in the literature (see, for example, Halvorsen and Pollakowski, 1981; Cropper *et al.*, 1988), the correct functional form for the HP function has received a great deal of attention in the literature, with a variety of different specifications suggested. The different functional forms such as linear, log-linear and log-log have been used by previous studies. However, the evidence does not indicate the superiority of any one functional form. It has been suggested (see, for example, Cassel and Mendelsohn, 1985) that the estimates of the environmental-variable coefficient may be more reliable with simple functional forms. Since the environmental variable (in most cases), plays a secondary role in determining the house price, complex mathematical transformation might result in less accurate parameter estimates (Palmquist, 1991). We tested the results of different functional forms in the present study and found that a simple log linear equation gave better results.

The main attributes used in this study and their expected signs on determining house values are presented in Table 1. The signs of the estimated coefficients will be positive if the characteristic has positive impacts on property values and negative if the characteristic contributes to reducing the house values.

Lacking any formal measure of house size, the number of bedrooms (*Bed*), bathrooms (*Bath*) and number of garage space (*Garage*) act as a proxy for the dimension of the house. This may vary independently of land size. The garage space is deemed important as many households are now frequently in the possession of more than one automobile. This variable includes both lock up garages and carports as both provide shelter and an additional level of security to car owners. *Area* is simply the size of the property and is measured in square meters.

Distance to supermarkets (D_*Shop*), high schools (D_*School*) and parks (D_*Park*) represent access to community amenities and

Table 1: Independent Variables Used in the HPM and Their Expected Signs

Variable	Sign
Structural characteristics	
Bed — number of bed rooms	+
Bath — number of bathrooms	+
Garage — number of garage spaces	+
Area — lot size (sq meters)	+
Pool — swimming pool, dummy:1 if available, 0 otherwise	
Brick — dummy:1 if primary building material is only brick, 0 = otherwise	+
Neighborhood characteristics	
D_School — road distance to nearest school (m)	$-/+$
D_Shop — road distance to nearest supermarket (m)	$-/+$
MHI — medium household income (AUS \$/weekly)	+
Environmental characteristics	
D_Park — Distance to nearest park (m)	$-/+$
D_Wildfire — Distance to the major source of wildfire – (m)	+
DM_2009 — dummy:1 if property sale took place after the wildfire	$-$
DM_2011 — dummy:1 if property sale took place after the flood	$-$
Other variables	
D_2006 — dummy:1 if property sale took place in 2006, 0 = otherwise	+
D_2007 — dummy:1 if property sale took place in 2007, 0 = otherwise	+
D_2008 — dummy:1 if property sale took place in 2008, 0 = otherwise	+
D_2010 — dummy:1 if property sale took place in 2010, 0 = otherwise	$-$
D_2011 — dummy:1 if property sale took place in 2010, 0 = otherwise	$-$
D_2012 — dummy:1 if property sale took place in 2012, 0 = otherwise	$-$
D_2013 — dummy:1 if property sale took place in 2013, 0 = otherwise	$-$

Note: The main attributes used in this study and their expected signs on determining property value are presented in Table 1. The signs of the estimated coefficient will be positive if the characteristic has positive impacts on property value and negative if the characteristic contributes to reducing the property value.

commercial areas. Parks, here refer to playgrounds and recreational areas. While supermarket and school proximity may be considered a simple convenience, the proximity to parks represents a community amenity. Distance to source of wildfire (Mt Archer National Park) is shown by D_Wildfire. We create two dummy variables to capture the *before* and *after* effects of natural disasters, namely wildfires and floods. This model is estimate separately and is shown as Model II for all the three suburbs. The first dummy captures the impact of wildfires from October 2009 on property values. We name it DM_2009. It is coded 1 if property sale took place after the wildfires. The second dummy is called DM_2011 which captures the impact of the floods from January 2011. Furthermore, the dummy variables for year of sale (D 2006, *D_2007, D_2008, D_2010, D_2011, D_2012 and D_2013*) are designed to capture price changes of the property market due to the two natural disasters, wildfires and floods. Year 2009 is set as the base year. This is because the major wildfire in Rockhampton occurred in 2009. Separate regressions models showing year dummies are estimated and are named Model I. It should be noted here that only "normal" real estate transactions were recorded for this study. Any transaction which listed a relationship between the buyer and seller or any government purchase of property was disregarded. Also disregarded were properties with land size greater than 3000 m². This approach follows Lewis *et al.* (2008) who also point out that by removing larger lots the problem of inadvertently capturing the prices of potentially developable sites is avoided.

The following log linear equation was found to give the best results. Accordingly, the model that is used to analyse the determinants of property values is given by Equation (3):

$$lnHP = C + \beta_1 Bed + Bath + \beta_3 Garage + \beta_4 Area + \beta_5 Pool$$
$$+ \beta_6 Brick + \beta_7 D_{School} + \beta_8 D_{Shop} + \beta_9 D_{Park}$$
$$+ \beta_{10} D_{Wildfire} + \beta_{11} MHI + DM\_2009 + DM\_2011$$
$$+ \beta_{12} D2006 + \beta_{13} D2007 + \beta_{14} D2008 + \beta_{15} D2010$$
$$+ \beta_{16} D2011 + \beta_{17} D2012 + \beta_{18} D2013 + U \qquad (3)$$

The analyses for the study are conducted in three stages. In the first stage, separate ordinary least squares (OLS) models are estimated for the three suburbs using year dummy variables (Model I) and without year dummies but including the *before* and *after* natural disaster dummy (Model II). In the second stage of the analysis, we test for spatial dependence or autocorrelation using the Moran's I statistic and a Lagrange Multiplier (LM) test. For this purpose, longitudinal and latitudinal data for each property were collected. They are then translated into geographical coordinates using Cartesian coordinates in order to estimate the spatial weight matrix. In the third stage we estimate the required spatial models.

Moran's I statistic provides proof of spatial dependence which takes into account the level of spatial clustering or dispersion patterns. Moran's I statistic ranges between -1 to $+1$ where -1 implies extreme negative spatial dependence (aggregation of dissimilar prices) and $+1$ implies extreme positive spatial dependence (clustering of similar prices). Moran's I is estimated using the following Equation:

$$Moran's\ I = \frac{n \sum_{i=1}^{n} \sum_{j=1}^{n} w_{ij}(y_i - \bar{y})(y_j - \bar{y})}{(\sum_{i=1}^{n}(y_i - \bar{y})^2 (\sum \sum_{i \neq j} w_{ij})} \tag{4}$$

In Equation 4, y_i is the market value of the property and $\bar{y}$ is its mean value. Furthermore, w, is the row standardised (row sum equal to unity) weight matrix where w is a $N \times N$ symmetric matrix and y is a $N \times 1$ column vector. Because of the potential presence of spatial dependence [which can be confirmed through the Moran's I statistic (a general test), and LM test (a more specific test)] an OLS regression analysis alone is insufficient to interpret results of the analysis. Therefore, it is important to detect spatial dependence through the Moran's I statistic and a LM test and correct for any potential spatial dependence using spatial models such as the spatial lag model (also known as SAR) and spatial error model (SEM) shown in Equations (5) and (6).

$$Z_{Li} = \rho W Z_{L-i} + X\beta + u \tag{5}$$

$$Z_L = \rho^* W^* Z_{L-i} + X^* \beta + u_L; \quad \text{where} \quad u_L = \lambda^* W^* u_{L-i} + e_i \tag{6}$$

In Equation (5), Z_L is the price of the property in location L and Z_{L-i} is the lag price of the adjacent locations. W has the properties of being row standardized, symmetric and is an inverse distance-based weight matrix. Failing to include this lag price variable as an independent predictor has a significant impact on the model specification when spatial dependence is present (Moran's I is significant). The spatial dependence parameter is shown by ρ. X is a vector of independent variables and β's are coefficients to be estimated. In Equation (6) the additional term u_L corresponds to the autocorrelation of independent variables across the selected boundary.

As shown by Anselin (1988), spatial dependence is one of the main consequences of using geographic data, especially when the properties are located close to each other. This spatial dependence occurs when the price of a property located in a particular suburb is determined both by its own characteristics as well as the characteristics of nearby properties. With such spatial dependence in mind we employ two spatial models which are determined by an LM test. The two appropriate spatial models used based on the LM test are namely the SAR and the SEM, the results of which are then compared with the OLS results.

This study uses data collected from several sources. House sales occurring between January 2006 and December 2013 are considered. The primary source of data was the subscription-based online real estate database, *RPdata* (http://rpdata.com.au). *RPdata* provides commercial and residential real estate information for Australia and New Zealand and is updated almost on a daily basis. The database covers 99 per cent of Australia and obtains its data directly from the Valuer Generals Office of each state. *RPdata* consistently provides information on house sale price, date, location, bedrooms, bathrooms and land size. Information regarding garage space and swimming pools is not consistently provided for every property transaction on the database. Where information regarding these factors was absent, pictures obtained from *RPdata* and Google maps were used to individually assess their presence and quantity (garages). Due to the extensive coverage of "google street view", obtaining this information for almost all transactions was possible. In a few cases this information could not be obtained and these sales transactions were dropped from the study sample.

All distance-based measurements used in the models were obtained using google maps Australia. Google maps allow users to calculate the road or walking distance between any two locations by entering each address into the directions tab on the website. For all socioeconomic data, the Australian Bureau of Statistics (ABS) 2006 census data was used. Data on median household income ($/weekly) was also obtained from the 2006 census data. A census collection district is the smallest geographical area for which census statistics are calculated, with each district containing 220 dwellings on average. All of the collected data was merged to create a unique and comprehensive data set. The final data set contains 593 dwellings for Frenchville, 473 for Park Avenue and 507 for Norman Gardens. This level of observations is large enough to satisfy the asymptotic assumptions of the OLS model and also conforms to the data limitation rules in conducting a LM test and running spatial models such as SAR and SEM.

5. RESULTS AND DISCUSSION

Tables 2, 3 and 4 present the descriptive statistics of the variables used to estimate the regression model(s). The minimum and maximum house values in Frenchville are $40,000 and $971,864 respectively. Mean house value for the same suburb is $376,114 while the average land size is 753 m^2. The average number of bedrooms and bathrooms are 3.5 and 1.5 respectively. Approximately 18 per cent of houses have swimming pools. The distance variables are particularly relevant to this study. Average distances to a high school and supermarket are approximately 1.7 Km and 2.3 Km respectively. The average distance to the nearest park is approximately 718 meters. These average figures can be compared with Park Avenue and Norman Gardens. The minimum and maximum house values in Park Avenue are $130,000 and $726,567 respectively, while they are $139,215 and $789,189 for Norman Gardens. Mean house values for Park Avenue are $283,132 and average land size is 748 m^2 while they are $392,498 and 728 m^2 respectively for Norman Gardens. The average number of bedrooms and bathrooms for Park Avenue are

Table 2: Descriptive Statistics of Estimated Variables for Frenchville

Variable	Minimum	Maximum	Mean	Std. dev.
HP	40,000	971,684	376,114	103,720
BED	2	6	3.46712	0.66221
BATH	1	4	1.51433	0.59293
GARAGE	0	5	1.75717	0.8148
AREA	455	2907	753.383	256.926
POOL	0	1	0.18381	0.38766
BRICK	0	1	0.58516	0.49311
D_SCHOOL	50	5300	1714.28	910.001
D_SHOP	45	5800	2382.61	981.378
D_PARK	20	2800	718.373	461.919
D_WILDFIRE	50	2200	1384.12	491.281
MHI	941	1678	1425.18	202.081
D_2006	0	1	0.13997	0.34724
D_2007	0	1	0.05396	0.22614
D_2008	0	1	0.17707	0.38205
D_2010	0	1	0.11973	0.32492
D_2011	0	1	0.08432	0.2781
D_2012	0	1	0.11467	0.31889
D_2013	0	1	0.13659	0.34371

Note: All Definitions of the Variables and Measurement Units are Shown in Table 1.

3 and 1.2 respectively while they are 3.6 and 1.5 for Norman Gardens. Nine per cent of houses in Park Avenue have swimming pools and 12 per cent in Norman Gardens. Average distances to high school and supermarket are 2.7 Km and 3.4 Km respectively for Park Avenue and 1.9 Km and 4.8 Km for Norman Gardens. The average distance to nearest park is 1 Km for Park Avenue and 800 meters for Norman Gardens. Note that distance to Mt Archer National Park (the source of wildfire) is not provided for Norman Gardens since only a small area of this suburb adjoins the national park and not many sales have occurred in the relevant area which could be included in the data analysed. Distance to Fitzroy River (the source of flooding) is not included for Park Avenue since this variable was not statistically significant.

As discussed, in the first stage of the analysis, separate OLS models were estimated for the three suburbs with year dummies

Table 3: **Descriptive Statistics of Estimated Variables for Park Avenue**

Variable	Minimum	Maximum	Mean	Std. dev.
HP	130,000	726,567	283,132	63,662
BED	1	6	3.03171	0.69277
BATH	1	4	1.21776	0.46617
GARAGE	0	5	1.43129	0.85124
AREA	312	2023	748.448	199.595
POOL	0	1	0.08879	0.28475
BRICK	0	1	0.18393	0.38784
D_SCHOOL	50	5400	2716.65	1517.34
D_SHOP	210	5500	3379.64	1084.92
D_PARK	40	3400	1002.26	592.148
MHI	790.7	1198	1047.68	112.094
D_2006	0	1	0.24524	0.43069
D_2007	0	1	0.13742	0.34466
D_2008	0	1	0.10571	0.30779
D_2010	0	1	0.09937	0.29947
D_2011	0	1	0.08668	0.28166
D_2012	0	1	0.08879	0.28475
D_2013	0	1	0.06765	0.25142

Note: All Definitions of the Variables and Measurement Units are Given in Table 1.

(Model I) and a *before* and *after* natural disaster dummy (Model II). The purpose of this analysis was to identify the impact of household, neighbourhood and environmental characteristics and year dummies (Model I) on property values in the study period. Once this analysis was completed, we introduced a *before* and *after* natural disaster dummy to estimate the same models. In this model the year dummies were replaced by the *before* and *after* natural disaster dummy (Model II). The results for each of the three suburbs are shown as Model I (with year dummies) and Model II (with natural disaster dummy and without year dummies) in Table 5. The regression results show that most of the estimated coefficients have their expected signs and most of them are statistically significant at 1, 5 and 10 per cent levels. Note that the distance to D_Wildfire is negative. This result is not unusual and has been observed in other studies such as Athukorala (2012). As they point out, residents clearly discount the possibility of their properties being affected or they believe that they

Table 4: Descriptive Statistics of Estimated Variables for Norman Gardens

Variable	Minimum	Maximum	Mean	Std. dev.
HP	139,215	789,189	392,498	103,179
BED	2	6	3.619329	0.690893
BATH	1	4	1.546351	0.521591
GARAGE	0	6	1.83432	0.802766
AREA	227	2023	727.9408	180.0282
POOL	0	1	0.12426	0.330204
BRICK	0	1	0.836292	0.370376
D_SCHOOL	100	5500	1884.734	1250.511
D_SHOP	400	8200	4740.592	2068.424
D_PARK	20	2800	818.8146	497.6255
MHI	1069	1712	1409.053	282.5291
D_2006	0	1	0.187377	0.390599
D_2007	0	1	0.108481	0.311294
D_2008	0	1	0.096647	0.295768
D_2010	0	1	0.037475	0.190111
D_2011	0	1	0.076923	0.266733
D_2012	0	1	0.106509	0.308793
D_2013	0	1	0.29783	0.457756

Note: All Definitions of the Variables and Measurement Units are Shown in Table 1.

have adequate insurance and have undertaken actions to self-insure. They are effectively making the trade-off to pay more to live in close proximity to green space at the risk of wildfires affecting their properties. Noted are the negative signs for year dummies for most of the years in the post disaster periods (Model I). Furthermore, the dummy variable for *before* and *after* variable (Model II) is also negative showing the negative impact on property values following the natural disasters. This holds for both Frenchville and Park Avenue.

5.1. *Spatial Analysis*

As mentioned in Section 4, it is important to check for potential spatial dependence using the Moran's I statistic and a LM test and correct for any such spatial dependence using the appropriate spatial models. An LM test provides the basis for choosing an appropriate

Table 5: OLS Regression Results of the Estimated HP Value Models

Variable	Frenchville Model I	Frenchville Model II	Park Avenue Model I	Park Avenue Model II	Norman Gardens Model I	Norman Gardens Model II	Norman Gardens Model III
Constant	11.94307****	12.2663****	11.54228****	11.84423****	11.94628****	12.1186****	12.11627****
Bed	0.0553713****	0.052703****	0.0974133****	0.1008836****	0.0326024*	0.0335522*	0.0335269*
Bath	0.1112085****	0.1141905****	0.0544669****	0.064562***	0.0962988****	0.0973689****	0.0969762****
Garage	0.02255***	0.0225938***	0.0197542***	0.018751***	0.0302755**	0.0315197**	0.0311859**
Area	0.0002248****	0.000235****	0.00000942	0.0000107	0.0005239****	0.0005117****	0.0005111****
Pool	0.068209****	0.0692439****	0.116588****	0.105345***	0.047861	0.0474283	0.04918
Brick	0.0739766****	0.0792724****	0.1313914****	0.1286344****	0.0699254**	0.0772249**	0.0778578**
D_school	0.0000268****	0.0000284***	-0.0000176***	-0.0000313****	0.000025*	0.0000258**	0.0000257**
D_shop	0.0000405****	-1.16E-05	0.000015*	0.0000213**	3.06E-06	8.52E-07	1.83E-06
D_park	-0.0000156	0.000024*	0.0000296****	0.0000394***	0.0000665**	0.0000636**	0.000063**
MHI	0.0001544***	2.20E-05	0.000531****	0.0002053***	-2.3E-05	-0.0001147*	-0.0001159*
D_WILDFIRE	-0.0000486**	-0.0001074****					
DM_2009		-0.033832***					
DM_2011				-0.0555885***		0.0201314	0.024298
D_2006	-0.1793688****		0.1230954****		0.001677		
D_2007	0.0505135*		0.0834272***		0.1090849**		
D_2008	0.0050217		0.0200749		0.069134		
D_2010	-0.0408926*		-0.0517598***		0.062266		
D_2011	-0.0631216***		-0.082785***		0.0798863*		
D_2012	-0.0179768		-0.0268149		0.071901		
D_2013	-0.1202321***		-0.0213432		0.039793		
Adjusted R²	0.56	0.55	0.47	0.43	0.38	0.38	0.38
N	593	593	473	473	507	507	507

Note: The asterisks ****, ***, **, and * denote significant variables under 1, 5, 10 and 20 per cent level of significance respectively.

Table 6:   Moran's I Test and LM Test for Spatial Dependence for the Three Suburbs

Test	Frenchville		Park Avenue		Norman Gardens	
	Statistic	P-value	Statistic	P-value	Statistic	P-value
Moran's_I	0.237	0.812	1.403	0.161	4.642	0
LM_Error (SEM)	10.496	0.001	0.504	0.478	18.105	0
Robust_LM_Error (SEM)	10.519	0.001	2.53	0.112	4.959	0.026
LM_Lag (SAR)	0.443	0.506	10.899	0.001	44.647	0
Robust_LM_Lag (SAR)	0.467	0.495	12.925	0.00	31.501	0

spatial regression model. The results of tests conducted for spatial dependence are shown in Table 6.

Moran I statistic and LM test for spatial correlation shown in Table 6 indicates that spatial dependence is not a major issue for the Frenchville and Park Avenue suburb data. However, both tests show the existence of spatial dependence at statistically significant levels for the Norman Gardens sample. Given that spatial dependence is likely in the Frenchville and Park Avenue suburb data, we use the most appropriate spatial models (based on Table 6 results) for all three suburbs for comparison purposes. The results of spatial models are shown in Table 7.

With 593 observations in Frenchville, the estimated model (Model I) is considered to be reasonably representative of the data profiles. The models explain about 56 per cent of variations in the property values. All the examined coefficients except the D_park variable under structural characteristics are significant at one and five percent levels. Result shows that brick houses are relatively more expensive than other structures. In this model the slope coefficients with respect to the number of bedrooms, number of bathrooms, number of garages, availability of swimming pool and size of the land area measure the individual contribution of each attribute to the price of the property subject to quasi-concavity. For example, the coefficients with respect to the number of bedrooms and bathrooms are 0.055 and 0.112 respectively. This implies that when the number

Table 7:   Regression Results of the Estimated Spatial Models

Variables	Frenchville Model I (Error Model)	Frenchville Model II (Error Model)	Park Avenue Model I (Lag Model)	Park Avenue Model II (Lag Model)	Norman Gardens (Model I) (Lag Model)	Norman Gardens Model II (Lag Model)	Norman Gardens Model III (Lag Model)
Constant	11.91432****	12.23934****	7.024469****	6.275344****	4.537067****	4.717535****	4.713441****
Bed	0.0557254****	0.0530694****	0.0940341****	0.0952496****	0.0296997*	0.0296552*	0.0296296*
Bath	0.1112252****	0.11424***	0.0523765***	0.0602747***	0.0767382***	0.0739193***	0.0741083***
Garage	0.0225119***	0.0225625***	0.0203805****	0.0203495****	0.0257114**	0.026078**	0.0264672**
Area	0.0002234****	0.0002336****	0.0000281	0.0000345	0.0004494****	0.0004347****	0.0004351****
Pool	0.0685592****	0.0695863****	0.111737****	0.0976286****	0.0596148**	0.061547**	0.0608665**
Brick	0.0740612****	0.0793592****	0.1236223****	0.1160086****	0.0625596**	0.0671523**	0.0663315**
D_school	0.0000273***	0.0000288***	-0.0000133**	-0.0000219****	0.0000159	0.000016	0.0000161
D_shop	0.0000404***	-1.18E-05	-5.65E-06	0.0000134**	-0.0000179	-9.84E-06	-0.0000105
D_park	-0.0000159	0.0000238*	0.0000168	0.0000221*	0.0000443**	0.000041*	0.0000414*
MHI	0.0001565***	2.37E-05	0.0003851****	5.88E-05	-0.0000652	-0.0001159*	-0.0001143*
D_WILDFIRE	-0.0000446*	-0.0001036****					
DM_2009		-0.034253***		-0.0623352***		-0.0249856	
DM_2011							-0.0273437
D_2006	-0.1798523****		-0.1009095****		0.0318294		
D_2007	0.0498475*		0.0851553****		0.1076623**		
D_2008	0.0050643		0.0201929		0.062407		
D_2010	-0.0419595*		-0.0506108**		0.0451673		
D_2011	-0.0631102***		-0.0758903***		0.0425666		
D_2012	-0.0184183		-0.069884*		-0.0041772		
D_2013	-0.1208603****		-0.0792521*		-0.0268203		
Rho/Lambda	0.000132 (Lambda)	0.000123 (Lambda)	0.3784469**** (Rho)	0.4585541**** (Rho)	0.6022523**** (Rho)	0.5943961**** (Rho)	0.597196**** (Rho)
N	593	593	473	473	507	507	507

Note: The asterisks ****, ***, ** and * denote significant variables under 1, 5, 10 and 20 per cent level of significance respectively.

of bedrooms and bathrooms increase by 1, property values will increase by 5.5 and 11.2 per cent respectively. Of the neighbourhood characteristics, median household income is significant. Distance to school variable is statistically significant at the 20 per cent level. Distance to park is significant, but has a positive sign. The positive signs of these two variables could be due to short driving distance to these amenities. This is especially the case with distance to high school where students can also use public transport. Distance to supermarket has a positive sign, but is not significant in the model. Distance to Mt Archer National Park (source of wildfires) variable is significant at 10 per cent and has a negative sign. This is contrary to whàt is expected but other studies also report a similar sign (see, for example, Athukorala (2012). This suggests that residents clearly discount the possibility of their properties being affected or they believe that they have adequate insurance, have undertaken actions to self-insure and are effectively making the trade-off to pay more to live in close proximity to green space at the risk of wildfires affecting their properties. We used 2009 as the base year for creating year dummy variables. It shows that house prices before 2009 (except for 2006) were positive. However, since 2009 property prices are negative for Frenchville. It should be noted here that the impact of the GFC on property values in 2010 should also be considered. However, property prices since then are also negative indicating the negative impact of wildfires on the suburb. The *before* and *after* natural disaster dummy in model II confirms this result.

We used 473 observations for the Park Avenue sample. This model (Model I) explains about 29 per cent of variations in the property values. The regression results show that most of the estimated coefficients have their expected signs and are statistically significant at the 1 per cent level. Of the neighbourhood characteristics, median household income is significant. Distance to school is statistically significant at the 20 per cent level with a negative sign. Distance to park is significant, but has a positive sign. As noted this result is not unusual. Similarly, distance to supermarket has a positive sign and is not significant in the model. As was done for Frenchville, we used 2009 as the base year for creating dummy variables. It shows that property prices before 2009 were positive except for 2006. However, since 2009 property prices have shown negative signs for most years with the fall in prices in 2010 most likely being attributed to the GFC. However, after the floods at the end of December 2010/January 2011, 2012 and 2013 the negative impacts can mostly be attributed to the floods. Model II confirms this result.

For the control site (Norman Gardens), 507 observations were used. Model I explains about 38 per cent of variations in the property values. For the control site, too, we used 2009 as the base year to create the dummy variables. It shows that before 2009, house prices were positive, barring 2006 and post 2009 house prices have been positive for 2010 and 2011. This is despite the GFC crisis of 2009 which had a temporary effect on property prices for around less than two years. However, the negative signs for year dummies for 2012 and 2013 show that property prices have declined. This could be due to the stigma attached from frequent natural disasters that have impacted on the two neigbouring suburbs from wildfires and floods. For example, since the 2009 wildfires in Frenchville, the suburb was affected once more by wildfires in 2012 (to a lesser extent) and Rockhampton area in 2011. Park Avenue was affected by floods at the end of December, 2010/January, 2011, 2012 and 2013. The frequent occurrence of natural disasters in the area could be a reason for the decrease in property values due to the stigma attached to such disasters. Model II and Model III that undertake a *before* and *after* analysis also show that property prices have declined since the natural disasters in Frenchville, Park Avenue and in the Rockhampton area.

As mentioned earlier, house values for the suburb of Frenchville in 2007 and 2008 were clearly higher than in 2009. According to the OLS and spatial analyses in Model II, house prices recorded negative signs in 2010, 2011, 2012 and 2013 for the suburb. This may be due to the stigma attached to the suburb as a wildfire prone suburb. Similarly, negative signs were also recorded in the spatial analysis for the suburb of Park Avenue (Model I) for the post flood years, 2011–2013. Once again this may be due to the stigma attached as a flood prone suburb. Negative signs imply that properties which were sold after the natural disasters in 2009 have recorded lower values. For example, the regression results show that the average property value loss in 2011 for Frenchville (wildfire affected suburb) was approximately $22,606. In other words, the results of this study provide evidence to conclude that wildfires decreased the average house values by 6.1 per cent in 2011 when compared to the average house prices in 2009. A similar trend is shown for Park Avenue (flood affected suburb). Model II conducted for Frenchville and Park Avenue also confirm that the natural disasters did have an impact on property values on the two suburbs. On the other hand, Norman Gardens (control site), which was not greatly affected by the natural disasters, show positive house prices in 2010 and 2011. Based on these results, it could be argued that residents are willing to pay a premium price to live in a suburb that is largely unaffected by natural hazards. However, the premium price effect disappears when the neighbouring suburbs continue to be subject to natural disasters. This is shown for years 2012 and 2013. The suburbs of Frenchville and Park Avenue have been frequently affected by wildfires and floods since October, 2009 and December, 2010/January, 2011 respectively.

6. CONCLUSIONS AND POLICY IMPLICATIONS

In the chapter we examined the impact of natural disasters (in relation to wildfires and floods) on house prices after such events. For this purpose we selected the Rockhampton region in central Queensland, Australia. This region is ideal for a study of this nature because wildfires and floods have occurred in the same locality, one year apart affecting different suburbs. Furthermore, these natural disasters have re-occurred in the same suburbs since then. A major wildfire affected the suburb of Frenchville (and a few other suburbs) in October 2009 and 2012 which was followed by floods at the end of 2010/beginning of 2011, 2012 and 2013 affecting suburbs adjacent to Frenchville, such as Park Avenue. For this study we selected two suburbs affected by natural disasters, namely wildfires (Frenchville) and floods (Park Avenue) to test our hypothesis that average house prices in the natural disaster affected suburbs are likely to be negative (at least in the short term) after such events. On the other hand, we hypothesized that those suburbs (in the same area) which suffer less damage are likely to witness an increase in average house prices simply because buyers will be willing to pay more to live in more secure areas. However, if natural disasters become more frequent in the neighbouring suburbs, then it is likely for the premium effect to disappear. The control site that was selected was Norman Gardens which borders the suburbs of Frenchville and Park Avenue. Only a small area of Norman Gardens was threatened by wildfires.

The regression results show that most of the structural variables are significant. These findings are consistent with other empirical studies (Weicher *et al.*, 1982; Sirpal, 1994; Des Rosiers *et al.*, 1996; Tyrvainen, 1997; Sirmans *et al.*, 2005; Hui *et al.*, 2007; Jim and Chen, 2009). The results show that in addition to the number of bedrooms, bathrooms and carports, the availability of facilities such as a swimming pool has a large impact on property prices. The results further show that brick houses are more expensive than timber houses. Interestingly, the distance to wildfire risk area (which is the Mt Archer National Park) has a negative sign. This implies that as the distance to green space (the national park) increases, the house values decrease. This result is not unusual and has been observed in other studies such as Athukorala (2012). What this result says is that residents discount the possibility of their properties being affected by wildfires or they believe that they have adequate insurance, have undertaken actions to self-insure and are effectively making the trade-off to pay more to live in close proximity to green space at the risk of wildfires affecting their properties.

Apart from the above results, the *before* (years 2006, 2007 and 2008) and *after* (2010, 2011, 2012 and 2013) results are interesting. The regression results in Model I show that house prices were positive *before* the two natural disasters (i.e. 2007 and 2008) in all the three suburbs. However, the results show that *after* the natural disasters (2010–2013), house prices have shown a decline in the affected suburbs of Frenchville and Park Avenue. Interestingly, the control site (Norman Gardens) continued to record positive prices in 2010 and 2011. These results provide some evidence to argue that buyers were willing to pay more to live in natural disaster secure areas and vice versa. However, it must be noted that this impact may be temporary if natural disasters continue to occur in the adjoining suburbs. We see such a trend for Norman Gardens in 2012 and 2013 where property values have ceased to increase and are showing a decrease. This could be attributed to the stigma attached to such disasters. Models I and II confirm the existence of such a trend.

As the published literature shows property prices in the affected areas are likely to recovery (and in some cases rapidly) if there are no major natural disasters in the next few years. In this case natural disasters in the region have been quite frequent. Furthermore, it is also likely that the rate of recovery of property values is dependent on factors such as the cost and availability of insurance, public infrastructure, socio-economic status of residents and wildfire and flood mitigation activities undertaken to minimize the damage to the suburbs from natural disasters.

The results have several policy implications. What the results show is that affected suburbs have lower property values. This means that in the case of wildfires, any avertive action taken (which lead to decreased wildfires) will result in increased property values of the suburb. Avertive action can include back burning for which a council levy for affected suburbs can be charged. Similarly, flood Levees could be constructed (have been recommended for Rockhampton) to minimize the damage from floods. Insurance companies could contribute towards mitigation efforts. Note that in the case of Frenchville, residents are willing to pay more to live close to Mt Archer National Park which interestingly is the major source of the wildfires. This has been observed in other studies such as Athukorala (2012). What this means is that residents clearly discount the possibility of their properties being affected or they believe that they have adequate insurance, have undertaken actions to self-insure and are effectively making the trade-off to pay more to live in close proximity to green space at the risk of wildfires affecting their properties. Hence, in the absence of a wildfire insurance policy, residents will continue to pay more to live closer to natural disaster areas such as wildfires.

In the case of flooding and wildfires it is also important to weigh the costs and benefits of rebuilding. For example, in the case of flooding it might be best to convert identified areas subject to frequent flooding into green spaces. Another important policy implication stemming from the study is the importance of disclosing natural disaster affected areas to potential buyers so that the purchase price reflects the true costs of living in natural disaster prone areas. Currently, no such mandatory requirement exists but rather relies on the principle of *caveat emptor*. Given the high degree of information asymmetry that exists (and hence market failure) this is an area that is worthy of government intervention.

REFERENCES

Anderson-Berry, LJ (2003). Community vulnerability to tropical cyclones: Cairns, 1996–2000. *Natural Hazards*, 30(2), 209–232.

Anselin, L (1988). *Spatial Econometrics: Methods and Models*. Dordrecht, The Netherlands: Kluwer Academic Publishers.

Anselin, L and N Lozano-Gracia (2009). Errors in variables and spatial effects in hedonic house price models of ambient air quality. In *Spatial Econometrics*, Arbia, G and BH Baltagi (Eds.), pp. 5–34. Physica-Verlag HD.

Athukorala, W, W Martin, and C Wilson (2012). Valuing Bushfire Risk Using a Spatial Hedonic Property Value Method. Paper presented at the 3rd Human Dimensions of Wildland Fire Conference program held in Seattle, Washington, April 17–19 2012.

Athukorala, W, W Martin, P Neelawala, D Rajapaksa and C Wilson (2016). Impact of wildfires and floods on property values: A before and after analysis. *The Singapore Economic Review*, 61(01), 1640002.

Beringer, J (2000). Community fire safety at the urban/rural interface: The wildfire risk. *Fire Safety Journal*, 35(1), 1–23.

Bockstael, NE (1997). Modeling economics and ecology: The importance of a spatial perspective. *American Journal of Agricultural Economics*, 78(5), 1168–1180.

Brunsdon C, AS Fotheringham and M Charlton (1996). Geographically weighted regression: A method for exploring spatial nonstationarity, *Geographical Analysis* 28, 281–298.

BTE (2001). Economic Cost of Natural Disasters in Australia. Bureau of Transport Economics, Canberra.

Cassel, E and R Mendelsohn. (1985). The choice of functional forms for hedonic price equations: Comment. *Journal of Urban Economics*, 18(2), 135–142.

Crompton, JL (2001). The impact of parks on property values: A review of the empirical evidence. *Journal of Leisure Research*, 33(1), 1–31.

Cropper, ML, BD Leland and KE McConnell (1988). On the choice of functional form for hedonic price functions. *Review of Economics and Statistics*, 70(4), 668–675.

Des Rosiers, F, A Lagana, M Theriault and M Beaudoin (1996). Shopping centres and house values: An empirical investigation. *Journal of Property Valuation and Investment*, 14(4), 41–62.

Donovan, G, PA Champ and D Butry (2007). Wildfire risk and housing prices: A case study from Colorado Springs, *Land Economics*, 83(2), 217–233.

Dougherty, C (2007). *Introduction to Econometrics* (3rd ed.). Oxford: Oxford University Press.

Eves, C (2004a). The impact of bushfires on residential property markets. *Pacific Rim, Property Research Journal*, 10(4), 420–443.

Eves, C (2004b). The impact of flooding on residential property buyer behaviour: An England and Australian comparison of flood affected property. *Structural Survey*, 22(2), 84–94.

Fisek, GO, N Yeniceri, S Muderrisoglu and G Ozkarar (2002). Risk perception and attitudes towards mitigation. In Proceedings from the Second Annual IIASA-DPRI Meeting Integrated Disaster Risk Management: Megacity Vulnerability and Resilience. Retrieved from http://www.iisa.ac.at/Research/RMS/dpri2002/Papers/fisek.pdf. Accessed on October 21, 2005.

Fothergill, A and LA Peek (2004). Poverty and disasters in the United States: A review of recent sociological findings. *Natural Hazards*, 32(1), 89–110.

Freeman, AM (1993). The Measurement of Environmental and Resource Values. Theory and Methods. Washington, DC: Resources for the Future.

Gilbert, JB (2004). The Bushfire Risk: Community Awareness and Perception on the Rural-Urban Fringe of Melbourne. London: Unit Dissertation, University College, London.

Google and Google Earth Maps (2012). Retrieved May, 2012, from http://maps.google.com.au/.

Greene, WH (1997). *Econometric Analysis* (3rd Ed). New Jersey: Prentice Hall.

Griffith, DA, DWS Wong and T Whitfield (2003). Exploring relationships between the global and regional measures of spatial autocorrelation. *Journal of Regional Science*, 43, 683–710.

Halvorsen, R and H Pollakowski (1981). Choice of functional form for hedonic price equations. *Journal of Urban Economics*, 10, 37–49.

Hui, ECM, CK Chau, L Pun and MY Law (2007). Measuring the neighboring and environmental effects on residential property value: Using spatial weighting matrix. *Building and Environment*, 42, 2333–2343.

Huh, S and S Kwak (1997). The choice of functional form and variables in the hedonic price model in Seoul. *Urban Studies*, 34(7), 989–998.

Jim, CY and WY Chen (2009). Value of scenic views: Hedonic assessment of private housing in Hong Kong. *Landscape and Urban Planning*, 91, 226–234.

Kim, Y and RL Johnson (2002). The impact of forests and forest management on neighboring property values. *Society and Natural Resources*, 15, 887–901.

Lamond, JE (2008). The impact of flooding on the value of residential property in the UK. University of Wolverhampton, PhD thesis. Retrieved from http://hdl.handle.net/2436/31427. Accessed on 20 September 2011.

Lamond, J (2009). What is the impact of flooding on property values? Some evidence from the UK. *FiBRE (Findings in Build and Rural Environment) series*. Retrieved from http://www.rics.org/site/download_feed.aspx?fileID=4025&fileExtension=PDF. Accessed on 14 September 2011.

Lamond, J, D Proverbs and F Hammond (2010). The impact of flooding on the price of residential propeety: A transactional analysis of UK market. *Housing Studies*, 25(3), 335–356.

Lamond. J, and D Proverbs (2006). Does the price impact of flooding fade away? *Structural Survey*, 24(5), 363–377.

Lewis, LY, C Bohlen and S Wilson (2008). Dams, dam removal, and river restoration: A hedonic property value analysis. *Contemporary Economic Policy*, 26(2), 175–186.

Lutzenhiser, M and N Netusil (2001). The effect of open spaces on a home's sale price. *Contemporary Economic Policy*, 19, 291–298.

McCaffrey, S (2004). Thinking of wildfire as a natural hazard. *Society and Natural Resources*, 17(6), 509–516.

McGee, TK and S Russell (2003). It's just a natural way of life: An investigation of wildfire preparedness in rural Australia. *Environmental Hazards*, 5(1), 1–12.

Palmquist, RB (1991). *Hedonic Methods in Measuring the Demand for Environmental Quality*. North-Holland, Amsterdam.

Queensland Government (2011). Understanding flood: questions and answers. The Estate of Queensland. Retrieved from www.chiefscientist.qld.gov.au. Accessed 3 October 2011.

Rajapaksa, D, C Wilson, S Managi, V Hoang and B Lee (2016). Flood risk information, actual floods and property values: A quasi-experimental analysis. *Economic Record*, 92(S1), 52–67.

Rambaldi, AN, CS Fletcher, K Collins and RRJ McAllister (2011). Housing shadow prices in an inundation prone suburb. Retrieved on http://www.uq.edu.au/economics/abstract/429.pdf. Accessed on 28 September 2011.

Rockhampton Regional Council, (2012). Regional Profile and Statistics. Retrieved from http://www.rockhamptonregion.qld.gov.au/Your_Community/Regional_Profile_and_Statistics. Accessed on 20 June 2012.

Rosen, S (1974). Hedonic prices and implicit markets: Product differentiation in pure competition. *The Journal of Political Economy*, 82, 34–55.

Sirmans, GS, DA Macpherson and EN Ziets (2005). The composition of hedonic pricing models. *Journal of Real Estate Literature*, 13, 1–43.

Sirpal, R. (1994). Empirical modelling of the relative impacts of various sizes of shopping centres on the values of surrounding residential properties. *Journal of Real Estate Research*, 9, 487–505.

Teague, B, R McLeod and S Pascoe (2010). 2009 *Victorian Bushfires Royal Commission, Final Report Summary*. Retrieved from http://www.fire.qld.gov.au/ http://www.royalcommission.vic.gov.au/finaldocuments/summary/pf/vbrc_ summary_pf.pdf. Accessed September 2012.

Tyrvainen, L (1997). The amenity value of the urban forest: An application of the hedonic pricing method. *Landscape and Urban Planning*, 37, 211–222.

Tyrvainen, L and A Miettinen (2000). Property prices and urban forest amenities. *Journal of Environmental Economics and Management*, 39, 205–223.

Weicher, JC and D Hartzell (1982). Hedonic analysis of home prices: Results for 59 metropolitan areas. *Research in Real Estate*, 2, 267–291.

Zhai, G and T Fukuzona (2003). Effect of flooding on Megalopolitan land price: A case study of the 2000 Tokai flood in Japan. *Journal of Natural Disaster Science*, 25(1), 23–36.

CHAPTER 7

DISASTER RISK REDUCTION AND DISASTER MANAGEMENT IN GOVERNMENT PLANNING AND POLICY AGENDA

Suman K. Sharma

Nanyang Technological University

Reflecting complex linkages between the natural, built, socio-economic and other environments, disasters' consequences can extend beyond the physical to economic, to social and psychological dimensions. Those dimensions complicate the task of impact estimation, and also, the undertaking of policies and actions — measures considered essential — to mitigate risks and threats to hazards and disasters. Furthermore, based on more recent events, the complexities surrounding a thorough understanding of disasters' impacts and consequences are growing as well as evolving; which underscore the reality that any attempt to mitigate potential adverse consequences can be a challenge to policymakers and development actors. This chapter aims to broadly assess how do policymakers and development partners — based on existing knowledge — devise and implement policies and actions not only in response to imminent and actual crisis events but also to mitigate economic damages and losses of potential disaster risks and in the meantime, pursue the sustainable development agenda they are committed to. We attempt to look into two broad questions (i) How well the governments in the region have progressed in terms of mainstreaming a DRR agenda into their development policies, strategies and activities not only at the national but also local levels?; and (ii) in the course of pursuing the DRR agenda, What are the gaps and issues that need to be addressed so as to achieve the goal of reducing risks to hazards and disasters and building resilience? We maintain a broad understanding that DRR agenda should ideally blend in risk reduction concepts and appropriate measures in undertaking development planning, policies and activities at the national, sectoral and local levels, thus requiring dissemination and sensitization of risk related knowledge and information to all stakeholders involved. Given that a multitude of priorities and actions are involved in this endeavor, we narrow down the efforts made and focus only on a few selected aspects considered relevant primarily highlighting the issues and challenges involved.

1. INTRODUCTION

Countries at all levels of development are seen to be increasingly vulnerable to natural hazards and disasters arising from a range of socio-economic factors and other anthropogenic drivers. Reflecting complex linkages between the natural, built, socio-economic and other environments, disasters' consequences can extend beyond the physical to economic, to social and psychological dimensions (Sharma, 2010). All of those factors, in turn, complicate the task of impact estimation, and consequently, the undertaking of policies and actions — measures considered essential — to mitigate risks and threats to hazards and disasters. Furthermore, based on disaster incidents over the last decade and half, the complexities surrounding a thorough understanding of disasters' impacts and consequences are growing as well as evolving (UN-ESCAP/UNISDR, 2012; Van Der Vegt *et al.*, 2015). In this imperfect world of comprehending disasters thoroughly, any attempt to mitigate potential adverse consequences can be a challenge to policymakers and development actors alike. It is, therefore, crucial to understand how do policymakers maintain a balance between existing comprehension (or lack thereof) of risks and threats surrounding crisis and disaster events (imminent as well as potential) and the corresponding policy measures and actions essential to mitigate adverse consequences. Chapter 7, therefore, aims to broadly assess how do planners, policymakers and development actors — based on existing knowledge — devise as well as implement disaster risk reduction (DRR) based policy measures and actions not only in response to imminent and actual crisis events but also to mitigate economic damages and losses of potential disaster risks so as to pursue the sustainable development agenda that most countries are committed to in recent times.[1]

Along this line, Chapter 7 attempts to look into a few related questions, such as, How do the governments in Asia and the Pacific fare in understanding risks and threats to hazards and disasters and their complexities? What are the broad measures adopted by policymakers and development strategists to address the challenges and risks associated with disaster risk management (DRM) in terms of mainstreaming disaster risk reduction (DRR) into overall development and planning agenda? Specifically, Have they identified regulatory and legislative measures to mandate disaster risk reduction (DRR) concerns in their planning and development strategies? Overall, Chapter 7 deals with two broad questions. First, How well the governments in the region have progressed in terms of mainstreaming DRR into their national development policies, strategies and activities not only at the national but also local levels? Second, in the course of pursuing the DRR agenda and aligning with a DRR focused governance structure, What are the issues and challenges that most countries encounter, which need to be addressed to achieve the goal of reducing hazard and disaster risks and building resilience?

While the need for incorporating DRR concerns into disaster risk management (DRM) process and overall development planning and sectoral policies are extremely timely not only to address imminent disaster risks but also to prepare for potential hazards and disasters in future, the actual task of accomplishing the goal appears to involve a painstaking process requiring a multitude of efforts and actions. Hence any attempt to make objective assessments of the progresses and achievements made towards mainstreaming DRR concerns into

---

[1]In the present context, a DRR agenda is understood as the one that expands previous approach and practice of disaster management, focusing on concepts, practice and measures that reduce disaster risks and vulnerabilities " ... by bridging and addressing complex cross-cutting issues, through a systematic effort that requires interdisciplinary and multi-level approaches" (Lim, Choun-Sian *et al.*, 2017).

development agenda can be a daunting one. In order to ensure an effective mainstreaming of DRR into development process, given the broadness of the goal (and consequently, activities to be undertaken thereafter), efforts must be needed in a variety of ways. To begin with, since disasters' impacts and consequences can be reflected in many different ways going far beyond the physical and economic sectors, a DRR agenda should ideally blend in risk reduction concepts and appropriate measures in undertaking development planning policies and activities at the national, sectoral and local levels, which, among others, requires dissemination and sensitization of risk related knowledge and information to all stakeholders involved (UNISDR, 2014; others). Given the multitude of priorities and actions involved in this endeavor alone, for instance, it is only practical to narrow down the efforts made by countries in the region and therefore, in this chapter we focus only on a few selected aspects considered relevant.

Evidences seen among nations indicate that in a broader national context, some of the general policy tools used in the process include enabling regulatory frameworks, legislative measures, budgetary allocations (with increased tax incentives for DRR focused investments) and risk mitigation measures promoting DRR agenda (Birch and Wachter, 2006; Wisner *et al.*, 2012; others). Furthermore, the growing complexities seen during aftermaths of recent disasters around the world and their consequences not only spilling over to various sectors but also, spanning over time, suggest that the policy measures can ensure a sustained outcome only when they involve a longer-term perspective and also, integrate both macro and micro measures with necessary supporting mechanisms built at the local governance level (in relation to accountability, transparency and equity). Along this framework, Chapter 7 begins with a broad discussion of some of the national level efforts made in the region towards incorporating DRR concerns in policy agenda followed by a brief account of some of the efforts and measures taken at the local level. As expressed earlier, since the task of successfully integrating DRR concerns into development planning and policy agenda could involve an enormity of challenges requiring a series of non-relenting efforts on the part of all stakeholders, only a few aspects are discussed. For example, we intend to broadly assess availabilities of some of the national level DRR related policy setting and measures, namely, enabling regulatory and legal framework; clearly identified mandates for resource allocation; integration of national strategies and sectoral development planning; development strategies linked with risk reduction activities; and similar aspects that reflect national commitments to achieving the goal of a meaningful mainstreaming of DRR into development agenda.

Prior to the 90s, governments in the region largely focused on achieving a higher growth rate so much so that most policies and programs rarely shed light on risk reduction concerns in the processes of conceptualizing, designing, implementing and monitoring phases of development planning and activities (Havidan *et al.*, 2007). Over the course of last two decades or so, it seems that the conceptual link between disaster risk reduction (DRR) and development planning has been established as the national governments in the region for the most part acknowledge that a DRR based development approach is essential to prepare for and cope with both imminent and potential hazards. However, the operational aspect — still in a state of infancy — seems to be a hard reality in case of most countries in the region (UN-ESCAP/UNISDR, 2012).

Disaster *pundits* often wonder why is it that a development agenda — embedded with a comprehensive risk planning and risk reduction measures to address imminent and future hazard and disaster risks and associated impacts — has still not achieved adequate priority with explicit motivation and commitment by key players — the government, non-government, business and corporate sectors and more importantly, political bodies? While recent evidences across the region reveal an increasing level of national commitments particularly in terms of awareness raising and incorporating DRR concerns into national policy agenda and at times, also in sectoral policies and planning framework, the overall lack of attention to DRR even by economic analysts and forecasters let alone corporate sectors and businesses is rather disappointing to say the least. Specifically, despite the efforts made particularly in more recent years, governments still lag far behind in integrating various DRR initiatives effectively at the national level that is truly embedded through a range of clearly defined mandates for implementation including strong political commitments, necessary legal and regulatory frameworks, adequate resource allocations and regular monitoring and evaluation mechanisms (UN-ESCAP, 2012; Wisner *et al.*, 2012; UNISDR, 2014).

While many evidences exist to support the claim that within the Asia-Pacific region, there is a long way to achieving a meaningful integration of DRR focused policies and development planning processes that would lead to measurable outcomes of such a merger, the efforts made and achievements seen (to be described partially later in the chapter), albeit in sporadic cases, must not be overlooked. Most countries in the region have made noteworthy attempts to incorporate the DRR concept reflecting their risk reduction priorities and resilience building in one or more national level policy documents while several countries have articulated the DRR spirit through their respective local development agendas as well. However, policy makers and program executers frequently seem to encounter a range of issues and challenges in translating the policy commitments into measurable actions. Furthermore, DRR initiatives in recent times are being closely viewed, and subsequently, the necessary efforts are meant to be undertaken, in terms of resilience building. However, the resilience concept, and consequently, the resilience building tasks have been understood in many different ways depending on the context and discipline under consideration. More importantly, operationalization of resilience building can exhibit complexities, and at times, also lead to ambiguities. In this context, apart from broadly assessing DRR mainstreaming in national policy agenda, we provide some thoughts and observations on application of resilience concept in the area of natural hazards and disasters from a national perspective followed by brief discussions on the role of communities in disaster risk reduction and disaster management practices.

2. DRM AND MAINSTREAMING DRR CONCERNS INTO DEVELOPMENT AGENDA: GENERAL OVERVIEW

During the 90s and thereafter, significance of a disaster risk reduction (DRR) approach in the disaster risk management and the national development agenda got a strong momentum and the DRR theme became focus of attention due mainly to initiatives taken by organizations like the United Nations and others, which facilitated the national governments and supported them in pursuing DRR focused planning and activities (UN-ESCAP, 2012). Since then national governments have been increasingly pursuing the agenda primarily in line with the Hyogo framework (where DRM constitutes five key components — risk identification, risk reduction, preparedness, financial protection and resilient reconstruction) to achieve the sustainable development goal through integrating disaster risk concerns into development planning, policies and practices (Ghesquiere and Mahul, 2010; UNISDR, 2015). Following the trend, governments and policy makers in recent years have increasingly busied themselves in devising ways to catch up with a paradigm shift from traditional disaster management methods focused more on post-disaster reconstruction and recovery processes towards risk reduction concerns as part of development planning reflected through policies, plans and legislation, including their impacts and legal implications (Wisner *et al.*, 2012; UNISDR, 2017). The impacts of major hazards and disasters in recent years, particularly the 2004 Indian Ocean Tsunami, Asian Floods, the 2011 Triple catastrophe in Japan, the 2013 Typhoon Haiyan in the Philippines, the 2015 Nepal Earthquake, the 2016 earthquakes (Japan and Ecuador), just to name a few, leading to increasing complexities in consequences especially in terms of spill-over cross-sectoral impacts (for instance, on supply-chain system during Thailand Floods and Japan's triple catastrophe, among others) clearly underscore the need for a DRR focused development agenda at the national as well as local levels.

Development approaches in the past, designed in most cases to achieve higher economic growth rates, largely turned out to be detrimental to DRR spirit as the unsustainable development practices and depletion of environmental resources eventually ended up increasing both the vulnerability and exposure to hazards thus leading to a realization that development planning and policies must be reoriented towards risk reduction concerns. Country level studies have revealed that such development practices, among other factors, have contributed to policies that have been detrimental to environment, increased marginalization of rural and vulnerable communities and worsened levels of vulnerability on multiple fronts (Havidan *et al.*, 2007; UN-ESCAP, 2012). While in recent times the DRR agenda has gained popularity among academia, professional communities and also, as reflected through policy commitments, the national governments and international communities, complexities associated with translating the commitments into implementation and actions appear to be a herculean task. Wider understanding prevails that the task of translating the necessary policy commitments into an effective set of implementable programs and actions requires a series of concerted efforts incorporating such components as legislative, regulatory and institutional mechanisms with clearly defined roles and responsibilities, information sharing and regular dialogues among stakeholders, resource provisions, genuine commitments at all levels and a sound system of monitoring and evaluation (Havidan *et al.*, 2007; UN-ESCAP/UNISDR, 2012; Wisner *et al.*, 2012; UNISDR, 2015; World Bank, 2017).

Given the enormity of the tasks involved to succeed in mainstreaming DRR into a sustainable development agenda, existing arguments prevail that the national governments provide necessary enabling environments including basic institutional and legislative framework; resource generation and allocation mechanisms; coordination and collaboration among stakeholders leading to a system aimed at institutional capacity building and an effective functioning of national platform for DRR agenda (Wisner *et al.*, 2012). Along this line of thought, the remaining paragraphs in this section look broadly into some of those aspects beginning with the legislative and institutional policy framework to support a DRR sensitive development approach in the region.

Legislative and institutional frameworks are meant to be the backbones based on which all other DRM plans, policies and decisions ought to be formulated. Once the legislative and institutional arrangements are set up, the next step is to assess how the national level official DRR strategies address key elements of DRM. Country cases on progress and challenges of DRR indicate that most countries in the region have clearly identified their DRR priorities in one or more official documents (UNISDR, 2014: Table 1.1a). While in most countries, basic institutional and legislative framework are in place and existing policies are there to support an effective DRM system, complexities of large scale disasters tend to undermine the existing organizational structure and its multiple layers leading to difficulties to come up with appropriate immediate response. A case in point is the Philippines following the aftermath of Typhoon Yolanda (or Haiyan) in November 2013 when local government bodies became overwhelmed with external support to such an extent that they were unable to manage on their own given the vastness and intensity of activities during the immediate aftermath of the event (United Nations Office for Coordination of Humanitarian Affairs, 2014).

Similarly, DRR based development agenda can hardly succeed until and unless the effort is backed and sustained through an effective system of resource generation and allocation mechanisms. However, most countries suffer from one issue or the other whenever resource generation and resource adequacy are concerned to implement DRR plans and activities. Most countries in the region, in general, suffer from resource inadequacy in budgetary allocations dedicated to risk reduction measures. More specifically, most countries overwhelmingly encounter complexities in calculating budget and track fund usage leading frequently either to failure to report DRM budget or inconsistencies arising from varying methodologies across countries. Furthermore, national governments frequently highlight certain practical issues in calculating DRR focused budget as DRR activities are often funded through sectoral investments consequently leading to serious discrepancies in budget monitoring system (UNISDR, 2014).

Another essential element for a successful DRR oriented development agenda is a system of effective coordination, collaboration and partnership among all stakeholders involved in DRM so as to strengthen national capacities. Broad consensus indicates that in order to successfully incorporate DRR concerns into national policy agenda and ensure a meaningful governance system with explicitly articulated DRR concerns, countries need to build a platform of collaboration — possible only through effective consultations — among all stakeholders in DRR practices relying on such core strategies as a comprehensive approach, combined with pragmatic policies, embedded with a sound system of implementation, monitoring and evaluation (Joon Young Hun, 2012). Hence in order to materialize the task of effective coordination and collaboration across all stakeholders involved in a DRR agenda, building and functioning of a national level platform with representations of multiple sectors — government, non-government, civil society, academia, private and others — is vital, and also, appears to have been well endorsed at various levels. Such national platforms have been set up in many countries with diverse objectives ranging from information sharing to coordination while in many cases roles and responsibilities of the agencies seem rather vague and unclear (UNISDR, 2014).

Similarly, the goal of sustainable development based on risk reduction policy measures may not necessarily lead to successful outcomes unless the DRR agenda receives a genuine commitment on the part of all, including political leaders and development workers, along with shift in peoples' mindset towards risk reduction mentality. In line with the Hyogo Framework for Action (HFA) 2005–2015, endorsed by 168 governments at the World Conference on Disaster Reduction held in Kobe, Japan, three strategic goals were agreed upon: the full integration of disaster risk reduction into sustainable development policies and planning; the strengthening of institutions and capacities to build resilience; and the systematic incorporation of risk reduction approaches into the implementation of emergency preparedness, response and recovery programs. The three strategic goals were further divided into five priorities for action, namely, (i) to ensure that risk reduction is a national and local priority supported by a strong institutional base, laws and policies and a budget; (ii) to identify assets and monitor disaster risks, and strengthen early warning systems; (iii) to turn knowledge into practical action; (iv) to reduce underlying risk factors; and (v) to strengthen countries' preparedness (UNISDR, 2005). As seen through the strategic goals and priorities for action, the underlying message is clear, first and foremost, there needs to be a huge shift in people's mindsets, including the mindset of political leaders (Van Der Vegt, 2015), if we are seriously committed to succeed. Changing the mindsets from the past — where disaster management measures focused largely on post-disaster emergency and recovery measures — to the pre-disaster risk reduction and preparedness measures can be a difficult and slow process and thus requires strong will, perseverance and commitments on the part of all stakeholders.

More recently, as a successor instrument of the HFA 2005–2015, the Sendai Framework for Disaster Risk Reduction 2015–2030 was adopted in March 2015 at the 3rd UN World Conference in Sendai, Japan. Building on elements to ensure continuity to the work under the HFA and also, broadening the scope of disaster risk reduction to include both natural and man-made hazards, the Sendai framework has been praised for a number of features, which include stronger emphasis on disaster risk management, setting up of global targets, identifying DRR as an expected outcome, identifying a goal focused on reducing new risk, preventing existing risks and increasing resilience (UNISDR, 2015; UNISDR, 2017).

While DRR approach has been acknowledged as a centerpiece of the development agenda in recent times and to a large extent, most countries have made efforts to steer development policies and strategies towards this direction, the outcomes for the most part seem to fall short of expectations. It is, therefore, timely to reflect upon how far we are on the success ladder, despite acknowledging that the implementation of DRR can be an open ended process, and subsequently, focus on issues and challenges that seem to disrupt the path of success. Before we get into the issues involved (later in

Section 4), in the next section (Section 3), we provide a brief account of the progresses made in terms of disaster risk management (DRM) by the national governments in the region followed by more detailed country level accounts in Indonesia and the Philippines.

3. DISASTER RISK MANAGEMENT AND NATIONAL GOVERNMENTS

a) Overview

Where do the national governments stand in terms of disaster risk management (DRM) and internalization of DRR concerns into development agenda? Or, following an alternative term commonly used in disaster literature,[2] How well the significance of disaster risk governance (DRG) is reflected in the national development planning and policy agenda?[3] While any attempts to provide definitive answers to these questions can be challenging and require open dialogues among stakeholders, the following paragraphs nonetheless aim to depict a broad understanding of some of the DRR initiatives in the region and challenges that lie ahead. We begin with a brief discussion of the progresses made followed by some broad issues involved while embracing a DRR agenda.

In recent years, national governments around the world have exhibited a growing acknowledgment of disaster issues and made attempts to reflect the sentiments through a DRR based development agenda and the respective policy matters in a variety of ways. In the Asia-Pacific region, it is fair to state that significant efforts have been made in order to incorporate DRR concerns explicitly into the national development planning and sectoral policies. In terms of integrating sectoral policies and strategies into disaster

---

[2]For instance, Gall *et al.* (2014); and others.
[3]Disaster literature in recent years has offered differing views on the exact meaning of the term "disaster risk governance" and what it constitutes of. While we appreciate the significance of such a debate, for the present purpose we stick with a more general understanding that disaster risk governance is a component of sustainable development at the local to national scales (Gall *et al.*, 2014).

management laws and program framework, Japan, for instance, has made remarkable progress in recent years through measures like integration of gender policies into DRR framework following the 1995 Kobe earthquake; and undertaking of significant efforts to encourage participation of a wide range of stakeholders in DRR decision making as well as program activities particularly following the 2011 Great East Japan Earthquake. Similar efforts are made in recent years in China both towards extending participatory approaches and incorporating sectoral policies on disadvantaged and marginalized groups into the DRR related specific policy directives (UN-ESCAP, 2012).

In Indonesia, following the aftermath of the 2004 Earthquake and subsequent Tsunami, in 2007, a major law (signed by the President) was enacted while in the Philippines, the institutional framework got major boost with new legal mechanisms in 2010 shifting from relief-oriented policies to DRR focused agenda with notable participation of NGOs and community-based organizations (CBOs) in DRR activities (BNPB, 2013; Disaster Risk Reduction Network Philippines, 2010).[4] In these two Southeast Asian countries — both highly prone to natural disasters — the national governments in recent years have taken some concrete steps in the institutional development aimed at strengthening national capacities since DRR appears to have been much more integrated into their respective development planning. While the Indonesian government has explicitly promulgated DRR concern as one of the nine national development priorities, the Philippines government too has been making similar mainstreaming efforts with participation of a wide range of stakeholders to ensure DRR becomes one of the top priorities in the development planning (BNPB, 2013; Disaster Risk Reduction Network Philippines, 2010; Disaster Risk Reduction Network Philippines, 2010). Similarly, Thailand has increasingly shown DRR commitments in its development agenda with major efforts towards adopting and integrating

---

[4]The following sections in the chapter discuss the achievements and challenges of country level experiences in greater detail in Indonesia and the Philippines.

disaster risk reduction into national development plans as well as sectoral plans. As revealed through the HFA progress report, Thailand has been making headways in terms of adopting and translating the commitments shown through the national disaster prevention and mitigation plan 2010–2014 in a more integrated manner aimed at promoting awareness raising measures as well as encouraging people's participation in DRR activities (PreventionWeb, 2015). In 2015, the Thai government announced details of a new five-year national disaster prevention and mitigation plan which incorporates the priorities for action of the Sendai Framework for Disaster Risk Reduction, largely focused on understanding disaster risk in all its aspects, improved risk governance, investment in disaster risk reduction and better preparedness (UNISDR, 2016; UNISDR, 2015).

In the neighboring Malaysia, disaster management is guided by the National Security Council Directive No. 20 — complemented by other sectoral legislation in forming a comprehensive framework, including the Land Conservation Act and Environmental Quality Act, which in turn prescribes the management mechanisms and determines the roles and responsibilities of various agencies to ensure effective coordination and resource mobilization in DRM. Although the Malaysian government has yet to formulate a national legislation for disaster management, several development approaches are worth noting, such as, implementation of poverty reduction efforts as part of DRR strategy, significant progress being made in integration between DRR and Climate Change Adaptation, approval of the National Policy on Climate Change in 2009 to mainstream climate resilient development where the Key Actions are very much DRR oriented through, among others, systematic harmonization and integration of DRR in existing and new legislation, policies and plans; mobilization of financing and technical assistance; as well as R&D and establishment of disaster database inventory (Malaysia Disaster Management Reference Handbook, Center for Excellence in Disaster Management & Humanitarian Assistance, 2016).

In South Asia, countries like Pakistan, Bangladesh, Sri Lanka and India have successfully taken several measures in formulating disaster risk management policies into their development agenda. Following the 2004 tsunami, noteworthy measures included introduction of new legislations and reforms in institutional development essential for disaster management. For instance, India passed a new Disaster Management Act in 2005 that established a National Disaster Management Authority under the Ministry of Home Affairs and a Disaster Mitigation Fund. In 2009, a National Policy on Disaster Management — comprehensive enough to identify roles and responsibilities of state vs. federal governments in different phases — was approved by the Indian government, based on which the central government's approach is to act as a facilitator in overall management of disaster risks in the country while the primary responsibilities of DRM rest with the state governments (Ahmad, 2013). India, considered to be one of the world's most disaster prone countries with disasters ranging from floods, droughts, cyclones, earthquakes, landslides, avalanches to forest fires, recognizes the importance of strengthening DRR efforts. While during most catastrophic incidences, the country's private sector actively participates in humanitarian emergencies till the response phase, it is not involved in disaster planning processes thus limiting private sector's role as important stakeholder (UNISDR, 2015).

Similarly, Pakistan, following the 2005 earthquake, which highlighted its vulnerability to disaster risks, demonstrated a clear policy shift from the existing response-focused to the current more proactive approach. In the following year, a National Disaster Management Authority Ordinance emerged (NDMO, 2006, replaced in 2010 by the current National Disaster Management — NDM Act). Currently, DRR efforts are embraced through the National Disaster Risk Management Framework (NDRMF) (2007–2012) that outlines a comprehensive national DRR agenda with a proactive approach by emphasizing particularly on risk assessment, risk mitigation and preparedness measures. By doing so, the document, for the first time acknowledged the existing inefficiencies in appreciating the underlying reasons behind hazards turning into disasters (National Ministry of Climate Change, Government of Pakistan, 2013). In case of Sri Lanka, the Disaster Management Act was passed in 2005 that established the National Council for Disaster Management and a Ministry of Disaster Management and Human Rights, which has the authority to direct all other government ministries in the provision of disaster response and assistance (Hapuarachchi, 2009, pp. 55–6). At present, a cabinet approved National Disaster Management Policy is in effect in Sri Lanka, based on which the National Disaster Management Plan followed by the action plan, Comprehensive Disaster Management Programme have been launched. Furthermore, based on the National Progress Report on the HFA, to some extent, DRR concerns have been given due consideration while formulating the national housing policy and the local government policy (Disaster Management Centre, Sri Lanka, 2015).

In Bangladesh, a country highly susceptible to multiple disasters like cyclones, flooding and sea-level rise, a national plan for Disaster Management (NPDM) 2010–2015 has provided clear mandates and policies essential for a meaningful DRR based development agenda (Hapuarachchi, 2009, pp. 55–6). The national plan appears to be making reasonable progress, among others, towards guiding the co-ordination work of the Disaster Management Bureau and the respective line ministries in cooperation with local communities and civil societies. The government's "Vision 2021" sets effective disaster management as a sub-goal while DRR has been emphasized in the annual budget 2014–15 under the relevant sectoral development plans. DRR oriented goals have been set as well as activities identified in various areas in conjunction with climate change adaptation (CCA) framework with a vision of resilience building (Prevention-Web, 2015c).

In other Asian countries, despite that the starting level in disaster management system has been more conventional they appear to be making progress towards showing DRR commitments albeit in sporadic ways (Wisner, 2012; UNESCAP, 2012; others).

b) Disaster Risk Management in Indonesia

In Indonesia, while disaster management framework had existed as guiding policy tools as early as the mid-60s, the system's top-down approach which largely focused on disaster relief rather than risk reduction measures, frequently showed its flaws, for instance, in managing resources and delaying while responding particularly to smaller and more frequent disasters. Also, the model was severely inadequate in addressing the human-induced component of hazards and vulnerabilities thus undermining the significance of risk reduction measures that could have mitigated disasters' adverse impacts in the first place (Wisner, 2012).

The 2004 Tsunami and its devastating consequences highlighted that Indonesia's existing National Disaster Plan lacked severely in dealing with major crisis events. Thereafter, the country embarked on the path of enhancing the existing system of disaster management, which was followed by a series of acts, laws and corresponding programs and policies. In the process, the government established a number of legal documents focused on a disaster risk reduction (DRR) approach. The recent DRR approach appears well supported by various regulatory as well as legislative measures. In most cases, the existing acts and laws highlight the intrinsic linkages between the legal frameworks for DM, the avenues where DRR approach can be used and broader development objectives such as the Millennium Development Goals (MDGs), and more recently, Sustainable Development Goals (SDGs), among others. The endorsement of the HFA, not only set the momentum for intense DRR advocacy but also represented a milestone in funding and the mainstreaming of DRR in development planning both at the national and the sub-national level (UNISDR, 2005; UNESCAP, 2012; UNISDR, 2015).

Following the HFA, the Disaster Management Law 24/2007, considered the most important Law designed to manage disasters, was signed by the then president in April 2007. The 2007 Law, aimed primarily at reducing disaster risks, can be considered a milestone as it provided a comprehensive basis for managing crises and disasters and introduced a fundamental paradigm shift from disaster response to risk reduction. Moreover, recognizing the need to increase hazard awareness and develop a more systematic and integrated approach to DRR, it formally acknowledged that DRR is an important part of the people's basic right to protection and needs to be mainstreamed within government administration and development. The Law itself deserves particular merit since the legislation appears to include most basic principles, namely, public participation, public-private partnership, international collaboration, a multi-hazards approach, continuous monitoring, national and local dimensions, financial and industrial dimensions, an incentive system, and education (ADPC, 2008; UNDP Indonesia, 2008a, b). Also, one unique characteristic of the legal reform approach of the 2007 Law was that the advocacy for reform was led by the civil society organization, the MPBI (the Indonesian Society for Disaster Management).

In 2008, a presidential regulation was issued to establish the National Disaster Management Agency (BNPB) followed by a Minister issued Decree No 46/2008 requiring mandatory establishments of Local Disaster Management Agencies (BPBDs) in all provinces. Consequently, DRM in Indonesia has been guided by various plans and policies including the first National Action Plan for Disaster Risk Reduction in 2006 (BNPB, 2006), followed by the National Guidelines for Disaster Management 2010–2014 and the National Action Plan for Disaster Risk Reduction 2010–2012 (BNPB, 2010a, b). The lead agency entrusted with DRR coordination is the National Disaster Management Agency (BNPB), which constitutes 19 permanent members, representing various government ministries and nine experts/professionals representing non-governmental stakeholders such as practitioners, researchers, NGOs and community-based organizations (CBOs). BNPB, therefore, maintains strong links to the administrative office of the Ministry of Home Affairs in relation to its sub-national role in developing local Disaster Management Agencies (BPBDs). The 2007 Law thus addresses and regulates the development and application of DM plans as well as DRR plans at the national and subnational levels (BNPB, 2010).

The present DRR approach to disaster management in Indonesia has been considered largely holistic in the sense that in addition to the BNPB, which reports directly to the President, and its local counterparts — BPBDs, local Disaster Management Agencies — the system not only recognizes the need for active multi-stakeholder collaboration and public participation but also provides an operational avenue through the establishment of a National Platform for DRR (Planas-PRB). The National Platform is represented by organizations of the United Nations DRR teams, universities, and national as well as international NGOs designed to build and maintain coordination among DRR stakeholders (Djalante and Thomalla, 2012; Guarnacci, U. 2012). Consequently, over the years, apart from efforts made by the National Platform, the government agencies have been increasingly lending support to pursue the DRR mainstreaming agenda, with cooperation from the international agencies, non-government organizations, civil societies, such as voluntary organizations and the private sector. During the last few years, government regulations have been regularly modified and adapted to evolving DRM related needs and environments, for instance, apart from encouraging greater role of civil societies and community based initiatives (e.g., volunteer response squads), the regulations have also mandated government line ministries and BNPB's responsibilities to enhance their response capacity (such as, through developing early warning systems).

On the whole, observations on Indonesia's progress on DRR path indicate that the performance record of BNPB's efforts are quite promising, for instance, in 2008, ASEAN adopted Indonesia's disaster responses in Aceh to respond to the Cyclone Nargis in Myanmar. Not surprisingly, Indonesian DRR efforts have been praised by other countries in the region. More importantly, in 2011, the United Nations hailed Indonesia as the first global champion of disaster risk reduction, and recently in 2016, the USAID has affirmed the country's growing significance as a role model for developing countries in disaster management. Consequently, Indonesia's role in disaster diplomacy seems to have been prominent and also growing. Over the years, it has taken initiatives through administering — mostly humanitarian — assistance to its neighboring countries during needs, for instance, the Philippines a number of times between 2011 and 2013 (including in response to typhoon Haiyan), the 2008 Sichuan earthquake, the 2010 Haiti earthquake, the 2015 Vanuatu tropical cyclone, and 2016 Ecuador earthquake and Fiji tropical cyclone.

In June 2016, acknowledging its competence in dealing with large scale disasters, Indonesia signed a Memorandum of Understanding (MoU) with Fiji on disaster management which encompasses, among others, exchange of knowledge and expertise in disaster risk reduction, prevention, and preparedness, human resource development, climate change adaptation and recovery, and joint trainings and workshops.

While assuming an active role at the ASEAN Coordinating Centre for Humanitarian Assistance on disaster management (AHA Centre), Indonesia's regional involvement further expanded as it took on the chairmanship of the ASEAN Committee on Disaster Management (ACDM), the subsidiary body that oversees the implementation of the ASEAN Agreement on Disaster Management and Emergency (AADMER) under the Conference of Parties (COP) starting 2016. Although the country could become a role model in disaster management efforts, its credibility needs to be strengthened through the improvement of its domestic working mechanisms since despite the tremendous efforts made and successes achieved the national progress report on the HFA implementation (2013–2015), is rather unflattering indicating a range of implementation issues hampering its disaster management efforts (PreventionWeb, 2015b).

In spite of a series of significant policy measures over the years, Indonesia has had to confront a range of issues and challenges in its efforts to translate the DRR commitments into actions due mainly to lack of institutional capacity, technical know-how, budget, and human resources at local level; lack of community participation and ownership in disaster risk reduction programs and decision-making processes; and lack of communication and coordination among government agencies and institutions. In recent times, for instance, concerns are being frequently raised particularly by its neighboring countries in the region regarding Indonesia's continuing battle with persistent forest fires leading to transboundary haze problems thereby raising serious questions over the effectiveness of its disaster management practices. Although there are powerful signs that the country is on its way to increasing its presence through civil-military responses to natural disasters at regional and international levels, the possibility of such presence can be materialized only when it is able to successfully address the gaps and challenges not only in its domestic disaster management efforts but also in its commitment to solve hazardous impacts that frequently spillover to neighboring regions, among others (Sembiring, *et al.*, 2016).

c) *Disaster Risk Management in The Philippines*

In the Philippines, one of the most disaster prone countries in Asia, institutional structure for responding to disasters was initiated in early 40s through a presidential order that was designed to formulate and implement policies and plans to assist the affected population and provide necessary support during emergency conditions (Wisner, 2012). In the following decades, several laws and executive orders were issued in order to strengthen the Philippine disaster control capability and to establish a national program for community disaster preparedness, which further provided momentum to the National Disaster Coordinating Council (NDCC) as the highest policy making body to oversee the disaster related issues in the country. The commitment to building a sound disaster management system was subsequently reinforced during the 1990s through the country's pledge to achieve the MDGs targets, and later in 2005, to building resilient communities when the Hyogo Framework for Action 2005–2015 (HFA) was adopted. More recently, various government declarations have suggested that coordination links on disaster related matters are being established from the lowest government units, the barangays, to the national level (AIPA, 2011).[5]

Currently, the Philippine Congress has been particularly guided by the Republic Act (RA) 2010, No. 10121, which was signed into law in 2010. The RA 2010, otherwise known as the Philippine Disaster Risk Reduction and Management Act of 2010 (also, the National

---

[5]Source: Philippines Country report on Disaster response management — 3rd Asean Inter-Parliamentary Assembly (AIPA) Caucus Report, Manila, the Philippines, 31 May–3 June 2011. Available at http://www.aipasecretariat.org/wp-content/uploads/2013/07/Philippines-Country-Report-Disaster-Management.pdf.

DRRM Plan), serves as the national guide on how sustainable development can be achieved through inclusive growth — aimed at promoting people's welfare and security towards, with a gender-responsive and rights-based approach, while building the adaptive capacities of communities — increasing the resilience of vulnerable sectors, and optimizing disaster mitigation opportunities. The law stresses on adopting a DRR oriented disaster risk management approach that is holistic, comprehensive, integrated and proactive in lessening the socio-economic and environmental impacts of disasters including climate change, and promoting the involvement and participation of all sectors and stakeholders concerned, at all levels, especially the local community. In addition, recognizing the link between DRR and the climate change, the Philippine Congress has also passed Republic Act No. 9729 or The Climate Change Act of 2009, which aims to mainstream climate change into the formulation of government policy by setting up a national framework strategy and program on climate change. The NDRRM Council has been continuing the DRR initiatives and activities in partnership with various national and local agencies in a wide ranging area including contingency planning for disaster preparedness, community level DRM, drills and other measures (NDRRMC, 2011).[6]

The 2010 Act has clear mandates for DRR components reflected in development of policies, plans and implementation of actions and measures pertaining to all aspects of disaster risk management including governance, risk assessment and early warning, knowledge building and awareness raising, reducing underlying risk factors and preparedness for effective response and early recovery (NDRRMC, 2011). As for the governance structure, four major institutional mechanisms for DRMM are provided under the 2010 law, which constitute (i) DRRMC networks from the national, regional,

---

[6]The NDRRMP has four Priority areas — prevention and mitigation, disaster preparedness, disaster response and rehabilitation and recovery — with four long-term goals and 14 objectives, which are designed to be realized through 24 outcomes, 56 outputs and a total of 93 Activities (NDRRMC, 2011; see Annex 1 for more).

provincial, city and municipal levels, and BDRRM Committee at the barangay level; (ii) Local Disaster Risk Reduction and Management Offices; (iii) Office of Civil Defense; and (iv) Disaster Volunteers. In addition, various interventions have been designed to ensure effective integration of DRR education in school level curricula, skill development programs and mandatory trainings for public sector employees. Also, a number of mechanisms exist to mobilize and coordinate international humanitarian assistance for DRR. As for the funding mechanisms, the Act has provisioned that resources will be made available mainly through the National DRM and Recovery Fund, Local DRM and Recovery Fund and Special Trust Fund. Furthermore, early warning systems (EWS) were established in selected priority areas in collaboration between the ILO, central government bodies and provincial and municipalities in the surrounding areas.[7]

In 2011, the Strategic National Action Plan (SNAP) on DRR 2009–2019 was adopted by the then President of the Philippines, designed as a road map indicating the vision and strategic objectives on disaster risk reduction of the country for the next ten years. The SNAP was based on (a) an assessment of the disaster risks, vulnerability and capacity; (b) gap analysis that identified and mapped out significant on-going initiatives; and (c) DRR activities based on the HFA considered (by stakeholders) as achievable priorities for the country, with adequate relevant resources and capacity for implementation. The development and implementation of SNAP was based on two guiding principles, namely, DRR is directly linked to poverty alleviation and sustainable development, and DRR entails the participation of various stakeholders in order to mainstream DRR in relevant sectors in the society (NDCC, 2009).

In recent years, however, despite the institutional strengths in the design of DRRM, its governance system has come under severe criticisms. For instance, following the Typhoon Yolanda (Haiyan) in

---

[7]Source: NDRRMC 2012, NDRRMC final version, Dec 2011. Available at http://www.ndrrmc.gov.ph/attachments/article/358/Final%20Report%20re%20TS%20Sendong,%2015%20-%2018%20December%202011.pdf.

2013, the government's response had been widely criticized for being slow and uncoordinated in dealing with the sudden chaotic situation. The Typhoon Yolanda (Haiyan) rehabilitation plan, for example, was only approved nine months after the super typhoon ravaged parts of the *Visayas*.[8] Lately, policymakers and program implementers have realized that although the NDRRMC was designed as a coordination body to oversee disaster preparedness as well as recovery measures, major gaps exist in the institutional capability for undertaking recovery and rehabilitation measures on the part of the Council (NDRRMC) as well as the local bodies as reflected through repeated creation of task forces for recovery after major disasters, thus indicating reliance on ad hoc solutions instead of a permanent and more sustainable one.[9]

Consequently, in early 2016, a bill (SB 2417) was filed that seeks to transform the NDRRMC into a separate government agency and give it more power to handle issues concerning major disasters. The bill, in addition, seeks to reorganize the current structure of the Office of Civil Defense (OCD), the office in charge of implementing RA 10121. As proposed, the new NDRRMA shall be headed by a director-general and three deputy director-generals with the following responsibilities, among others: (i) formulate and implement the NDRRM Plan, submitted to Congress for approval; (ii) develop and ensure the implementation of national standards in carrying out DRRM programs; (iii) ensure that Local Disaster Risk Reduction and Management Officers (LDRRMOs) adhere to national standards; (iv) provide technical assistance and necessary resources to increase LGU capacity; and (v) establish DRR learning institutes. As envisaged under the bill, the NDRRMC — composed of cabinet secretaries — will still have supervisory powers over the NDRRMA. The council will develop the country's DRRM framework while

---

[8]The **Visayas** is one of the three principal geographical divisions of the Philippines, along with Luzon and Mindanao. It consists of several islands, primarily surrounding the Visayan Sea, although the Visayas are considered the northeast extremity of the entire Sulu Sea, its inhabitants are predominantly the Visayan people.
[9]Retrieved in December 2016. Available at http://www.rappler.com/move-ph/70835-new-senate-bill-new-drrm-agency.

NDRRMA will be tasked to implement it (Disaster Risk Reduction Network Philippines, 2016).[10]

Over the past several years, the Philippines' government, following the Republic Act 2010 — considered a milestone to set the tone and lead the basis for a paradigm shift from disaster preparedness and response to risk reduction — has shown serious commitments through significant efforts and various measures in the area of legal and institutional setup and in policy formulation in line with a DRR focused development agenda. In addition, it has been widely praised for taking a leadership role in pursuing a DRR agenda and considered a model by international communities for governments, community organizations and local communities. The country is particularly credited in taking various steps to encourage, support and coordinate DRR related activities to encompass various NGOs, civil societies and community and volunteer organizations on similar footing not only in the event of a disaster but also during preparedness measures (Gaillard *et al.*, 2014). However, translating those effectively into lowering peoples' risks and vulnerabilities and improving their lives has proven to be a difficult task.[11] Despite the efforts made on several fronts including the instrumental role of government in bringing together a range of stakeholders, challenges still remain not only in minimizing risks to hazards and disasters but also sustaining the positive outcomes and scaling them up to exert meaningful impacts on the lives and livelihoods of the majority of the population.[12] Numerous incidents including the four major typhoons in recent years, Sendong 2011, Pablo 2012, Yolanda 2013 and Glenda 2014,

---

[10]Additional sources were retrieved in October 2016 from http://www.rappler.com/move-ph/70835-new-senate-bill-new-drrm-agency, and http://www.rappler.com/move-ph/issues/disasters/preparedness/74139-ocd-pama-disaster-management-reforms.

[11]The Philippines Country report on Disaster response management — 3rd (and 4th) Asean Inter-Parliamentary Assembly (AIPA) Caucus Report, 2011 (and 2012): Available at http://www.aipasecretariat.org/wp-content/uploads/2013/07/Philippines-Country-Report-Disaster-Management.pdf.

[12]Source: Philippines Country report on Disaster response management — 3rd ASEAN Inter-Parliamentary Assembly (AIPA) Caucus Report, Manila, the Philippines, 31 May — 3 June 2011. Available at: http://www.aipasecretariat.org/wp-content/uploads/2013/07/Philippines-Country-Report-Disaster-Management.pdf.

underscore that the root causes of disasters lie far beyond isolated DRR initiatives.[13]

There has been a growing realization among disaster communities that any attempt to understand a lackluster performance of DRR agenda must reflect on the question: Where do we stand in terms of understanding (or lack thereof) of peoples' risk, vulnerability and exposure to hazards and disasters? The Philippines' case, a common scenario in most countries, suggests that the underlying causes of people's vulnerability have yet to be fully recognized and addressed. Significant efforts are constantly needed — both in terms of mindset and policy action — to shift from post-disaster response and recovery mechanisms of the past towards preparedness measures such as identifying hazard prone areas and other socio-economic barriers likely to contribute to hazard risks and exposure. The general understanding among policymakers is that constant efforts are needed to transform from past development plans and policies, which incorporated neither the risk analysis nor focus on building people's capacities, towards truly believing that disasters are indeed a function of people's vulnerability. This further underscores an urgent need to develop a DRR system to ensure disaster risk assessments (hazards, vulnerability, exposure) are conducted in a regular and sustained manner, and the information utilized properly into preparation of development plans, risk management, DRR activities, sectoral policies (like social, economic, environmental and infrastructural), which will address the underlying causes of people's vulnerabilities (NDRRMC, 2012).

4. ISSUES AND CHALLENGES IN MAINSTREAMING DRR DEVELOPMENT AGENDA

To date, most countries in the region have outlined their legislation and institutional arrangements reflecting the commitments, albeit

---

[13]Gallard *et al.* (2014). Available at http://www.eastasiaforum.org/2014/08/08/a-hard-act-to-follow-disaster-risk-reduction-in-the-philippines/.

on paper, to a DRR-focused development agenda. More importantly, most countries have clearly identified their DRR priorities in one or more official documents such as the national DRM policies, other central authority or area action plans or Strategic National Action Plan for DRR.[14] However, over the years, a number of issues and challenges are reportedly encountered while translating those commitments into implementable actions. Disaster studies on national level policy achievements have frequently identified various factors responsible for lackluster performance in achieving a successful integration of DRR into development in practice some of which include inadequate institutional and legislative structure, inadequate information on risks and exposure to hazards and disasters preventing people from taking necessary measures, deficiency in resource generation mechanisms, lack of proper coordination among program implementers, unclear roles and responsibilities of agencies designated to undertake and manage disaster risks and inadequate capacity — both technical and financial — to deal with disaster risks and exposure particularly in terms of risk implications of development projects and activities (Wisner *et al.*, 2012; UN-ESCAP/UNISDR, 2012; Rao, 2013; UN-ESCAP, 2012; UNISDR, 2014; World Bank, 2017). The paragraphs below discuss some of those issues.

Insufficient clarity in existing legislative/institutional environment requiring an integrated approach with greater commitment

Review of country cases indicate that the major obstacles relating to the legislative and institutional aspects of a DRR development agenda include obsolete institutional and legal framework and/or those with insufficient clarity leading to lack of understanding on the part of program implementers; framework with limited focus on DRR and greater focus on relief and recovery methods; lack of

---

[14]Source: Various country level documents (such as those cited in UNESCAP 2013, UNESCAP 2014) including Ahmad (2013).

commitment and political will to undertake a proactive risk reduction approach; and framework with little coordination — both at the interagency and intra-agency levels — that are entrusted with the task of actually implementing DRR focused programs and activities.

Exact nature of consequences of any disaster can rarely be predicted in advance. Despite this it is essential that an institutional DRM system identify detailed procedure in the event of an imminent disaster, for example, list of actions to be carried out in response to a varying degree of losses and complexities. However, most country cases indicate that the procedure outlined by laws and regulations are not detailed enough and therefore not necessarily applicable in the aftermath of a major disaster with complex cross-cutting consequences. For instance, in case of Indonesia, despite significant measures taken by the government, the country still suffers from lack of understanding of risk reduction concept at all levels; a factor thus identified as one of the main issues hampering the DRR implementation process. Furthermore, various examples — both in Indonesia and most other countries — have shown that the central governments are not able to comprehensively engage local communities and disseminate/communicate key DRR policies within all districts/cities and constituencies. The problem appears more common in developing countries where the situation at the local level in many instances can be far worse (UNISDR, 2014).

Unlike the countries, say, Indonesia and the Philippines, each with a comprehensive set of DRR laws and regulations, interestingly a country like China despite achieving a remarkable economic progress in recent times, still does not seem to have a comprehensive disaster reduction laws and regulations mainly due to existing legal system of "one law for one event". The situation therefore, at times, has led to lack of relevant supporting policies, inadequate implementation of laws and regulations, and more importantly, difficulties in coordinating DRR activities all of which seem to be working against an integrated approach to DRM and DRR development agenda. Arguments for an integrated method of managing disaster risks have been expressed both by governments and academicians in the region calling not only for rigorous and multi-factor risk assessments but also greater reliance on institutional support systems identifying regulations and procedures for an effective intervention. Consequently, in practice, this underscores the need for a multi-disciplinary approach involving a wide-ranging team of individuals representing key sectors — the academic and practitioners, policy makers in all spheres, national, regional, NGOs, community organizations and civil societies. However, the slow progress achieved thus far indicates that despite the commitments expressed in several forms by most countries, it has been increasingly clear that it is rather difficult to translate the concept of DRR development agenda into practice in terms of operationalizing the relationship between risk reduction, economic growth and disaster impacts given their inter-active relationships (Amendola *et al.*, 2008; UN-ESCAP/UNISDR, 2012; UN-ESCAP, 2012; UNISDR, 2014).

This does not, however, mean that DRR concerns are not inte-grated properly into national development planning and policies in the region. In fact, significant improvements have been made towards the integration process in recent years in several country cases but inconsistencies are seen both at the conceptual and operational levels. A case in point is the Philippines' DRR agenda and CCA (National Climate Change Act), both in the conceptual and operational terms. Despite that both approaches aim at increasing people's capacity to adapt to the changes and hazards brought about by the climate and reducing their vulnerabilities, as seen in the Philippines and other country cases as well, the two approaches are largely isolated not only in terms of institutional arrangements but also operational aspects. Furthermore, at the operational level, since the DRRM and CCA, in most cases, are not viewed within a sustainable development framework, programs are developed intermittently, or on ad-hoc basis, for instance, only when a disaster occurs. The problem seems common in many country cases and programs and projects are not sustained because they are not mainstreamed into the development plans and more importantly, into national and local policies — both of which will secure sustained funding and political support (UNISDR, 2014; Bang, 2013; and others). In a broader sense, therefore, a more practical issue commonly observed across

countries relates to roles and responsibilities of existing authorities
and their respective institutional alignments. For example, in many
country cases, there seems to be a lack of a central agency responsible
for taking the lead in DRR activities and coordinating activities
of sectoral organizations (UNISDR, 2014). The issue can be more
pressing particularly during major crisis events.

Overall, DRR focused acts and plans do exist in several countries
in the region, however, lack of consistency and coordination between
different laws and plans seem to be hindering implementation of
DRM activities in a comprehensive manner (Bang, 2013; and others).
In Indonesia, for instance, there is an urgent need to synchronize
and harmonize laws and regulations across sectoral agencies as
well as at different government levels. Similarly, embedded culture
of post-disaster recovery focused on emergency management and
relief require shifting mindsets. Furthermore, even with a sound
legal framework, an effective enforcement can be hampered due
to lack of regulatory power, capacity (human and financial), and
awareness/coordination across sectors and with different government
levels, for instance, Bangladesh does have some sound DRR policies
and frameworks but lacks capacity on all fronts, technical, financial
and human, to implement those.

Poor coordination and lack of cooperation at multiple levels

Systemic nature of poor coordination and lack of cooperation during
DRM stages — not only across agencies and disaster stakeholders
but also within various levels of a single line agency — can hamper a
DRR agenda as mainstreaming of DRR into development programs
requires existing disaster management mechanisms be integrated
to ensure effective and sustainable outcomes. However, common
scenario across countries indicates that most stakeholders suffer
from poor coordination and lack of cooperation during most stages
of disaster management and the problem can get more severe
during emergency response (UNISDR, 2014; World Bank, 2017).
Furthermore, during the implementation phase of policy measures,

it is important that the roles and responsibilities of stakeholders especially those involved in service delivery are clearly identified to ensure effectiveness. For instance, Indonesian case suggests that when multiple channels are involved, there is a danger of duplication of efforts without proper coordination thus complicating the immediate actions to be undertaken by local bodies (BNPB, National Agency for Disaster Management, 2014). Similarly, the poor coordination issue became evident in the Philippines following the 2013 Typhoon Yolanda (Haiyan) where local bodies, overwhelmed with foreign assistance, were barely able to manage the newly acquired resources on their own.

A pertinent concern, therefore, is: how to balance roles and responsibilities of the national governments *vis-à-vis* external actors, as far as their respective roles as key players in DRR development agenda are concerned. In several Asian countries, external actors are known to have dominating roles, and at times, they can be imposing upon domestic ones seeking influence as well as publicity, which could undermine existing local wisdom and capacity in managing crisis events. So the challenge lies in devising a reasonable way to balance out roles/responsibilities across implementing agencies while pursuing the DRR agenda. On the one hand, coordination within the government sector, both horizontally and vertically, is essential to oversee existing disaster management system given the complexities of the issues involved. At the same time, wisdoms, capacities and resources available at local bodies and adjacent institutions and civil societies are far too crucial and need to be properly utilized to develop resilience to hazards and disasters in future.

Within a government system, an effective coordination mechanism across agencies must prevail virtually at all levels so as to ensure a smooth functioning of DRR programs and activities leading to measurable outcomes. As an example, lack of coordination across line agencies can result in inconsistencies in disaster impact information. In Indonesia, as is commonly seen elsewhere, data on disaster victims, number of people affected and numbers of people needing immediate help and so on is rarely consistent and suffer from omissions as well as duplications leading to problematic responses. One case in point is difference of data in terms of survivors that are injured and the types of injury they suffer will make it difficult to allocate medical personnel and equipment, including medicines needed to treat disaster survivors. Similarly, differences in data concerning damaged houses and public infrastructure will hamper calculation of the needs for rehabilitation and reconstruction, thus slowing down the overall recovery of the disaster affected communities. The data inconsistency issues like these, among others, can mislead the situation on the ground so much so that the genuine needs of affected peoples and communities cannot be identified and addressed properly (BNPB, 2014; PreventionWeb, 2015b; PreventionWeb, 2015c).

Consequences of recent disasters and the complexities involved, therefore, have increasingly shown that perhaps it is time to modify and/or amend prevailing DRM systems among most governments in the region (for instance, NDRRM in Indonesia and the Republic Act 10121 in the Philippines, among others) to transition towards a more coordinated system of DRR focused measures. There have been increasing calls that existing rules of laws, in many instances, appear to exhibit less prominence on disaster preparedness compared to disaster response, which the governments need to seriously reflect upon to improve DRR mechanisms (NDRRMC, 2015).

Paradigm Shift from emergency management to risk reduction: a mirage?

It is ironic that more than a decade after the HFA endorsement most countries in the region still seem to have difficulties in transitioning from a greater focus on post-disaster mentality to undertaking risk reduction and preparedness measures. As an example, despite the paradigm shift approach of the 2007 Law on disaster management in Indonesia, the number of disaster risk reduction plans and programs is still severely inadequate, a common reality in most Asian countries. Overall, in its current form, therefore, disaster management seriously requires institutional orientation as it still tends to place greater emphasis on emergency response rather than disaster prevention and risk reduction. The challenge now is to materialize the new paradigm of risk reduction approach and create a sustained system through necessary disaster policies, regulations and operating procedures at all levels including the lowest level of governance. DRR paradigm needs to be advocated among decision makers, so that all development policies and programs are designed with a risk reduction perspective. More specifically, development programs need to adopt a risk reduction perspective in all aspects of planning including disaster risk mapping, local land use, temporal as well as spatial planning, for instance.

Inadequate information and capacity to manage hazard and disaster risks

A related area of concern consists of inadequate information, capacities and skills essential for risk management at all levels. A significant share of population in many countries still tends to reside in hazard prone areas — a hard reality around the globe. This shows that vulnerable groups of people are either unaware of and/or unable to benefit from various awareness raising activities in many instances. Greater focus on targeted measures is essential to disseminate risk awareness measures including regular risk reduction training and simulations, distribution of materials highlighting hazard risks, establishments of emergency rapid response teams at the community level, establishing and coordinating volunteer organizations. Furthermore, at the government level, provinces, districts and cities should establish their local disaster management bodies and allocate those with required resources and personnel thus making them aware of the relative importance of risk-sensitive development planning and programming *vis-à-vis* emergency and recovery measures. For example, despite that Indonesia has passed numerous rules/regulations in DRR and DM from the central to district/city levels, capacities both at the central and particularly district/city levels are still inadequate to ensure successful outcome. The key challenge, among others, is identified as lack of coordination across stakeholders and lack of clarity in roles and responsibilities between BNPB and national actors and BPBDs and local actors (Pristiyanto, 2015) leading to inadequate capacities to successfully carry out awareness raising and risk reduction measures. Similarly, in the Philippines, following the recent crisis events like 2013 typhoon Yolanda (Haiyan) and others (the 2014 tropical storms Mario and Seniang, 2015 typhoon Lando and the December 2016 typhoon Nina), various observations and assessments suggested that despite a comprehensive regulating DRM framework in the country, the local bodies are not adequately equipped in capacity to handle destruction and casualties in the event of a major disaster (CARITAS/Global Risk Forum, 2014; and others[15]). Call for raising awareness has been increasingly emphasized in recent times and the target groups include private citizens, the business community, and even the youth sector, among others (NDRRMC, 2015).

At the same time, however, awareness raising measures may not necessarily lead to measurable outcomes right away and at times raising awareness can simply be easier said than done; as various case studies across Asia suggest that achieving the goal of risk reduction with a lowered level of vulnerability still appears to be a far cry in practice. In most country cases, for instance, including the Philippines and Indonesia in the Southeast Asia and countries in South Asia, despite that a number of awareness raising DRM materials are produced, most of the recommendations seem to emphasize more on disaster preparedness and response measures rather than reducing peoples' vulnerabilities and exposure to disaster risks such that the underlying messages of risk reduction hardly get conveyed to the majority of people nor do their potential contribution towards a sustainable risk reduction reflected. In view of this, awareness raising efforts should rather be aimed at institutionalizing the knowledge development mechanisms, conveying the complementarity between DRR focused activities and those for disaster response, and sharing and knowledge management system so as to ensure

---

[15]Retrieved on 22 February 2017. Available at https://en.wikipedia.org/wiki/List_of_retired_Philippine_typhoon_names.

a sustained DRR agenda in practice (Riyanti D and F Thomalla, 2012).

Furthermore, country level progress reports on DRR development agenda indicate that amidst the huge need for capacity building in many countries, ironically, the budgetary provisions and resource availabilities essential for carrying out DRR focused measures are largely inadequate. In terms of resource allocations towards risk reduction vs. emergency and recovery measures, data on national level budgetary allocations, in most cases, demonstrate that relatively larger portions of budgets are still allocated to post-disaster response and recovery measures compared to a DRR focused development approach aimed at reducing risks and vulnerabilities (UNISDR, 2014; World Bank, 2017).

Building National Resilience: Inadequate attention or operational complexities?

In recent times, there is a growing realization that disaster risk reduction efforts ought to be closely undertaken along with resilience building. Disaster researchers, therefore, have increasingly placed greater focus on capacity of nations and communities to recover from and cope with unpredictable events thus requiring a stronger emphasis on risk reduction measures aimed at resilience enhancement rather than vulnerability reduction (IFRC, 2004). While the concept of resilience building has been gaining immense popularity in recent years, the applicability and resulting variations, and at times, complexities surrounding it, are far too crucial to be overlooked. Over the years, the resilience concept has been understood and applied in many different ways depending on the context and discipline one may be referring to. More importantly, operationalization of resilience building at the national scale can involve a series of concerted efforts on multiple fronts and thus exhibit complexities leading at times to ambiguities. In the present context, our question of interest is: What exactly is meant by resilience in disaster research and how do nations operationalize the resilience building concept into reducing risks to hazards and disasters while pursuing a DRR development agenda?

Following the recent thinking on the literature on disasters, we consider three common elements of disaster resilience, based on which resilience is defined as a country's ability to (i) withstand or resist disaster impacts; (ii) bounce back after being impacted; and (iii) learn from experience and modify its behavior and structure to adapt to future disaster threats. Along this line, the next section provides some thoughts and observations on the application of resilience concept in the area of natural hazards and disasters. Specifically, Section 5 begins with a detailed literature review of the concept and measurement of disaster resilience followed by some insights on complexities involved in understanding and monitoring the extent of resilience among nations.

5. DISASTER RISK REDUCTION AND BUILDING NATIONAL RESILIENCE

Introduction and Literature Review

The concept of resilience has gone (and continues to go) through a multitude of debates/refinements crossing various disciplinary boundaries, namely, ecology, physics, psychology and psychiatry during the early days while disaster management and other areas in more recent times. In the context of natural hazards and disasters, resilience has been defined in many ways, sometimes bearing closer relationship with vulnerability while at other times an altogether different type or less strong relationship with vulnerability (Manyena, 2006). For instance, resilience is known to have two components — inherent and policy-induced. Given that the inherent component of resilience is considered an obverse of vulnerability (Briguglio, 2003), a higher level of (inherent) resilience means a lower degree of vulnerability. However, due to the policy-induced component of resilience, which does not necessarily depend on vulnerability, various definitions used by researchers in a wide range of areas suggest that resilience is not the opposite of vulnerability. Although even today, no consensus on the definition of resilience exists, and therefore, its relationship with vulnerability is still being debated.[16]

The consensus among disaster researchers today is that disasters' consequences are affected by measures taken before, during and after their occurrence. This realization has led to a greater focus on mitigation measures in order to reduce disasters' losses and to lessen the overall burden (Mileti, 1999; Rose, 2004; and others). Mitigation measures are considered important as they can lower both the probability and magnitude of disaster losses by reducing the vulnerability of manmade environment. However, even in the absence of mitigation, a nation can have the ability to cushion or reduce loss and its impact through enhancing its resilience (Rose, 2004). The resilience concept, in this context, is used to refer to the ability of a system (or a nation) to withstand, and also, recover from the effects of an external shock. According to Timmerman (1981; cited in Mayunga, 2007), resilience measures "a system's or part of the system's capacity to absorb and recover from occurrence of a hazardous event", while Wildavsky (1991) defines resilience as "the capacity to cope with unanticipated dangers after they have become manifest, learning to bounce back." Unlike the focus of mitigation on pre-disaster measures, resilience emphasizes resource strengthening and capacity enhancement measures applied before, during and after an event. Also, resilience places greater emphasis on behavioral and institutional aspects.

The early focus of disaster studies was on analysis of measures aimed at lessening a disaster's adverse consequences after its occurrence. The post-disaster measures emphasized on relief, reconstruction and recovery efforts primarily through fiscal/budgetary restructuring. Over time, the emphasis shifted to mitigation measures, which are considered more cost-effective compared to post-disaster measures, as disasters were increasingly being viewed as a result of natural and man-made behavior, thus calling for a

---

[16]For example, Alexander (2013) has examined how the term resilience came to be adopted in disaster risk reduction, and also, made attempts to resolve some of the conflicts and controversies that have arisen in the process.

need to address vulnerabilities of physical structures as well as socio-economic factors. Most mitigation studies have concentrated on reducing vulnerabilities of physical structures but a growing body of disaster researchers and practitioners has recognized the need for increasing capacities of societies and nations to withstand and recover from adverse effects of natural disasters indicating a greater focus on resilience building. Focusing our discussion on understanding of resilience and measurement of a nation's resilience in the area of hazards and disasters, in the following paragraphs, we discuss some of the vulnerability and resilience indicators commonly used.

Cutter, Boruff and Shirley (2003) and Cutter, Emrich and Burton (2008) have computed Social Vulnerability Index and Disaster Resilience Index, respectively, for all the US counties based on which vulnerability (at the county level), and correspondingly, resilience index (at the county level), are measured through several socio-economic and demographic variables including personal wealth, age, density of built environment, housing status, race/ethnicity, infrastructure dependence and single sector economic dependence. As for the national level computation of vulnerability index, one significant contribution was made by Briguglio (2003) with the goal of vulnerability reduction among the Pacific Island nations. However, the primary focus in this exercise was on measuring economic vulnerabilities in the context of a Small Island Developing State (SIDS), which under the circumstances, dealt with assessing vulnerabilities caused by external forces and not the consequences of domestic policies. Similarly, the United Nations (UN) has provided a comprehensive framework on building a Social Vulnerability Index (SVI) for the Caribbean region. The UN model focuses on five components: education, health, security and social order, resource allocation and communications architecture, each measured by relevant indicators. However, the actual computation of SVI is yet to be finalized due mainly to lack of data (UN-ISDR, 2007).

As for the measurement of disaster resilience, existing literature indicates that the resilience concept has been applied into the areas ranging from the level of a firm/business, to community, city and a nation. For instance, Rose (2004) has measured economic resilience, defined as "the inherent and adaptive responses to disasters that enable individuals and communities to avoid some potential losses", to analyze the behavior of individuals, businesses and markets through applying a computable general equilibrium (CGE) modeling framework.

Most of the initiatives on measurement of resilience appear to focus at the community level. In most cases, these community level approaches are limited to examining the resilience concept, providing assessment methods (Sea Grant, NOAA, 2008), and proposing frameworks to compute a resilience index (for example, Cutter *et al.*, 2008; UNISDR, 2013b; among others). As an example, Mayunga (2007) has proposed a conceptual and methodological framework for measurement and mapping of a community level disaster resilience using a capital-based approach. His framework to construct a resilience index is based on five major forms of capital: social capital, economic capital, human capital, physical capital and natural capital, each of which can be measured by a combination of different indicators. Similarly, Bruneau *et al.* (2003) present a conceptual framework to define seismic resilience of communities and provide quantitative measurements of resilience based on three complementary measures: reduced failure probabilities, reduced consequences from failures and reduced time to recovery. The framework integrates those measures into four dimensions of community resilience- technical, organizational, social and economic-, all of which can be used to quantify measures of resilience for various types of physical and organizational systems.

Simpson and Katirai (2006) have examined issues in measuring disaster preparedness and resilience at the community level and proposed a framework for creating a Disaster Preparedness Index (DPI) and Resiliency Index (DRi). In their model, Disaster Resiliency Index (DRi) is defined as the ratio of Preparedness Index (PI) to Vulnerability (V). Based on their framework, both the indexes, DPI and DRi, can be computed using the formula $DRi = Pi/V$; where P, the preparedness measure, can be computed based on various community level preparedness measures undertaken before a disaster occurs. Similarly, vulnerability (V) is defined as the product of hazard, probability of risk, hazard frequency and vulnerability measures. Based on this specification, a community is considered more resilient when the value of DRi exceeds one, while a less than one value would mean less resilient. The study provides a comprehensive list of suggested indicators for creating both DPI and DRi for possible inclusion in building the indexes.

Cutter *et al.* (2010) have developed a methodology to measure baseline characteristics of communities that foster resilience. Focusing specifically on the inherent component of resilience, their index is based on five dimensions — social resilience, economic resilience, institutional resilience, infrastructure resilience and community capital — each measured by relevant community level variables. They have later applied the methodology to several South-eastern counties of the United States making it possible to monitor changes in resilience over time and across places.

Some other studies on resilience measurement have focused at the city level, particularly those located around urban coastal areas. For instance, Chang and Shinozuka (2004) have computed index to measure resilience to earthquake disasters at the city level. Focusing on earthquake resilience, they have considered four dimensions — technical, organizational, social and economic performance of a city under consideration — each comprising of several indicators (with the city level data) in building a resilience index.[17] Similarly, researchers at the Kyoto University have computed Climate Disaster Resilience Index (CDRI) for 16 Asian urban cities with main focus on climate-induced disasters. Based on five resilience dimensions — natural, physical, social, economic and institutional- each measured by several city level indicators — the CDRI values are standardized using a ranking method ranging from 1 (a poor level of resilience) to 5 (the highest resilience) (IEDM/Kyoto University, 2008). The UNISDR launched a "Making Cities Resilient" campaign in 2010 to support sustainable urban development by promoting resilient

---

[17]For instance, technical performance (of water system) is measured through the number of major pumping stations lost in an earthquake.

activities and increase understanding of disaster risks at the local level. A number of outcomes of the campaign demonstrate the success as well as relevance of the project deemed valuable for policymakers, which mainly include three successful DRR components: (i) a dedicated institutional body of increased political commitment to DRR; (ii) projects geared towards improving infrastructure, retrofitting building or construction of safe schools are the next most important components of resilience building; and (iii) resilience indicators need to be locally developed vis-à-vis the city's own risks and current governance systems (UNISDR, 2013b, p. 7).

Existing literature on measurement of disaster resilience at the national level is scarce. Although Briguglio and others (2008) have computed both vulnerability index and resilience index at the national level, their focus is primarily on economic resilience, which is defined as the policy-induced ability of an economy to recover from or adjust to the negative impacts of adverse exogenous shocks and to benefit from positive shocks. In their framework, the resilience index is based on four major components, namely, macroeconomic stability, microeconomic market efficiency, good governance and social development, each measured through several economic, social and institutional variables (Briguglio *et al.*, 2008).

As per the more recent disaster literature, resilience concept has been adopted as a guiding principle behind an effective hazard risk management since even the major international organizations are leaning towards Index building exercises by quantifying hazard and disaster risks (Mayunga, 2007; Benson and Twigg, 2004; UNISDR, 2014). For example, recognizing the importance of mainstreaming disaster risk reduction within broader development agenda, organizations like the UNDP, World Bank and others have taken initiatives to develop indicators of national and sub-national disaster risk. Examples include, UNDP's Disaster Risk Index, a global assessment of national disaster risk, which calculates the average risk of deaths per country in large-scale and medium-scale disasters associated with earthquakes, tropical cyclones and floods. Similarly, The Hotspots Project, jointly initiated by the World Bank and ProVention Consortium, a global, sub-national assessment of risk calculated for grid cells rather than for countries as a whole, aims to provide a rational basis for prioritizing risk reduction efforts and highlighting areas where risk management is most essential. The project has calculated risks of both mortality losses and economic losses as a function of the expected hazard frequency and expected losses per hazard event (Center for Hazards & Risk Research, 2005). These indicators are primarily designed to allow development partners to judge the relative importance of disaster risk in decisions on country programming, to provide an initial basis for identifying requirements for strengthening disaster risk management, and to facilitate monitoring and evaluating program performance (Benson and Twigg, 2004).

More recent resilience indexes are intended to be used at the city level. The ACCCRN framework (Tyler *et al.*, 2014), for instance, has been developed for the purpose of local planning and monitoring changes in climate resilience in an urban context. Though the approach acknowledges that neither adaptation nor resilience can be measured directly, and that indicators are only proxies, the indicators and matrices are structured around key vulnerability issues within specific cities, thus emphasizing on building collaboration between city-level partners and the national-level program coordinators in order to implement climate resilient interventions (Tyler *et al.*, 2014).

Another recent initiative is the UN/ISDR Disaster Resilience Scorecard for Cities (UN/ISDR, 2014b), which is a tool for cities to assess their baseline level of "disaster resilience", defined as the ability of a city to mitigate and recover from an extreme event. This is further described as "the ability of a city to understand the disaster risks it may face; to mitigate those risks; and to respond to disasters that may occur, in such a way as to minimize loss of or damage to life, livelihoods, property, infrastructure, economic activity and the environment" (UN/ISDR, 2014b). The Scorecard includes 85 evaluation criteria, which are grouped in a range of categories like research (including evidence-based compilation and communication of threats and needed responses); organization (including policy, planning, coordination and financing); infrastructure (including critical and social infrastructure and systems and appropriate development);

response capability (including information provision and enhancing capacity); environment (including maintaining and enhancing ecosystem services); and recovery (including triage, support services and scenario planning) (UN/ISDR, 2014b).

Given that the resilience term has been used and understood in the context of a variety of disciplines, one can naturally wonder as to the applicability and usefulness of the concept at the operational level. The existing literature on disaster resilience shows that despite the ongoing debates on the conceptual aspect of resilience, its operational aspect still appears to be at its infancy stage (Mayunga, 2007). This is primarily due to the reason that complexities in the area of disaster resilience exist at multiple levels. For instance, at the operational level, difficulties exist in modeling individual, group and community behavior in a single framework while at the empirical level data availability can be the constraining factor (Rose, 2004). Similarly, resilience has been examined in relation to physical infrastructure and/or the structure of institutions (Manyena, 2006). Various researchers (Rose, 2004; and others) highlight that resilience building measures can be applied at the level of the firm, household, market, regional economy and the macroeconomy as a whole. Overall, the literature on disaster resilience indicates that despite the recent significance given to resilience in disaster risk management, the challenge is to transform the resilience concept into an operational tool for policy and management purposes, which is still not resolved despite the academic debate for more than three decades (Klein *et al.*, 2003).

Disaster Resilience: Operational Aspect and Complexities

The natural aspect of disasters, in terms of their location, intensity and frequency cannot be avoided, for the most part. Still, a country can make efforts through appropriate policy measures to prepare for, cope with, and recover from disasters; and this is where resilience thinking comes in. Unlike the early focus of disaster management on relief, reconstruction and recovery efforts aimed at reducing disasters' impacts after their occurrences, there is now a greater emphasis on resilience building to improve capacities of nations and communities.

The resilience concept, therefore, appears to be well acknowledged by all in various disciplines including disaster risks. The operational aspect of resilience, however, is easier said than done. Complexities can exist at multiple fronts. What are the factors that resilience depends on? What makes a country more (or less) resilient? What are the avenues that policymakers should consider in the process of building resilience? The answers can be complex. For illustration purpose, the paragraphs below attempt to highlight briefly the complexities involved in operationalizing the disaster resilience concept while measuring resilience in terms of five national level dimensions, namely, natural, physical, economic, social and institutional.

In the national context, for instance, resilience — expressed in terms of a nation's ability to manage and sustain basic functions and structures, and recover after a disaster occurs — can be understood by examining its state of natural environment, physical infrastructure and lifelines, economic development, social development and institutions, collectively referred as the five dimensions of resilience. The natural environment determines the extent to which a country faces different types of natural hazards (earthquakes, typhoons, floods, etc.). A country with a well-developed physical infrastructure designed to sustain the forces imposed by all the natural hazards affecting it is better able to withstand these events and their resulting effects, and is thus considered resilient. For instance, the contrasting situations (and the following aftermaths) in Haiti and Chile, both hit by major earthquakes during early January of 2010, underscore this point. A country with a higher level of social development is more likely to have citizens with better knowledge and skills to understand disaster-related risks, and therefore, take measures to better protect themselves. A higher economic development strengthens resilience through solidifying economic stability and ensuring resource availability; whereas sound institutions are essential for an economy to function, manage and govern properly and be resilient. In situations where good governance and rule of law are missing, a large disaster might lead to economic and social disorder. Consequently, an attempt to grasp a full understanding of a country's resilience requires understanding of each of the five resilience dimensions, which in turn, depend on a host of other factors. This is what makes understanding, application and measurement of resilience a challenging task.

To emphasize the operational complexities involved in measuring the national level disaster resilience, the above concepts are illustrated here through a cursory attempt to examine the situation in Indonesia. Indonesia suffers immensely from natural hazards as it lies near the intersection of shifting tectonic plates making it highly prone to earthquakes and volcanic eruptions. In recent years, natural disasters cause the country an estimated annual damage of over US$2 billion. Indonesia's physical infrastructure fares reasonably well compared with other Asian countries, for instance, more than 60% of its total road is paved, 97% of its population has access to electricity and 87% of its population has access to improved water source (US Global Investors, 2011; WHO/UNICEF, 2016; Trading Economics, 2017).[18] At the same time, the construction quality of its physical infrastructure, specifically dwellings, is inadequate considering the severity of earthquakes that strike Indonesia.

Based on social development, Indonesia ranks higher than most Asian nations with a 94% of adult literacy rate and about 69 years of life expectancy at birth,[19] thus suggesting a greater resilience. How it translates to a greater public awareness and interacts with other social factors in terms of actions taken by individuals and communities to make themselves more disaster resilient is still an open question. In terms of economic development, varying degrees of

---

[18]Based on Morgan Stanley research published by US Global Investors 2011. Retrieved from http://www.usfunds.com/investor-library/frank-talk/policy-reforms-pave-way-for-indonesia/#.WH3DetR95kg. (Accessed 17 January 2017). Data on improved water source is based on WHO/UNICEF Joint Monitoring Programme (JMP) for Water Supply and Sanitation (wssinfo.org) Retrieved from http://data.worldbank.org/indicator/SH.H2O.SAFE.ZS.

[19]According to the national estimates reproduced in the 2017 World Development Indicators published by the World Bank.

resilience can emerge, when measured through several factors such as GDP growth, savings rate, fiscal position, trade diversification, etc. Indonesia fares reasonably well in terms of national level economic indicators but a matter of concern is the absolute poverty faced by 27.8 million of its inhabitants (Statistics Indonesia, BPS 2017).[20] A similar varying and sometimes conflicting conclusion can be reached by examining Indonesia's institutional dimension, typically measured by governance, legal and political structure, security of property rights, and other factors.

As shown by Indonesia's example, examining a country's resilience to hazards and disasters is complex. Only by establishing the factors and identifying appropriate indicators to measure their contributions will policy makers be able to properly manage the threat of natural disasters, and therefore, strengthen a nation's resilience. Additionally, addressing the gap between academicians and practitioners working in disaster management is a challenge as practitioners tend to focus on ex-post top-down approaches while academicians tend to take a broader view highlighting interlinkages among the five resilience dimensions. For example, the institutional capacity is manifested in, among other things, land use planning, however, various themes of land use — density, location and type of use — which are key aspects of resilience, not taken into account adequately by land use planners. Understanding resilience and devising policy to strengthen national resilience are challenges that all countries face; how each country responds to these challenges determine the level of threat posed by natural disasters.

Perhaps given the complexities involved in applying the national level resilience concept into practice, its application at the local level — community, city — has largely appealed many both in research and policy arena — as exhibited by a growing popularity of the community (or city) level resilience measures that seem to

---

[20]In Indonesia, based on the latest data of the statistical agency BPS, as of March 2017, roughly 10.6% of its population of 261 million were estimated to be living in absolute poverty. Available at https://www.indonesia-investments.com/news/todays-headlines/poverty-in-indonesia-absolute-poverty-up-relative-poverty-down/item7995?.

better appreciate local/community level specificities within a society. Consequently, to underscore the point emphasized earlier in this section, most of the initiatives on resilience measurement focus at the community or city level through examining the resilience concept and proposing frameworks to compute resilience indexes (Bruneau *et al.*, 2003; Simpson and Katirai, 2006; Mayunga, 2007; NOAA, 2008; Cutter *et al.*, 2008; Cutter *et al.*, 2010; Tyler *et al.*, 2014; UN/ISDR, 2014). While significance of understanding resilience at the local/community level cannot be emphasized enough, it will make sense only when the policy measures and interventions aimed at building community resilience are taken in conjunction with measures to appreciate and promote community role in pursuing the DRR agenda, in the first place. It is, therefore, timely to understand: What are the mechanisms that would build on existing local level resource base including the knowledge and wisdom to mobilize community strengths in building resilience to hazards and disasters? To put the question in perspective, we look into the community role in disaster risk reduction and disaster management in the next section.

6. DISASTER RISK MANAGEMENT AND COMMUNITY INVOLVEMENT

Role of communities in disaster risk management: Introduction and Literature Review

Community based disaster management is commonly understood when communities themselves are at the forefront of managing such efforts as disaster preparedness, response and recovery measures not only during the aftermath of a disaster event but also preparing for potential disaster threats. It represents a situation when national governments formulate disaster management policies and pursue DRR agenda where the planning process clearly identifies potential hazards and threats within a community and also determines existing vulnerabilities. In addition, the process will incorporate mechanisms for resource generation and network building among community members so as to strengthen community resource base in dealing with imminent disasters as well as potential threats (MercyCorps et al., 2009; Mercer, 2010; Shaw, 2012a; Wisner et al., 2012; Zakour, and Gillepsi, 2013; ITC/OECD, 2015).

In recent times, a community-based disaster risk reduction and management approach seems to be gaining popularity. Even though the community concept has been used in a variety of ways in different contexts, the notion by itself conveys a positive message due to its emphasis on the role of communities in development and disaster management practices. As the community concept is closely linked with local participation -an essential element of modern day DRR mechanisms-, lately, a greater emphasis is being sought for an increasing involvement of local people in dealing with disaster management and addressing issues associated with disaster consequences (Delica-Willison and Gaillard, 2012). One of the obvious reasons of the growing popularity of community role in disaster management lies in its relevance in vulnerability reduction and disaster management strategies since the approach itself is associated with a policy trend that values the local knowledge and local capacities, and also, builds on local resources, including social capital (Allen, 2006). For instance, whenever a crisis event strikes the role of individuals and local communities in the area, who are exposed to hazard/disaster risks, can never be overemphasized for the simple reason that they are the ones who mostly have to deal with the immediate blow. This also means that communities are the ones to gain in the first place provided DRR measures and actions are taken in advance to reduce potential hazards and threats. No wonder in recent times, community based DRR approach under which communities are at the center of disaster management has been advocated widely although it is believed that the approach itself has existed since ancient times.

Although community involvement has been seen largely during post-disaster instances, a variety of case studies (at the global level) have shown that actions taken through community initiatives are also, at times, combined with measures of reducing risks and threats to hazards and disasters. Evidences exist to further substantiate that immediately following the aftermaths of disasters, community members tend to exhibit unique capacities to respond on their own provided they have adequate resources. Review studies worldwide have immensely praised community roles in disaster management indicating that local people and communities can at the same time prepare for, plan and act so as to minimize the potential disaster threats thus vindicating the role of communities in promoting and sustaining a DRR approach (Pelling, 2007; MercyCorps *et al.*, 2009; Wisner, 2012; Practical Action, 2009; IFRC, 2012; Zakour and Gillepsi, 2013; Centre for International Studies and Cooperation, 2014).

While policies and strategies — formal or informal — emphasizing the significance of community level DRR agenda have existed worldwide at various levels, the CBDRR approach received a momentum following the HFA 2005–2015, which prioritized DRR at the local and national levels and called for establishment of strong and functional institutions to manage disasters (UNISDR, 2005). The HFA action plan explicitly identifies the assessment of disaster risks, early warning systems, enhancement of community resilience, hazard risk reduction and preparedness strategies and activities at all levels. Consequently, since then most countries in the region have enacted various acts and regulations in an effort to highlight planned implementation of disaster management both at the national and local levels. This section discusses some of the principles and concepts related with the community level management of disasters commonly understood across the region.

Based on existing literature, the CBDRR approach primarily relies on the principles of people's participation and their empowerment, linkage of DRR activities with development, sensitivity to existing local knowledge and practices, and application of a multi-stakeholder DRR approach (Havidan *et al.*, 2007). Participation of communities can be ensured and members empowered only when community based activities undertaken through community organizations are conducive to an environment where communities are the ones who are able to define problems and express needs/priorities as well as design and implement necessary measures. Hence a participatory community based disaster management

(CBDM) model — properly integrated with development oriented activities that benefit everyone in a community or society — tends to incorporate community members' perception of vulnerability and capacity provided it is inclusive enough in true sense such that even poorer and marginalized are not left behind. Policies and activities, therefore, need to be designed and executed through addressing the root causes of people's vulnerabilities so as to increase their capacities to assess risk beforehand, and identify, prioritize, plan and implement risk reduction measures (for example, MercyCorps *et al.*, 2009; Mercer, 2010; Wisner *et al.*, 2012; Shaw, 2012a; Shaw, 2012; IFRC, 2012; ITC/OECD, 2015).

Several case studies on the community level DRM initiatives across the region have indicated that in many societies — ranging from various states of development — CBDRR has been employed through a variety of approaches usually depending on local contexts, wisdom, needs and priorities (Havidan *et al.*, 2007; Mercer, 2010; NDRRMC, 2015). For instance, according to local level progress report on HFA priorities, in Indonesia, following the 2006 Yogyakarta earthquake, a number of disaster recovery models were introduced of which one model — based on local wisdom with strong local cultural characteristics (in Bantul district) — is particularly significant. The model deserves genuine praise due to its participatory nature in which people themselves, for instance, decide on details of reconstruction of their own houses even though the area has been resource poor to begin with. The recovery measure applied in this case provides support to the argument that even with minimum assistance from the local government, a community DRM model can still demonstrate promises and eventually lead to successful outcomes provided it is sensible to local wisdom and culture with sufficient participation of the very people it is intended to benefit in the first place.[21]

Similar examples exist across Asia with a variety of approaches largely based on the basic principle of a participatory CBDRM.

---

[21]Prevention Web 2013; Local progress report on the implementation of the Hyogo Framework for Action (First Cycle). Available at http://www.preventionweb.net/files/31749_LGSAT_5HFA-Bantul-District(2011-2013).pdf.

In Japan, community involvement in disaster risk management has been formally recognized and supported by local as well as national authorities such that appropriate coordinating mechanisms have been built across a range of institutions to facilitate the necessary preparedness and recovery measures, as and when needed (Wisner *et al.*, 2012; Cabinet Office Japan, 2015). Consequently, various approaches exist countrywide such as *Jishu-bosai-soshiki (jishubo,* in short) where local governments persuade communities to organize and participate in DM activities (Bajek *et al.*, 2012). In Japan, the strengths of volunteer organizations have been perceived as immensely useful in recent times particularly following the aftermath of the Great East Japan Earthquake (GEJE) 2011, when several volunteer organizations managed to save numerous lives, thus underscoring their roles in managing crisis situations locally. Similarly, in Vietnam, a number of CBDRM initiatives — with a strong participatory component — have been operating focused on a wide ranging activities such as (i) mobilization of children's strengths towards risk reduction measures as part of the "Continued strengthening of community capacity in child-focused disaster preparedness and response" project; (ii) building resilience of vulnerable communities living in disasters prone communes (in Ha Tinh province), and a project focused on reducing flood and storm vulnerability in Quang Ngai Province (Centre for International Studies and Cooperation, 2014).

A CBDRR model is known to succeed well in a system where disaster planning and prevention are largely integrated into the overall national development plans and projects for sustainable development, for example, in Malaysia, the community model is further strengthened by the involvement of District and State Disaster Management Committees and authorities in developing as well as implementing overall emergency response plans. An excellent Malaysian case in point is a community-based disaster preparedness approach designed to develop a tsunami emergency response plan, which demonstrates that community setting has large potential to provide opportunities to build on traditional organizational structure like community leaders, volunteers and existing informal

DRR practices. The initiative, with a major focus on resilience building among others, particularly emphasizes on the strengths and wisdom of disaster survivors who in fact are in a position to turn disaster around as an opportunity (Aini Mat Said *et al.*, 2011; Wisner *et al.*, 2012). Similarly, community initiatives are seen to be tremendously useful to reduce vulnerability and build resilience and coping mechanisms through several success stories in the region (MercyCorps *et al.*, 2009; Mercer, 2010; Shaw, 2012a; Shaw, 2012; IFRC, 2012; ITC/OECD, 2015). For instance, community initiatives appear crucial in a coastal Bangladesh community, susceptible primarily to cyclones, as a study exploring vulnerability to cyclone hazards — using first-hand coping recollections from prior to, during and after the events-, has shown that beyond extreme cyclone forces, localized vulnerability is defined in terms of response processes, infrastructure, socially uneven exposure, settlement development patterns, and livelihood (Alam and Collins, 2010; IFRC, 2012).

Role of multi-stakeholder platforms and cross-sectoral collaborations are considered prerequisites for a community based DRR model to make a meaningful contribution towards a sustainable development path. In recent years, growing significance of a multi-stakeholder approach has been greatly appreciated and put into practice widely by communities worldwide as seen through the country reports on DRR progress demonstrating noteworthy examples in countries like Japan, Malaysia, Indonesia, the Philippines, and also, Bangladesh. Also, there are evidences to indicate that when a mechanism of multi-stakeholder platforms (MSPs)[22] is formalized, those MSPs can play an increasingly important role in DRR measures (Djalante, 2012; Shaw, 2012). The multi-stakeholder platform concept has been gaining momentum in other countries as well. For example, in a Timor Leste town, collaboration begins with coordinating community members through forming disaster

---

[22]Multi-stakeholders platforms (MSPs) are interpreted as a multiplicity of organizations starting from the global to local levels working more towards a series of coordinated and integrated actions in DRR (Djalante, 2012).

management (DM) committees and initiating the orientation of Participatory Disaster Risk Assessment (PDRA) teams. The DM committee members consequently constitute a multi-stakeholder team, which includes the government sector — both central and local — NGOs, civil societies and "at risk" community members. The outcomes of such collaboration seem to have helped not only create a management body within the community but also contributed to ensuring sustainability of the DRR process through community ownership (Mercer, 2012; Wisner *et al.*, 2012; Shaw, 2012).

Recent trend in the CBDRR approach calls for a growing need to focus more on the individuals and community members that engage in DRR, with an increased appreciation of inherent diversities. The approach will succeed when respective needs, views and interests of everyone in a society are understood, and also, peoples' experiences on risk perception and others, are acknowledged and accommodated accordingly (Centre for International Studies and Cooperation, 2014). Apart from risk mitigation and preparedness measures — crucial to reduce potential threats — a participatory CBDRR approach can sustain if it begins with an attempt to understand the importance of existing DRR measures including response and coping mechanisms within a community (Shaw, 2012). While in practice, CBDRR efforts need to be mindful of existing social, political, cultural, beliefs and understanding that might be influencing factors in view of common hazards and threats, caution must be taken to ensure all are treated fairly so as not to favor only a few privileged. Given the irony of unequal power relations prevalent in most societies, the spirit of CBDRR makes sense and can lead to success only when needs and concerns of all — even those at the bottom of social and economic strata — are appreciated and accommodated to minimize the risk of undermining the principle of targeting the most vulnerables to reduce risks and potential threats they face. In view of a range of interventions envisaged under a CBDRR agenda, we turn next to a few pertinent questions, such as, What role should the government bodies — local as well as national — assume so as to facilitate the process of CBDRR in achieving the ultimate goal of reducing and mitigating disaster risks? What is the relevance of CBDRR approach in an urban setting in terms of risk reduction and resilience building?

Role of Government in Community DRM and Recent Trend

Disaster risk reduction efforts, not surprisingly, involve a range of ambitious tasks and responsibilities that needs to be channeled and executed towards a coherent, effective and sustained path, which can easily overwhelm a single local (or even a national) body. Building on strengths of a multi-stakeholder approach, a successful execution of the CBDRR goal and necessary interventions, therefore, requires supports from all, and most importantly, the local and national governments who not only provide basic services and primary assistance during crisis events but also need to be involved in carrying out DRR measures including risk assessments and vulnerability reductions. Furthermore, the role of central government authority is essential to mandate as well as enforce legislative and regulatory measures to ensure existing development policies and practices are conducive to the spirit of a DRR development agenda through enabling environment for carrying out necessary risk reduction measures.

Policy makers, therefore, have a crucial role to play on multiple fronts, for example, building a clearly identified framework to execute DRR measures as well as to facilitate resource availabilities as financial backbones. In addition, policy makers and government bodies at all levels are in a position to demonstrate their strengths through knowledge dissemination and advocacy measures, for instance, through encouraging and scaling up the CBDRR successes by investing in community resources, local DRR planning, appropriate management structures and implementation and coordination mechanisms (UN-ESCAP, 2012; Wisner, 2012). Also, only with a meaningful backing from the government side (in terms of legislative, financial and others, for instance), the notion of a multi-stakeholder participation, as discussed earlier, is expected to materialize effectively.

In recent times, a growing role of CBDRR in urban areas has been seen as cities have been increasingly integrating DRR considerations into other local government activities, including education, livelihoods, health, environment, and planning, either by incorporating risk concerns into existing activities or initiating projects that address multiple issues simultaneously. Evidences exist worldwide as increasing number of population are living in cities in modern times suggesting an ever growing relevance and need for CBDRR in urban settings (UNISDR, 2013; UNISDR, 2015; UNISDR, 2017). One important initiative, for instance, was the 2010 Making Cities Resilient Campaign introduced with the goal of localizing the objectives and implementation of the HFA and also highlighting role of CBDRR in urban setting. The Resilient Campaign and the experiences gained have shown useful insights for DRR policy makers and practitioners including the emergence of a diverse set of resilience building aspects like the administrative and institutional framework for resilience, development of a dedicated body, and a political commitment to disaster risk reduction. Similarly, findings of the activities performed under various projects hold several implications for policymakers, for example, since the DRR priorities of local governments are context-specific, resilience indicators must be locally developed based on the risks as well as the governance systems at the local level. Overall, to a large extent, the conceptual link between DRR and sustainable development is vindicated such that the issues involved present mutually dependent challenges, which require collaborative, integrated planning and strategies, governance structures with innovative solutions (Frank Thomalla *et al.*, 2006; UN-ESCAP, 2013; UNISDR, 2015).

In the next paragraphs, we look into the evolution of the CBDRR approach in the national agenda using the examples of Indonesia and the Philippines, to be followed by common issues and challenges encountered in the region while applying the CBDRR agenda in practice.

CBDRR Approach in National Agenda: Indonesia and the Philippines

Evidences are seen that several countries in the region have increasingly demonstrated keen interest in involving the local communities in DRR initiatives through adopting significant measures to achieve proper policy level blending of the national DRR agenda with the local ones. In this section, we cover brief accounts of CBDRR developments in the context of Indonesia and the Philippines primarily in terms of national priority and activities undertaken.

(i) CBDRR in Indonesia:

In Indonesia's case, community role in managing disasters — both in terms of risk reduction and recovery measures — is far too crucial particularly given the country's vast diversities on several fronts — geographical, cultural, ethnic and linguistic, just to name a few. A single national DRR approach based on a top-down model would not only be hugely inadequate but also a greater reliance on national model would mean difficulties in comprehending the true nature of hazard and disaster risks arising from problems in risk mappings and detection of local level hazards, and also, problems and delays in reporting as well as monitoring of smaller scale disasters (IDEP Foundation, 2006). As such, significant measures have been taken to ensure that the national DRR agenda are properly integrated with the local initiatives in many respects.

Following the aftermath of the 2004 earthquake and Indian Ocean tsunami, the Indonesian government started working with various organizations to introduce community-based risk reduction initiatives as recovery measures to the affected communities. One of many such examples is the Integrated Community Based Risk Reduction (ICBRR) program, which aimed at building disaster-resilient communities in the targeted villages. The program activities included forming of community organizations for disaster risk management; participating in risk analysis, planning and implementation of activities; recognizing the need for innovative and context specific risk reduction strategies; sharing of resources from different stakeholders and empowering community members. The program implementation, therefore, ensured active participation of villagers in detailed assessments and implementation of various risk-reduction measures and monitoring of disaster risks to reduce vulnerabilities to potential hazards (Kafle, 2012); (Guarnacci, 2012).

Additional measures were taken following the 2006 Yogyakarta earthquake, as the Indonesian government realized that there was an urgent need to introduce disaster preparedness measures into school curriculum in order to educate people to better prepare for potential disasters. Consequently, the Indonesian National Commission for UNESCO chose to target the secondary school students as the focus group to address the most prevalent natural disasters such as earthquakes, tsunamis, floods, landslides, volcanic eruptions and hurricanes. Activities like production and distribution of educational materials played an important role in disaster preparedness measures by empowering both the teachers and students through improved knowledge of disaster threats and necessary preparedness measures. Furthermore, following the 2006 earthquake, the government had implemented infrastructure rebuilding strategy, which ended up being quite successful both in meeting housing and infrastructural needs and also subsequently addressing economic recovery (World Bank, 2011; BNPB, 2013).

In Indonesia, an excellent case in point that demonstrated the community level strength in the national level disaster management was seen in 2007 when the 2007 Law was passed. As noted earlier in the Chapter, a civil society group — the Indonesian Disaster Management Society (MPBI) — was the main driver that became instrumental behind the passing of the 2007 law in the first place, to be accompanied by regulations, plans and activities at the sub-national levels thereafter. In addition to establishing the National Disaster Management Agency (BNPB), the Minister of Home Affairs issued a Decree (No 46/2008) making mandatory establishments of Local Disaster Management Agencies (BPBDs) in all of the provinces with budget line for DM at the provincial government level. Following the establishments of the local DM agencies (or BPBDs), even though the central authority assumes responsibility and accountability in

DRR to prepare for, mitigate, respond, and rebuild in the DRR mainstreaming process, increased collaboration with local bodies and civil societies have evolved significantly thereafter (BNPB, 2012; BNPB, 2014).

Similarly, in 2009, the civil society group formally launched the National Platform for DRR, as mandated from The University Forum (Forum PT), a consortium of tertiary and research institutions, designed to be the lead provider of technical and information services to the government line ministries in implementing the DRR agenda. Apart from the leadership role in the National Platform for DRR — essential to the credibility of the platform — the University Forum also deserves merit through its provision of technical expertise in various dimensions of DRR agenda (BNPB, Government of Indonesia, 2012).

The CBDRR strategies under various projects, from 2011 onwards, had gradually shifted to accommodate local contexts and specificities better. For instance, in some cases the community members themselves could decide the location of their new permanent residential site on their own land. The changes were introduced in conjunction and consideration with several factors such as the development priorities, changes in the use of land, infrastructure investments and other investments to increase the resilience of the villages during the event of a natural disaster with the intensive involvement of local government bodies. The goal was to increase community awareness while choosing safer locations to lower disaster risks, for instance, the Government of Yogyakarta Special Region — together with *Rekompak*, the community initiative — had allowed residents to choose to relocate their dwellings in a safer area through providing a House Fund Aid.[23] Apart from

---

[23] In Indonesia, *Rekompak* is the innovative community-based model designed for post-disaster housing reconstruction during 2005–2012, created and adapted through the Multi Donor Fund for Aceh and Nias (MDF) and the Java Reconstruction Fund (JRF). It was created as a consequence of the many devastating natural disasters that struck Indonesia between 2004 and 2010. Available at https://openknowledge.worldbank.org/handle/10986/17640.

other benefits, the practice helped increase the community ability to build earthquake-resistant dwellings, improved DRR capacity through better preparedness measures, and developed neighborhood infrastructure affected by natural disasters (BNPB, 2012; BNPB, 2014; BNPB, 2016).

More recent community level DRR initiatives, with necessary support — legislative, infrastructure, technical and financial — from government, non-government and donor organizations, are largely centered on a number of tasks which mainly include providing immediate support during the aftermath of a disaster, undertaking various preparedness measures like mapping of local risks and hazards, planning mitigation measures to address local risks through building on local knowledge and capacities and providing necessary support during DRR focused recovery measures (IDEP Indonesia, 2010; Guarnacci, 2012; Pristiyanto, Djuni, 2015; BNPB, 2016).[24] Some of the successful activities include incorporation of knowledge in school curriculum, awareness raising programs and forming of EWS in various ways. For instance, one of the more recent local DRR initiatives deserves additional praise for the reason that several government regulations continue to address the role of civil society in forming volunteer response squads. Apart from being a civil society community based initiative, this also highlights the significance of government role and responsibility in forming volunteer squads — now headed by the BNPB (Disaster Management Agency) Head — and building their capacity. More specifically, common guidelines have been developed to help cross-fertilize the volunteer squads, which include a set of common training modules for — SAR, Damage and Loss Assessment, Logistics Systems, Information Management and contingency planning (BNPB, 2016). In coordination with the National Disaster Management Authority (BNPB), the Local Disaster Management Agency (BPBD) undertakes various preparedness measures like early warning systems and others against

---

[24]Source: IDEP Foundation, Indonesia, Helping People to Help Themselves 2016. Available at http://www.idepfoundation.org/en/.

potential disasters. One such recent initiative was taken in Jawa Timur, Surabaya, where the local BPBD installed the sign and information board related with volcanic eruption hazard encouraging the community to be alert in the event of potential threats (BNPB, 2016).[25]

(ii) CBDRR in the Philippines

In the Philippines, historical accounts indicate that community-based and participatory DRR initiatives were active even during the 1970s and 1980s driven by local organizations primarily aimed at helping those most vulnerable to disasters. The DRR agenda within the country has largely thrived as a result of separate as well as concerted efforts and actions on the part of government agencies, NGOs, CSOs and local communities dedicated to fostering DRR at all levels of society. Besides, over the years, its leadership in DRR efforts has been widely acclaimed by the local, national as well as the international organizations (Wisner *et al.*, 2012; Gaillard *et al.*, 2014).

The DRRM Act of 2010 (Republic Act 10121) mandates the establishment of Local Risk Reduction and Management Councils and offices — responsible for setting the directions, developing, implementing and coordinating the DRR and management plans, programs and projects within their territorial jurisdiction — at the provincial, city and municipal levels. These offices are designed to undertake fairly comprehensive risk reduction measures and responsibilities including various technical tasks like risk assessments and vulnerability analyses, integration of Hydro-Meteorological and geological hazard plans into land-use plans, design of early warning systems and evacuation centres. In recent years, a large number of community organizations and NGOs have been working with national government agencies as well as external agencies in promoting and implementing the CBDRM agenda. The key CBDRM

---

[25]BNPB, July 2016. Available at http://www.bnpb.go.id/berita/3019/bnpb-dan-bpbd- jawa-timur-pasang-rambu-dan-papan-informasi-tingkatkan-kesiapsiagaan-hadapi-ancaman-erupsi-gunungapi.

elements designed to recognize the diversities in the Philippine society have been identified as community ownership, use of local knowledge of hazard risks, recognition of communities as ultimate beneficiaries, multi-stakeholder participation, education and capacity building, complementarity between community-based and top-down approaches, sensitivity towards gender, culture and local structures and potential for resilience building (Allen, 2006; ADPC, 2008; Gaillard *et al.*, 2014).

In recent times, a multitude of local level DRR initiatives are seen to be ongoing in the Philippines. For instance, following the Typhoon Pablo in 2012, the NDRRMC organized national platform involving all stakeholders both at the national and local levels to devise a massive campaign in order to discuss various ways of dealing with disasters and natural calamities. The campaign also recognized officially the DRRM Council at the provincial level for its outstanding achievements in DRR practices as well as humanitarian assistance (OCD, 2013: the Civil Defense Gazette, 2013). Furthermore, the CBDRM approach is seen well embedded while managing DRR activities in cases of coastal urban communities. More notably, as highlighted earlier, there is a growing trend of cities integrating risk reduction measures into other local government activities like education, health and environment (UN-ISDR, 2013; UN-ISDR, 2014). It is, therefore, encouraging to see that despite the frequent occurrences of natural disasters in the country, a number of local government bodies, taking opportunities offered by the new institutional framework based on community-based DRR model, have demonstrated positive results. Examples include the exemplary evacuation work undertaken by the San Francisco Municipality in Cebu in 2013, thus saving all of its inhabitants. Similarly, the city of Dagupan of Luzon, with its unrelenting efforts, manages to avoid major disasters despite recurrent typhoons and flooding events in the region (Gaillard *et al.*, 2014). One of the most recent projects is in the city of IloIlo, namely, the Community-Based Adaptation and Resilience Against Disasters Project or CBARAD. Backed by the city government with the ultimate goal of making the city climate change resilient through its disaster risk reduction and management programs, the CBARAD project undertakes a number of activities including resource mobilization; volunteer mobilization; awareness raising; team building; and educating communities about climate change, hazard and disaster risks. The project has been particularly praised for its participatory component such that every individual in the community — including the elderly and children and vulnerable — represents a resource base rather than helpless victims during and after disasters (reliefweb, 2017).

7. COMMUNITY BASED DISASTER RISK MANAGEMENT: ISSUES AND CHALLENGES

Over the years, worldwide experiences indicate that community based disaster risk reduction and disaster risk management model[26] demonstrates its appeal and strengths to empower local peoples and communities to help them better manage hazard and disaster risks they face. Consequently, the concept has received a growing popularity among all including the national governments, aid organizations, academics and development actors. However, despite the ever growing interest in the CBDRR agenda and encouraging success stories, a widening variety of approaches have emerged increasing the complexities and challenges that policy makers and implementing partners encounter while implementing the CBDRR model and at the same time preserving the significance of community spirit and empowerment.

Various case studies have shown a number of issues and challenges while translating the CBDRR concept into a meaningful set of priorities and actions. The typical constraints that are seen to arise in the application process mainly include (i) lack of ownership and adequate capacity and authority at the local level (including the community and volunteer sector); (ii) societal systemic and structural factors; (iii) ad hoc and sporadic activities of local agencies and NGOs leading to unsustainability and poor coordination;

---

[26]For simplicity, the two terms, disaster risk management and disaster risk reduction, are used interchangeably in the present context.

(iv) lack of resources and commitments both at the central and local levels; and (v) lack of accountability and transparency and difficulties in ensuring longer term sustainability of DRR activities (Wisner *et al.*, 2012; UN-ESCAP, 2012; Shaw, 2012; UNISDR, 2014; UNISDR, 2017). Given the nature of broadness and extent as well as cross-cutting components across various domains of the issues and challenges, including the structural factors, among others (Passerini, 2001), thereby extending the complexities further and requiring a unrelenting series of efforts on the part of all stakeholders in operationalizing the CBDRR concept, only a few aspects are discussed in the present context.

Existing case studies indicate that in several instances even though the CBDRR initiatives were locally-based, community members for the most part did not feel the ownership as such since project inception and outcomes were largely claimed by external funding agencies, a familiar notion of experiences shared by communities in most developing countries. Success of a model requires that communities feel a sense of ownership and accomplishment as part of the project implementation process, which cannot be achieved without a meaningful local participation not only during implementation but also conceptualization and planning to ensure a feeling of genuine local ownership without external imposition (Bang, 2013). At the same time, the notion of local ownership might get complicated and even misunderstood due to inadequate capacity at the local level be it financial and/or technical. Consequently, it is essential that various awareness raising measures are undertaken such as through disseminating information and ways on how to build capacity of local people to enable them to assess risk beforehand, and identify, prioritize, plan and implement risk reduction measures at the community level (UNISDR, 2013; UNISDR, 2015).

Despite a growing focus on the community initiatives in the region, there are times when complications and challenges can arise due to systemic and structural factors. In the Philippines, for instance, most disaster events have shown that whenever a disaster strikes the peoples residing around the coastal regions suffer the most in terms of adverse consequences. However, based on the accounts of government authorities, there have been numerous cases when individuals in those communities seem reluctant to relocate to safer areas despite imminent threats as they fear they might not only lose their livelihood (fishing, for instance) but also get into unknown risks. Similar situation was reported during the 2008 volcanic eruption at Mt. Merapi in Yogyakarta, Indonesia, when many people in the area refused to leave their homes despite repeated warnings. Furthermore, changing peoples' mindsets is an evolving process and takes time as both in the Philippines and Indonesia, as well as in several other country cases, examples have revealed that despite various efforts by government agencies, and NGOs, many local government officials are not entirely aware of the opportunities and resources offered by the new institutional framework and still tend to rely more on disaster relief and response rather than risk reduction measures (UNISDR, 2014, 2015). This also reveals that existing methods of risk communication are far too inadequate without sufficient level of practical guidelines that are essential to carry out risk reduction measures in a participatory manner to better communicate the risk situation to those who are threatened or at risk to help manage their livelihood options better. Due to the remnants of past development approaches — based on top-down model for the most part with very little power delegation to local levels-, complexities associated with the task of translating the very notion of community participation and empowerment into practice becomes immense. This reiterates that a meaningful level of local participation cannot be achieved without a tremendous scale of awareness raising efforts to disseminate the role of community spirit to all involved and thus empower the communities in a gradual, effective and sustainable manner.

At the same time, it is essential that while communicating disaster related risks and threats, policy makers and implementing partners be mindful and appreciative of some of the deep-rooted structural issues and realities that prevail in most societies till this day. The task of awareness raising and community empowerment, for instance, can get complicated and at times easier said than done due to inherent power relations, often discriminatory against the oppressed, that exist within societies and communities — largely segregated into multiple hierarchies. Under those circumstances, there may be instances when certain people within a community with privileged background, such as, those with ample social and political clout, tend to interfere such that voices and grievances coming from the most vulnerable are not heard. Despite a growing homogeneity in most societies in recent times, with a greater sensitivity towards participatory and inclusive approaches, the issue is rather a systemic one, which, therefore, requires a continuous series of sustained efforts to change the inherent mindsets of all those involved. Successful execution of DRR measures, consequently, requires appreciation of existing norms and values within a society and understanding of the inherent relations among its members. This also means that program implementers frequently face challenges, at times, perhaps immense pressure, for instance, in terms of striking a balance between seeking cooperation with local elites and empowering the oppressed and marginalized within a community, thus requiring a tireless series of efforts on everyone's part.

Another constraint commonly encountered in ensuring an effective implementation of a community based DRR model is lack of coordination among various stakeholders both in terms of policy formulation and actions. Proper coordination across various DRR policies and programs at all levels specifically in terms of clarity in roles and responsibilities assigned to multiple agencies is essential for a successful implementation of the DRR agenda while lack of such institutional integration can be damaging. For example, in the Philippines, following the immediate aftermath of the 2013 typhoon Yolanda (Haiyan), and the subsequent effects, the situation at the local administrative bodies — reportedly chaotic — particularly in managing resources locally, revealed that the revised institutional arrangements between the government and NGOs on local level recovery efforts severely suffered from lack of proper integration across various policies and program activities — largely originated by inadequate attention and prioritization during conceptualization.[27]

---

[27]For instance, various media sources including local newspapers reported that DRR measures in some cases, such as a comprehensive land use plan, were reportedly prepared

Another issue commonly encountered during CBDRR implementation is an inadequate level of funding and resource capacity at the local level constraining the sustainability of DRR initiatives. Development actors and practitioners in modern times appear in a variety of forms representing various level agencies, such as, the external, national (government plus nongovernment), and subnational. Numerous cases exist where funding are provided however attached with non-flexible priorities and conditionality not always favorably adjusted to local needs and priorities. The bottom line is external dependence for the sake of DRR at the local level activities should be as little as possible so that similar activities can be carried out internally with little external support in the long-run. Too much dependence of programs and activities on short-term external funding and expertise also means that there will be little effort to provide adequate opportunities to empower people with skills and resources, which is commonly evident among NGO workers who implement the projects. Furthermore, case studies reveal that projects relying on short-term external funding (national as well as external) usually take longer timeframe compared to locally funded ones, which include projects incorporating elements of participatory risk assessment and mitigation and preparedness measures (Wisner, 2012; UN-ESCAP, 2012; Centre for International Studies and Cooperation, 2014).

CBDRR models in many societies are known to suffer additionally due to lack of a genuine political will. One of the most important components essential for a community based DRR model to succeed and thrive is the political will and commitment on the part of local leaders since they are the ones equipped with direct mandates to undertake and promote necessary preparedness measures to reduce hazard risks and build resilience. In view of the existing societal norms, with discriminatory power relations among community members at times, political and social elites

---

without proper consultations with those who were to be involved in executing the plan(s) in the first place.

must be willing to evaluate the current system and attempt to model those in conjunction with the concept and spirit of a true community DRR model such that there is ample room for new and progressive policies and practices as well as voices for all including grassroots organizations, civil societies and those most vulnerable and marginalized (ADPC, 2008; Neeling, 2013; UNISDR, 2015).

Furthermore, at the conceptual level, as compelling as the argument for a community managed DRR system appears, there are possibilities that in practice the validity of a community model can raise serious questions unless necessary measures are thought through and planned for in advance to address potential issues in relation to management, leadership, accountability and transparency to ensure a smooth functioning (Shaw, 2012). Several case studies have shown that a community based model can fail to achieve the goal in the absence of proper accountability and transparency at the local level primarily in terms of resources — both sources and allocation (Wisner, 2012; IJDRR, 2012; UNISDR, 2014).

Overall, to ensure a successful execution of the CBDRR agenda leading to meaningful outcomes along the sustainable development path, the role of national as well as local government bodies is essential both to mandate and enforce laws and regulations such that development policies and practices are intertwined with necessary risk reduction measures. Besides, the implementing bodies — at all levels — ought to demonstrate a genuine commitment, over-all accountability in terms of information sharing in all respects including project rationale, service delivery approaches, transparency methods and performance indicators to justify the needs and interests of all stakeholders concerned in an equitable manner.

REFERENCES

Alam, E and AE Collins (2010). Cyclone disaster vulnerability and response experiences in coastal Bangladesh. *Disasters*, 34(4), 931–954.

Alexander, D (2013). Resilience and disaster risk reduction: An etymological journal. *Natural Hazards Earth Systems Science*, 13, 2707–2716.

Allen, K (2006). Community-based disaster preparedness and climate adaptation: Local capacity-building in the Philippines. *Disasters*, 30(1), 81–101.

Amendola, A, J Linnerooth-Bayer, N Okada and P Shi (2008). Towards integrated disaster risk management: Case studies and trends from Asia. *Natural Hazards*, 44, 163–168.

Ahmad, M (2013). Disaster Management Initiatives Policy Perspectives and Effective Response Mechanism in India. Paper presented at the 28th ALNAP Meeting, 04 March 2013, Washington DC. Available at http://www.slideshare.net/ALNAP/disaster-management-initiatives-in-india.

Alam, E and E Collins (2010). Cyclone disaster vulnerability and response experiences in coastal Bangladesh. Available at: file:///C:/Users/Sony/Downloads/60433-Collins-RJ1-AC2-RJ2.pdf.

AIPA (2011). Philippines Country report on Disaster Response Management — 3rd ASEAN Inter-Parliamentary Assembly (AIPA) Caucus Report, Manila, the Philippines, 31 May–3 June 2011. Available at http://www.aipasecretariat.org/wp-content/uploads/2013/07/Philippines-Country-Report-Disaster-Management.pdf.

Asian Disaster Preparedness Centre (ADPC) (2008). Monitoring and Reporting Progress on Community Disaster Risk Management in the Philippines. ADPC April 2008. Available at: http://www.adpc.net/v2007/programs/CBDRM/INFORMATION%20RESOURCE%20CENTER/CBDRM%20Publications/2008/final_crphilippineshires_23nov.pdf.

Bang, HN (2013). Governance of disaster risk reduction in Cameroon: The need to empower local government. *Jamba: Journal of Disaster Risk Studies*, 5(2), 1–10.

Briguglio, L (2003). The Vulnerability Index and Small Island Developing States: A Review of Conceptual and Methodological Issues, paper prepared for the AIMS Regional Preparatory Meeting on the Ten Year Review of the Barbados Programme of Action, Praia, Cape Verde.

Briguglio, L, G Cordina, N Farrugia and S Vella (2006). Economic Vulnerability and Resilience Concepts and Measurements, (unpublished paper).

Benson and Twigg (2004). Measuring Mitigation, Methodologies for assessing natural hazard risks and the net benefits of mitigation — a scoping study. The International Federation of Red Cross and Red Crescent Societies, The ProVention Consortium. Available at: http://proventionconsortium.net/themes/default/pdfs/MM_synthesis.pdf.

Birch, E and Wachter (2006). Growing Greener Cities, Urban Sustainability in the 21st Century. Philadelphia: University of Pennsylvania Press.

Briguglio, L, G Cordina, N Farrugia and S Vella (2008). Economic Vulnerability and Resilience Concepts and Measurements. United Nations University and World Institute Development Economics Research (UNU-WIDER). Research Paper No. 2008/55. Available at https://www.um.edu.mt/library/oar/bitstream/handle/123456789/18143/oA%20-%20%20Economics%20Vulnerability%20and%20Resilience%20Concepts%20and%20Measurements.pdf?sequence=1&isAllowed=y.

Bruneau, M, SE Chang, RT Eguchi, GC Lee, TD O'Rourke, AM Reinhorn, M Shinozuka, K Tierney, WA Wallace and D von Winterfeldti (2003). A

Framework to Quantitatively Assess and Enhance the Seismic Resilience of Communities. *Earthquake Spectra,* 19(4), 733–752.

BNPB, (2010). *Indonesia: National progress report on the implementation of the Hyogo Framework for Action (2009–2011).* National Agency for Disaster Risk Management (BNPB), Government of Indonesia.

BNPB (2011). Disaster Management in Indonesia, National Agency for Disaster Management (BNPB). Government of Indonesia.

BNPB (2012). *Indonesia: National progress report on the implementation of the Hyogo Framework for Action (2011–2013).* National Agency for Disaster Risk Management (BNPB). Government of Indonesia.

BNPB (2013). *National Assessment Report on Disaster Risk Reduction 2013 Redefining Indonesian Disaster Management Strategy.* National Agency for Disaster Management (BNPB). Government of Indonesia.

BNPB (2014). *Indonesia: National progress report on the implementation of the Hyogo Framework for Action (2013–2015).* National Agency for Disaster Risk Management (BNPB), Government of Indonesia.

BNPB (2014b). *National Disaster Management Plan 2010–2014.* Disaster Management in Indonesia, National Agency for Disaster Management (BNPB). Government of Indonesia.

National Agency for Disaster Management (BNPB) (2015). *Indonesia's Disaster Risk Management Baseline Country Status Report 2015.* Disaster Management in Indonesia. National Agency for Disaster Management. Government of Indonesia.

BNPB (2015b). BNPB and East Java BPBD: Posting signs and information boards to Face Threats Increase Preparedness Volcano Eruption). Available at: http://www.bnpb.go.id/berita/3019/bnpb-dan-bpbd-jawa-timur-pasang-rambu-dan-papan-informasi-tingkatkan-kesiapsiagaan-hadapi-ancaman-erupsi-gunungapi.

BPS (2016). (or *Badan Pusat Statistik,* in Indonesian language). *Statistik Indonesia* 2016. Available at: https://www.bps.go.id/publikasi/view/4238.

Cabinet Office Japan (2015). White Paper Disaster Management in Japan Summary 2015. Available at: http://www. bousai.go.jp/kaigirep/hakusho/pdf/WPDM2015_Summary.pdf.

CARITAS (a Swiss NGO)/GRF (Global Risk Forum) (2014). Disaster Risk Reduction and Management in the Philippines. A desk study conducted by the Swiss NGO DRR Platform following typhoon Haiyan, Luzene, July 2014.

Centre for International Studies and Cooperation (2014). Framework for Community Based Disaster Risk Reduction in Vietnam. Joint Advocacy Networking Initiative in Vietnam. Available at http://peacewindsamerica.org/wp-content/uploads/2014/02/CBDRM-Framework.pdf.

Chang, S and M Shinozuka (2004). Measuring improvements in the disaster resilience of communities. *Earthquake Spectra,* 20(3), 739–755.

Center for Excellence in Disaster Management & Humanitarian Assistance (2016). Malaysia Disaster Management. Available at https://reliefweb.int/sites/reliefweb.int/files/resources/disaster-mgmt-ref-hdbk-Malaysia.pdf.

Cutter, S, B Boruff and W Shirley (2003). Social Vulnerability to Environmental Hazards. *Social Science Quarterly*, 84(2), 241–261.

Cutter, Emrich and Burton (2008). Baseline Indicators for Disaster Resilient Communities. Hazards and Vulnerability Research Institute, University of South Carolina, Columbia, CARRI Workshop. Available at http://www.resilientus.org/wp-content/uploads/2013/03/Susan_Cutter_1248296816.pdf.

Cutter, S, L Barnes, M Berry et al. (2008). A place-based model for understanding community resilience to natural disaster. *Global Environmental Change*, 18(4), 598–606.

Cutter, SL, CG Burton and CT Emrich (2010). Disaster Resilience Indicators for Benchmarking Baseline Conditions. *Journal of Homeland Security and Emergency Management*, 7(1). DOI: 10.2202/1547-7355.1732.

Delica-Willison, Z and JC Gaillard (2012). Community action and disaster. In *Handbook of Hazards and Disasters*, Wisner, B, JC Gaillard and I Kelman (Eds.), pp. 711–722. New York: Routledge.

Disaster Management Centre, Sri Lanka, (2015). PreventionWeb (2015). Sri Lanka National progress report on the implementation of the Hyogo Framework for Action (2013–2015). Available at http://www.preventionweb.net/english/hyogo/progress/reports.pdf.

Disaster Risk Reduction Network Philippines (2010). Online publications. Available at http://www.aksyonklima.ph/members/drrnetphils/.

Disaster Risk Reduction Network Philippines (2016). The Disaster Risk Reduction and Management Bill. Online publications. Available at https://www.preventionweb.net/files/11448_PDCdrrmbillprimer.pdf.

Djalante, R and F Thomalla (2012). Community resilience to natural hazards and climate change impacts: A review of definitions and operational frameworks. *Asian Journal of Environmental Disaster Management*, 3, 339–355.

Gaillard, JC, JRD Cadag and RCP Vaido (2014). A Hard Act to Follow: Disaster Reduction in the Philippines. East Asia Forum, University of the Philippines Diliman.

Gall, M, SL Cutter and K Nguyen (2014). *Governance in Disaster Risk Management*. IRDR AIRDR Publication No. 3. Beijing: Integrated Research on Disaster Risk.

Guarnacci, U (2012). Governance for sustainable reconstruction after disasters: Lessons from Nias, Indonesia. Environmental Development, 2, 73–85. Available at http://dx.doi.org/10.1016/j.envdev.2012.03.010.

Ghesquiere, F and O Mahul (2010). Financial Protection of the State Against Natural Disasters A Primer. Policy Research Working Paper 5429, World Bank. Available at http://documents.worldbank.org/curated/en/227011468175734792/pdf/WPS5429.pdf.

Government of Pakistan, Ministry of Climate Change (2013). *National Disaster Risk Reduction Policy*. National Disaster Management Authority. Ministry of Climate Change, Government of Pakistan. Available at http://preventionweb.net/go/32321.

Hapuarachchi, B (ed.) (2009). *South Asia Disaster Report 2008: Disaster and Development in South Asia*. Colombo. Sri Lanka: Duryog Nivaran and Practical Action.

Havidan, R, LK Enrico and RD Russel (2007). Handbook of Disaster Research. New York: Springer Science + Business Media LLC.

IDEP Foundation (2006). Community Based Disaster Management, Indonesia Development of Education and Permaculture (IDEP) Foundation. Available at https://brownschool.wustl.edu/sites/DevPractice/Haiti%20Reports%20of%20Development%20Agencies/CBDM%20report-%20Ricos.pdf.

IEDM Team, Kyoto University (2009). Climate Disaster Resilience: Focus on Coastal Urban Cities in Asia. Human Security Engineering for Asian Megacity, Kyoto University Program.

IFRC (2004). World Disasters Report 2004: Focus on Community Resilience. International Federation of Red Cross and Red Crescent Societies (IFRC), Geneva.

IFRC (2012). The long road to resilience Impact and cost-benefit analysis of community based disaster risk reduction in Bangladesh. International Federation of Red Cross and Red Crescent Societies (IFRC), Geneva.

IJDRR (2012). International Journal of Disaster Risk Reduction (Editorial). *Disaster risk reduction: An alternative viewpoint*. 2 (2012), 1–5. Available at https://www.researchgate.net/publication/257744190_Disaster_Risk_Reduct ion_An_Alternative_Viewpoint.

ITC/OECD (2015). Examples of Successful DRM Reforms and the Role of International Cooperation, Discussion Paper. ITC and OECD, July 2015. https://www.oecd.org/ctp/tax-global/examples-of-successful-DRM-re forms-and-the-role-of-international-co-operation.pdf.

Joon Young Hun (2012). *Disaster management from the perspective of governance: Case study of the Hebei Spirit oil spill*. Disaster Prevention and Management. 21(3), 288–298. Available at: http://www.emeraldinsight.com/journals.htm?articleid=17038772.

Kafle, SK (2012). *Measuring disaster-resilient communities: A case study of coastal communities in Indonesia*. Canadian Red Cross. *Journal of Business Continuity & Emergency Planning* 5(3), 316–326.

Kusumasari, B and Q Alam (2012). Local Wisdom-based disaster recovery model in Indonesia. *Disaster Prevention and Management*, 21(3), 351–369. Emerald Group Publishing Limited.

Klein *et al.* (2003). Resilience to natural hazards: How useful is this concept? *Environmental Hazards*, 5, 35–45.

Lim, C-S, MIH Reza and SAAG Aziz (2017). Unit & Module Title: DRR and Cross Cutting Issues. *Sustainable Development and Climate Change*. Available at http://www.ayvpukm.com.my/wp-content/uploads/2017/08/Module-2-Disaster-Risk-Reduction-and-Cross-Cutting-Issues-Mr-Lim-Chou n-Sian.pdf.

Manyena, SB (2006). The concept of resilience revisited. *Disasters*, 30(4), 433–450. Overseas Development Institute.

Mayunga, JS (2007). Understanding and applying the concept of community disaster resilience: A capital-based approach. Draft working paper prepared for the summer academy for social vulnerability and resilience building, 22–28, July 2007, Munich, Germany.

Mercer, J (2010). Disaster Risk Reduction or Climate Change Adaptation: Are we reinventing the wheel? *Journal of International Development*, 22, 247–264. DOI: 10.1002/jid.1677.

Mercer, J et al. (2012). *Community-based disaster risk reduction in Timor-Leste*. In Community, Environment and Disaster Risk Management, 10, 233–254, Shaw R, (Ed). Emerald Group Publishing Limited.

MercyCorps et al. (2009). Community Based Disaster Risk Reduction Contribution to Hyogo Framework of Action Nepal Case Study Kailali Disaster Risk Reduction Initiatives. European Commission, Mercy Corps and Nepal Red Cross Society. Available at https://www.mercycorps.org/sites/default/files/nepal_disaster_risk_case_study.pdf.

Mileti, D (1999). *Disasters by Design: A Reassessment of Natural Hazards in the United States*. Washington DC: Joseph Henry Press.

Neeling, M (2013). Post 2015 Framework for DRR Consultation with parliamentarians. Session report. Global Platform for Disaster Risk Reduction. Available at http://www.preventionweb.net/files/globalplatofrm/entry_ outcome"post2015frameowrkfordrrconsultationparliamentarians[1].pdf.

NDCC (2009). Strengthening Disaster Risk Reduction in the Philippines: Strategic National Action Plan 2009–2019. The National Disaster Coordinating Council, Office of Civil Defense, Planning Division, The Philippines. Available at http://www.adrc.asia/countryreport/PHL/2009/PHL_attachment.pdf.

The National Disaster Risk Reduction and Management Council (NDRRMC). (2011). The National Disaster Risk reduction and Management Plan 2011–2028, Republic of the Philippines. Available at http://www.ndrrmc.gov.ph/attachments/article/41/NDRRM_Plan_2011-2028.pdf.

The National Disaster Risk Reduction and Management Council (NDRRMC). (2015). Philippines National progress report on the implementation of the Hyogo Framework for Action (2013–2015), Republic of the Philippines. Available at https://www.preventionweb.net/files/43379_PHL_NationalHFA Progress_2013-15.pdf.

NOAA (2009). Advancing Coastal Community Resilience: A Brief Project Overview. Paper presented at Resilience Research Workshop, Natural Hazards Center, University of Colorado and the Community and Regional Resilience Institute, Colorado, July 14, 2009.

Office of the Civil Defense (OCD) (2013). The Civil Defense Gazette, Office of the Civil Defense, NDRRMC, The Philippines. 1(1). Jan–Mar 2013. Available at http://www.ocd.ndrrmc.gov.ph/attachments/article/151/Gazette%20Vol% 201%20Issue%201.pdf.

Philippines, the final version 23 April (2015). Available at: http://www.pre ventionweb.net/english/hyogo/progress/reports/v.php?id=43379&pid:223.

Pandey, B and K Okazaki (2004). Community Based Disaster management: Empowering Communities to Cope with Disaster Risks. United nations Centre for Regional Development, Japan. Available at http://citeseerx.ist. psu.edu/viewdoc/download?doi=10.1.1.467.1932&rep=rep1&type=pdf.

Passerini, E (2001). Who is to blame for the failures of sustainable reconstruction projects. *Natural Hazards Review*, 2(45), 45–53. Available at http:// ascelibrary.org/doi/abs/10.1061/(ASCE)1527-6988(2001)2% 3A2(45).

Pelling, M (2007). Learning from others: The scope and challenges for participatory disaster risk assessment. *Disasters*, 31(4), 373–385.

PreventionWeb (2015). Thailand National progress report on the implementation of the Hyogo Framework for Action (2013–2015). Available at http://www. preventionweb.net/files/41674_THA_NationalHFAprogress_2013-15.pdf.

PreventionWeb (2015b). Indonesia National progress report on the implementation of the Hyogo Framework for Action (2013–2015). Available at http:// www.preventionweb.net/files/41507_IDN_NationalHFAprogress_2013-15.pdf.

PreventionWeb (2015c). Bangladesh National progress report on the implementation of the Hyogo Framework for Action (2013–2015). Available at: http://www.preventionweb.net/files/40155_BGD_NationalHFAprogress_2013 -15.pdf.

Practical Action (2009). *Disaster Risk Reduction Nepal.* Online Publications. Retrieved on 28 February 2017 from http://practicalaction.org/disaster-risk-reduction-nepal.

Pristiyanto, D (2015). Indonesia: National progress report on the implementation of the Hyogo Framework for Action (2013–15). A National HFA Monitor update published by PreventionWeb. Available at http://www.prevention web.net/english/hyogo/progress/reports/.

Riyanti D and F Thomalla (2012). Disaster risk reduction and climate change adaptation in Indonesia: Institutional challenges and opportunities for integration. *International Journal of Disaster Resilience in the Built Environment*, 3(2), 166–180.

Riyanti, D (2012). Adaptive governance and resilience: The role of multistakeholder platforms in disaster risk reduction. *Natural Hazards Earth System Science*, 12, 2923–2942.

Robert, B, Y Matsuda and Y Okada (2008). Japan's Jishu-bosai-soshiki community activities: Analysis of its role in participatory community disaster risk management. *Natural Hazards: Journal of the International Society for the Prevention and Mitigation of Natural Hazards*, 44, 281–292.

Rajib Shaw (ed.) (2012). *Community, Environment and Disaster Risk Management.* Emerald Group Publishing Limited.

Rao, S (2013). Disaster risk governance and subnational levels. GSDRC Helpdesk Research Report 991. Birmingham, UK: GSDRC, University of Birmingham. Available at http://gsdrc.org/go/display&type=Helpdesk&id=991.

Reliefweb (2017). Philippines: Stronger community-based disaster preparedness plan for Iloilo up. Retrieved from https://reliefweb.int/report/philippines/ philippines-stronger-community-based-disaster-preparedness-plan-iloilo.

Rose, A (2004). Defining and measuring economic resilience to disasters. *Disaster Prevention and Management*, 13(4), 307–313.

Rose, A (2009). Economic Resilience. Paper presented at Resilience Research Workshop, Natural Hazards Center, University of Colorado and the Community and Regional Resilience Institute, Colorado, July 14.

Said, AM, FR Ahmadun, AR Mahmud and F Abas (2011). *Community preparedness for tsunami disaster: A case study*. Disaster Prevention and Management, 20(3), 266–280. Available at: http://www.emeraldinsight.com/journals.htm?articleid=1937591&show=abstract.

Sea Grant and NOAA (2008). Coastal Resilience Index: A Community Self-Assessment-A Guide to Examining How Prepared Your Community is for a Disaster. Draft publication of the Sea Grant Consortium and National Oceanic and Atmospheric Administration.

Sembiring, M and JA Lassa (2016). International Disasters in Asia Pacific: Indonesia's Civil-Military Responses. RSIS Working Paper (series No. 174/2016; 12 July 2016).

Sharma, SK (2010). Socio-Economic Aspects of Disaster's Impacts: An Assessment of Databases and Methodologies. Submitted to the Economic Growth Centre, Division of Economics, School of Humanities and Social Sciences, Nanyang Technological University, Singapore. Available at http://www3.ntu.edu.sg/hss2/egc/wp/2010/2010-01.pdf.

Shaw, R (2012a). *Overview of Community-based disaster risk reduction*. In *Community, Environment and Disaster Risk Management*, (Volume 10) Chapter 1, pp. 3–17. Emerald Group Publishing Limited.

Simpson, D and M Katirai (2006). Indicator Issues and Proposed Framework for a Disaster Preparedness Index (Dpi). Working Paper 06-03, Center for Hazards Research and Policy Development, School of Urban and Public Affairs, University of Louisville, September.

Thomalla, F, T Downing, E Spanger-Siegfried, G Han and J Rockström (2006). Reducing hazard vulnerability. Towards a common approach between disaster risk reduction and climate adaptation. *Disasters*, 30(1), 39–48. Available at http://citeseerx.ist.psu.edu/viewdoc/download?doi=10.1.1.546.5629&rep=rep1&type=pdf.

Trading Economics (2017). Available at: https://tradingeconomics.com/indonesia/access-to-electricity-percent-of-population-wb-data.html.

Tyler, S, E Nugraha and Nguyen (2014). Developing Indicators of Urban Climate Resilience. ISET. Available at http://i-s-e-t.org/resources/working-papers/wp2-climate-resilience.html.

UNISDR (2005). Hyogo Framework for Action 2005–2015: International Strategy for Disaster Reduction Building the Resilience of Nations and Communities to Disasters. The United Nations Office for Disaster Risk Reduction (UNISDR).

UNISDR (2007). *A Guide Note on Indicators for Assessing Progress on Disaster Risk Reduction*. United Nations International Symposium for Disaster Risk Reduction, Unpublished draft.

UN-ESCAP/UNISDR (2012). *Reducing Vulnerability and Exposure to Disasters The Asia-Pacific Disaster Report 2012.* UN-ESCAP and the United Nations Office for Disaster Risk Reduction, United Nations. Available at http://www.unisdr.org/files/29288_apdr2012finallowres.pdf.

UNISDR (2013). Global Assessment Report (GAR) on Disaster Risk Reduction 2013, United Nations Office for Disaster Risk Reduction, the United Nations.

UNISDR (2013b). Making Cities Resilient: Summary for Policymakers A global snapshot of how local governments reduce disaster risk. United Nations Office for Disaster Risk Reduction. Available at http://www.prevention web.net/files/33059_33059finalprinterversionexecutivesu.pdf.

UNISDR (2013). The Pacific experience in developing policy and legislation on disaster risk reduction and climate change adaptation. The United Nations International Strategy for Disaster Risk Reduction (UNISDR), Regional Office for Asia and the Pacific (UNISDR AP). Available at http://www.unisdr.org/files/34003pacificexperienceonlegislation.pdf.

UNISDR (2014). Progress and Challenges in Disaster Risk Reduction: A contribution towards the development of policy indicators for the Post — 2015 Framework on Disaster Risk Reduction. Geneva, Switzerland. The United Nations Office for Disaster Risk Reduction (UNISDR).

UNISDR (2014b). Disaster Resilience Scorecard for Cities. Working Document. United Nations International Strategy for Disaster Risk Reduction (UNISDR). Available at http://www.unisdr.org/2014/campaign-cities/Resilience%20Scorecard%20V1.5.pdf.

United Nations Office for Coordination of Humanitarian Affairs (2014). *IASC Inter-agency Humanitarian Evaluation of the Typhoon Haiyan Response.* Prepared on behalf of the Inter-Agency Humanitarian Evaluation Steering Group, October.

UNESCAP (2015). Overview of Natural Disasters and Impacts in Asia and the Pacific, 1970–2014. United Nations ESCAP Technical Paper, March.

UNISDR (2015). Sendai Framework for Disaster Risk Reduction 2015–2030. The United Nations Office for Disaster Risk Reduction (UNISDR), Geneva, Switzerland. Available at: http://www.preventionweb.net/files/43291_sendaiframeworkfordrren.pdf.

United Nations (2015b). Global Assessment Report (GAR) on Disaster Risk Reduction 2015 Making Development Sustainable: The Future of Disaster Risk Management. The United Nations International Strategy for Disaster Risk Reduction, New York.

UNISDR (2016). Thailand Adopts Sendai Framework. United Nations International Strategy for Disaster Risk Reduction (UNISDR). Retrieved from https://www.unisdr.org/archive/44955.

US Global Investors (2011). Based on Morgan Stanley research published by US Global Investors 2011. Retrieved from http://www.usfunds.com/investor-library/frank-talk/policy-reforms-pave-way-for-indonesia/#.WH3DetR95kg, 17 January 2017.

Van Der Vegt, G, P Essens, M Wahlstrom and G George (2015). *Managing Risk and Resilience: From the Editors*, 58(4), 971–980. Lee Kong Chian School of Business. Singapore Management University.

Wildavsky, A (1991). *Searching for Safety*. New Brunswick, New Jersey: Transaction Publishers.

Wisner *et al.* (2012). *Handbook of Hazards and Disaster Risk Reduction*. Routledge Publications. Available at http://discovery.ucl.ac.uk/id/eprint/1332844.

The Brookings Institution (2013). The Brookings Institution — London School of Economics Project on Internal Displacement. The Year of Recurring Disasters: A Review of Natural Disasters in 2012, by Elizabeth Ferris, Daniel Petz and Chareen Stark. Available at http://www.brookings.edu/~/media/research/files/reports/2013/03/natural%20disasters%20review/brookings_review_natural_disasters_2012.pdf.

The World Bank (2011). Java Reconstruction Fund Progress Report. The World Bank, Washington DC.

The World Bank (2013). World Development Report 2014. Risk and Opportunity Managing Risk for Development. The World Bank, Washington DC.

The World Bank Group (2017). Unbreakable Building the Resilience of the Poor in the face of Natural Disasters. Climate Change and Development Series. World Bank Group, International Bank for Reconstruction and Development, Washington DC.

WHO/UNICEF (2016). WHO/UNICEF Joint Monitoring Programme (JMP) for Water Supply and Sanitation. Retrieved from http://data.worldbank.org/indicator/SH.H2O.SAFE.ZS.

Zakour, M and D Gillepsi (2013). *Community Disaster Vulnerability Theory, Research and Practice*, Springer Publications.

CHAPTER 8

DISASTER RISK REDUCTION AND SUSTAINABLE DEVELOPMENT: GOING FORWARD

Suman K. Sharma
Nanyang Technological University

As seen through various chapters in this volume, disasters can have severe consequences on peoples' income, wealth, health, and social state. They can have equally damaging effects on various income groups in a society, and for the most part, the adverse impacts can persist for a much longer time. As discussed in Chapter 7, national governments in the region have employed various measures to translate their understanding of disasters into respective policy agendas and pursue a sustainable development path aimed at risk reduction. However, available evidences indicate that despite making significant progress in, for example, identifying satisfactory level of DRR focused development programs and policy agendas, most countries in the region still lack severely in terms of translating effectively the DRR agenda into practice due to various issues and challenges that require immediate attention. This concluding chapter briefly weighs in our outlook on the status of existing DRR development agenda in practice, particularly, in view of our understanding of disasters and the issues and challenges involved in operationlizing the agenda, and provides some thoughts and reflections on how best to mobilize our efforts and address the challenges through building on available supportive environments.

1. INTRODUCTION

Evidences around the world indicate that economic losses and damages caused by crisis and disaster events seem to be continuously growing. According to the 2015 Global Assessment Report (GAR) on Disaster Risk Reduction, economic losses worldwide from natural disasters like earthquakes, tsunamis, cyclones and flooding average around US$250–US$300 billion annually and expected annual losses in future are estimated as US$314 billion in terms of the built environment alone, which provides an indication of the amount countries should set aside to meet losses annually (UNISDR, 2015b). Similar sentiments are echoed through the 2016 United Nations Report on Disaster Risk Reduction (UNISDR, 2017). More distressing findings are presented in another recent research (The World Bank, 2017), indicating that devastating consequences of disasters go far beyond financial losses as they tend to push communities further down the poverty line with as many as about 26 million people globally forced into poverty every year. The report cites numerous cases where natural disasters' impacts are known to be severely detrimental to ending global poverty; such as the 2013 Typhoon Haiyan in the Philippines (costing $12.9 billion and plunging one million into poverty); the 2010 Cyclone Aila in Bangladesh coastal areas (spiking unemployment and poverty rates to 49% and 22%, respectively); and many others (The World Bank, 2017). At the least, something is clear — apart from a huge amount of average annual losses globally (for instance, an estimated $300 billion or more according to the World Bank 2017 report), major disasters have the potential to severely affect peoples' lives and worsen their economic and social well-being. The grim reality needs to be understood and addressed undoubtedly, and therefore, requires urgent attention on the part of all stakeholders — more importantly, policymakers, development actors and communities alike.

In recent years, existing knowledge on disaster events, based on a variety of case studies available worldwide, has consistently emphasized the underlying link between disaster risk reduction and sustainable development, and consequently, explored prospective, corrective and compensatory risk reduction and risk management approaches as a way to integrate these into development activities, so as to avoid further risk generation and accumulation. Furthermore, in the process of integrating disaster risk management into development priorities, a growing number of interventions are seen to emphasize that managing risks cost less than managing disasters. As such the focus of disaster risk reduction needs to move away from managing disasters towards managing risks so as to contribute to making development sustainable (UNISDR, 2017; World Bank, 2017; UNISDR, 2012; UNISDR, 2015b; among others). While the significance of a risk reduction approach in achieving the goal of a sustainable development appears to have been vindicated by all, at least conceptually; as far as the actual task of implementing a DRR-focused development agenda is concerned, the disaster community certainly has a long way to go.

As seen through various chapters in this volume, disasters can have severe consequences on peoples' average levels of income, wealth, health, and social state. The severe damaging effects of major disasters are seen to have varying impacts on different income groups, and also, the overall adverse impacts of major disasters can persist over a much longer time. In addition, we have seen cases where occurrences of disasters can damage the property market. Furthermore, adverse impacts of a major disaster can create a situation where the longer-term effect results in a steady decline of per capita GRP in the region. In terms of hazard and disaster risks, the case studies covered in the book have shown that certain common social factors can determine peoples' susceptibility to hazards demonstrating that factors that generate hazard and disaster risks are often interrelated with varying contributions. Although recent disaster impact studies have made noteworthy efforts, studies for the most part are hampered by a range of issues including those related to data, methodology and the available estimation techniques, and therefore, face enormous challenges in attempting to adequately comprehend disasters' impacts in their entirety. Complexities are too many such that major disasters' consequences not only tend to interact with a range of socio-economic factors and intersectoral attributes but also appear to be evolving over time sometimes leading to unknown risks thus further complicating the task of impact estimation.

Against this backdrop, Chapter 7 discussed some of the key measures employed by the national governments in the region to translate their understanding of disasters into the respective policy agendas and pursue a sustainable development path aimed at risk reduction. In addition, the chapter discussed role of communities in disaster risk reduction so as to mobilize community strengths in building resilience to hazards and disasters. As highlighted in the chapter, available evidences indicate that despite making significant progress in, for example, identifying satisfactory level of DRR-focused development programs and policy agendas, most countries in the region still lack severely in terms of translating effectively the DRR agenda into practice due to a range of issues and challenges that require immediate attention. This concluding chapter briefly weighs in our outlook on the existing status of DRR development agenda in practice, particularly, in view of our understanding of disasters and the issues and challenges involved in operationlizing the agenda, and provides some thoughts and reflections on how best to mobilize our efforts and address the challenges through building on available supportive environments.

In the remaining sections of Chapter 8, we outline the background information on where do national governments stand in terms of their progress on the DRR development path, to be followed by some thoughts and reflections considered relevant in operationalizing the agenda primarily focusing on such initiatives as risk identification, risk communication and risk transfer mechanisms. We end this concluding chapter by outlining a number of available supportive environments to build on the DRR agenda. Specifically, Section 2 outlines a few aspects that portray, to some extent, the current status regarding implementation of the DRR development agenda from a national perspective; Section 3 offers some reflections attributed to the limited progress seen in implementing the DRR agenda; while Section 4 lists down the available positive enabling environments to support the cause despite the issues and challenges. The chapter ends with a brief concluding note in Section 5.

2. DRR AND SUSTAINABLE DEVELOPMENT AGENDA: WHERE DO WE STAND?

Recognition of DRR-focused Development Agenda: While available evidences worldwide convey that countries are increasingly vulnerable to natural disasters and their devastating consequences, the recognition of which is also growing and thus opening avenues to address not only the underlying issues at present but also new and emerging future risks better. As such based on numerous declarations, commitments, policy formulations, program implementations at multiple levels — national, regional, local, and international — general consensus indicates that today DRR is universally recognized as a development issue (UNISDR, 2014).

Looking back at the earlier years, the DRR spirit was nicely articulated through the HFA framework as early as in 2005 and subsequently endorsed by most nations during the following years. More notably, the underlying themes and messages of the framework have been in some sense largely internalized at various levels — the national, international and in some cases local. The DRR sentiments in recent years have been reinforced through the Sendai Framework for DRR (SFDRR), which recognizes that disasters have potential to hinder progress towards sustainable development (UNISDR, 2017; UNISDR, 2015). So at the moment, it seems reasonable to assert that the role of DRR in aligning towards a sustainable development path is widely acknowledged. To go with the spirit, at the operational level, there are numerous DRR based initiatives around the world busy at work and frequently making headlines demonstrating their significance publicly at various levels. The efforts made and successes achieved thus far are adequate reasons for the development communities to seriously reflect on the lessons learned from available experiences and evaluate the progress made (or lack of it) along the DRR path.

Operational Complexities and DRR Progress: Through a cursory look at a few country cases plus some general observations as discussed in Chapter 7, we have seen that in most countries,

DRR policies, plans and actions appear to be in place but at the operational level they haven't been adequately implemented indicating a slow, at times painful, progress towards a sustainable development path. Specifically, despite that in most country cases, DRR policies and planning mechanisms are identified into the development agenda, the available policy and planning documents suffer from lack of coordination and frequent fragmentation at multiple levels, for instance, in many cases, poor linkages between legislation and policy documents are far too common. At the operational level, among other factors, program implementing agencies frequently seem to suffer from inadequate level of coordination both at the inter-agency and intra-agency levels, which at times appear severe enough to derail the progress. Besides the obvious issues that can be identified in most country cases, disaster communities frequently encounter some systemic issues originating from factors that seem more structurally inherent within societies and nations.

Development Projects and Risk Assessments: *Inadequate Attention:* DRR advocates have long been troubled, and consequently, in recent times, become increasingly vocal about an irony that seems too deep rooted to be addressed properly as demonstrated through numerous cases when government actions — as good intentional as they could be — end up increasing disaster risks. For instance, when government authorities implement policies and actions relating to issuance of building structure, dams, building codes and land use, most of which are not well adjusted to local needs and priorities. Such actions, among others, are usually not based on risk assessments and potential environmental and other hazards. Preceding any development project, therefore, it is essential that assessments are undertaken to ascertain whether the building and construction of bridges, roads, dams end up increasing the risks of affected communities, which in many instances are the marginalized groups. To achieve the goal of sustainable development outcome, development projects must be assessed in advance in terms of their potential impact on DRR development agenda to ensure risk reduction is achieved and resilience is strengthened.

If nations are serious and committed indeed to pursuing a DRR-focused development path in a sustained manner, they ought to move towards undertaking development measures aimed at reducing disaster risks and build and strengthen resilience — at all levels from the community to the national level. For instance, while pursuing the path of economic growth and sustaining its pace, development programs and policies need to be aligned along the spirit of DRR-focused agenda, such that DRR measures must be undertaken early on and potential risks and threats of all projects must be assessed, identified and subsequently addressed to in a timely manner. Only with proper risk identification of hazards and potential disasters and necessary preparedness and mitigation measures in advance, can a development endeavor lead to success in achieving the goal of a sustainable development. However, the issues and challenges based on various case studies along with the lessons learned indicate that there is an urgent need to reorient the development projects such that necessary risk reduction measures are undertaken, in advance, at all levels.

Increased Disaster Risks (Resulting from Urbanization, Globalization, among others): Furthermore, as seen through various chapters in this volume, risks and threats to natural hazards and disasters appear to be growing as well as evolving over time. The trend of increasing risks and threats — for a variety of reasons — seems consistent based on more recent global studies as well. For instance, according to the Global Assessment Reports 2015 and 2016, as the process of globalization advances, so does the pressure of urbanization, which also means that investments tend to concentrate at locations that offer comparative advantages, and as a result, can lead to increased hazards as well as increased exposure of economic assets to those hazards. The role of growing hazard and disaster risks and their complexities, combined with lack of appreciation of risk-generating factors on the part of policy makers and development actors, leading to the limited success in implementing a DRR development agenda has been underscored by various recent case studies and findings. For example, despite the achievements made over the years in disaster preparedness measures, among others, the progress has been limited in most countries in terms of managing the underlying risks, as development decisions are still being made without much appreciation of risk-generating factors thus generating and accumulating new risks at a faster rate than reducing existing risks (UNISDR, 2015b; UNISDR, 2017; World Bank, 2017). Hence it is time more than ever to reflect upon the big question: Why are we still noticeably behind in terms of implementing the DRR-focused development agenda — embedded with necessary risk reduction measures-, despite, seemingly, the unanimous acknowledgment it commands among the disaster communities?

3. REFLECTIONS ON EXISTING DRR APPROACH AND WAYS TO ADVANCE DRR AGENDA

As highlighted repeatedly, despite the realization of a close link between the DRR and sustainable development agenda, the rate of progress in translating the agenda into practice, in most countries, have been far slower than envisaged. At the minimum, judging through various legislative and institutional developments, policies, programs and actions aimed at risk reduction, we all seem to agree that national governments have come a long way on the sustainable DRR development path. Yet given the limited progress so far it is time to reflect on some fundamental questions: Despite seemingly good intentions and considerable attempts and some progress thus far, why are we still so behind in our attempts to manage the underlying risks and threats and not able to make a significant dent in achieving the goal of risk reduction? More specifically: Apart from the issues and challenges identified in this volume, are there other factors that we might be overlooking or not daring enough to come forward and pinpoint, some of which could be too sensitive politically or otherwise?.

Now is the time to reflect on some fundamental questions as to what exactly is going on despite the worldwide acknowledgment and vindication as well as major efforts demonstrating the significance of DRR development agenda in achieving the goal of sustainable development. Does the lack of progress originate from the existing deficiencies that we have identified — in this volume — and are visible to most of us, or does it convey some deep rooted systemic issues suggesting inherent deficiencies in the very structure of a society? The answers perhaps require some serious reflections and discussions across various disciplines with sufficient level of ingenuity, honesty and even soul searching in every sense of the word.

By now, policy makers and disaster communities all alike have realized that the root causes of hazards and disasters including their adverse consequences lie much deeper than what seems obvious on the surface. Hazard and disaster risks and threats are growing, evolving as well as leading to greater complexities, thus highlighting the need for undertaking proper risk assessment methods, in advance, of all development programs and activities so as to minimize their potential risks and threats and enhance resilience. In addition to undertaking risk identification and risk assessment measures, it is essential to carry out necessary awareness raising measures aimed at risk communication and risk transfer mechanisms so that the available information on — risks and threats of potential hazards as well as available options of risk transfers — are conveyed to all.

For example, policy makers and practitioners, therefore, need to seriously examine and reflect upon the following: How well the risks associated with hazards and disasters are communicated to the majority of people including those belonging to the excluded groups and bottom socio-economic strata who may have different priorities concerning their day-to-day subsistence and little knowledge and incentive to prepare for potential future disasters? Have they widened their outreach sufficiently to cover all affected communities with necessary measures to educate them properly with tools like early warning systems, and so on, supported by proper monitoring and evaluation measures in place? In a broader sense, therefore, now is the urgency to evaluate some basic questions such as: do people have access to information in the first place? For instance, how many people in Southeast Asia are aware of the pollution related risks and threats they face in recent times? Are the public authorities disseminating and the media reporting the necessary information in an objective, honest, easily understandable and non-partition manner, or is it being manipulated by certain interest group(s) motivated politically or otherwise? At the same time, even if disaster risks are communicated to most of the population, it is equally relevant to examine: Is the risk communicated at a level that ordinary people and the local communities can comprehend easily or is it full of technical jargon? Are the risk reduction measures available to all including those who do not possess sufficient social, economic or political clout to lean on? More importantly, risk related information must be accompanied by alternative measures of risk-reduction; else information on risk alone may not suffice in most cases if no risk reduction alternatives are made available to at-risk groups. For instance, trainings on encouraging people to move away from hazardous areas by relocating elsewhere may not be enough unless alternative livelihood options are available to all. A case that illustrates this point is the situation that developed during the 2010 Mt Merapi volcanic eruption in Yogyakarta, Indonesia, when many people in the vicinity of the volcano refused to move away from hazardous areas due mainly to the fear of losing their livelihood permanently.

It seems that to date, for the most part, policymakers and development partners have been reluctant either to explicitly discuss or to take account of the underlying risk factors into their planning processes and policy actions — some of which might need non-conventional methods. Some risk factors can be too sensitive — politically or otherwise — to be discussed, while if overlooked might have severe implications and could end up exacerbating risks among certain groups within a society. These issues among others require open dialogues among all that would pave ways to assessing risks and concerns such as those including (i) Increased vulnerability of marginalized groups excluded on certain grounds either by societal biases and in some cases even national biases; (ii) Media biases in honestly portraying the true circumstances of peoples' vulnerability and exposure to threats; (iii) Rapid population growth threatening to damage the environmentally fragile region leading to increased risks (e.g., of health epidemic) due to government policy inaction and lack of enforcement; (iv) Rapid urbanization leading to peoples being victimized as they are forced to reside in fragile and hazard prone environments; and (v) Governments' inability, and/or reluctance, to properly communicate and address such issues as risks and threats caused by radicalization, terrorism and human rights abuses. The list can be much longer, unfortunately; the bottom line is: disaster communities, for the most part, have been largely shying away from discussing such underlying risk factors openly, some of which might require daring moves, so as not to antagonize certain interest groups or governments. In the past few years there have been examples of DRR advocates making cases and occasionally pleading to national as well as international policy makers and practitioners to resort to more open and honest discussions about the entirety of risks and threats (for example, Alexander, Davis, 2012). However, given the negligible progress in this direction, the current DRR development strategy urgently requires a radical and non-conventional momentum such that all types of risks and threats, existing as well as potential — examples include those related to media biases, rapid urbanization, corruption, terrorism, radicalization, human rights abuses, nuclear threats and cyber crimes — are openly discussed, information and knowledge properly disseminated to all and sincere risk reduction efforts are made and measures devised and executed to address those accordingly.

4. DRR AND SUSTAINABLE DEVELOPMENT AGENDA: ENABLING ENVIRONMENTS TO MOVE FORWARD

At the same time, thankfully, we are able to highlight several positive steps taken at various levels to encourage governments as well as other disaster communities to look and assess beyond the risks and threats that are obvious. As an example, it is commendable to observe that over the past few years in particular, international agencies like the United Nations, the World Bank, and others, have increasingly called upon the national governments to make sure that people have rights to information that are related to risks, threats and exposure to hazards and disasters, and therefore, such knowledge be made available to all concerned. The information could include, for instance, disaster loss estimates vis-à-vis potential benefits of DRR based development initiatives thus demonstrating not only the significance of DRR agenda but also economic arguments for risk reduction with resilience building.

However, despite significant efforts made by most countries in favor of DRR-focused development agenda through numerous risk assessment studies, policy level commitments as well as actions, lack of coordination among those in many cases have led to fragmentation and duplication of efforts. Consequently, to overcome the issue and strengthen the line of communication and coordination, a series of bold, daring and honest discussions and assessments are essential among all concerned in a periodic manner so the underlying elements responsible for lackluster performance of DRR policy actions emerge and become open to the disaster community as well as the public at large. This will pave the way for follow-up honest discussions on, say: how well the development projects are coordinated (or lack thereof) so as to bridge the gap between growth oriented projects and sustained DRR efforts? How to create a reasonable balance such that the underlying risks and threats do not end up derailing the DRR path? In the process, it is essential that national governments stick with the underlying goal, namely, to pursue the path of a sustainable development while ensuring that development projects ultimately end up reducing risks, building resilience, and also, minimizing potential hazard and disaster risks in future. Provided genuine commitment to their goal, national governments, in fact, now are in much better position today than in the past and have greater capacity, thus exhibiting a greater scope to devise measures to facilitate various platforms upon which such dialogues take place that seem more essential than ever particularly in view of the growing threats around the world including those caused by climate change, global warming, among others. The growing trend of recognition of those issues, at the same time, presents opportunities for all to pursue a sustainable development path and not to engage in actions that might not only be unsustainable but also threaten the very spirit of the DRR development in the first place.

Also, we acknowledge that a multitude of DRR-focused initiatives have indeed been taken at various levels by policy makers and development communities and in several cases reasonably encouraging outcomes have been witnessed particularly in more recent times. For this very reason, among others, we sincerely believe that although the DRR-focused development process has been challenging, the underlying issues can effectively be addressed provided the policy makers and development actors engage in constructive discussions with stakeholders and devise necessary measures and act in a concerted manner openly and honestly as well as patiently. Several noteworthy steps have been taken in this direction over the years, and enabling environments created, some of which are outlined below.

Available Legislative/Institutional Framework for DRR: In recent times, one crucial achievement is that most countries in the region have now been able to identify that a supportive legislative and regulatory framework is essential for undertaking disaster management. Although the challenges for successfully managing disasters are enormous, there are many opportunities that the legislative and regulatory framework is able to offer that may be taken advantage of to carry on and speed up the DRR agenda. Governments, therefore, are now in a much better position to build on this crucial opportunity, namely, a growingly supportive policy environment. In several country cases, it is seen that necessary disaster management laws and associated decrees are supported by various regulations at multiple levels, indicating that the regulatory framework has been in effect in a steady manner, thus offering an environment — immensely favorable — for governments to take the DRR agenda forward.

Along with the necessary legislative and regulatory framework for managing disasters, most countries currently also possess supportive institutional framework designed to carry the DRR agenda into action. For instance, in several country cases, the institutional aspect of disaster management has been strengthened through the establishment of national as well as local, city or, at times, provincial level agencies. Consequently, most governments now are in a better position to employ the institutional strength of disaster management at all levels for advancing their DRR paradigm. This will pave the way for governments to consider setting up disaster management agencies as autonomous bodies in future, so as to ensure better management of disasters and disaster related risks, issues and concerns.

Increasing Attention to DRR and Greater Collaboration among Stakeholders: In a broader context, compared to past development approaches, we cannot deny that in present times, most countries seem to be devoting a greater time and energy and attention towards a risk reduction based sustainable development agenda. This recognition in itself, namely, the growing attention national governments place on the issue of DRR, can be taken as a giant step and certainly be labeled as one more opportunity of crucial relevance. Furthermore, at the country level in several cases, increased attention to DRR has been shown through the establishment of various national forums and platforms to facilitate open dialogues and discussions among stakeholders to carry the agenda forward. The presence of such platforms and forums encourages the multi-stakeholders, including the private sector and academia, to actively participate in disaster management efforts, strengthening the efforts made thus far.

On the implementation side, equally compelling argument for a supportive environment is seen through the commitment of disaster management actors not only in implementing DRR measures in general but also taking part in emergency response and recovery measures. A few country cases have shown, for instance, that cross-sectoral collaboration that involves the government, the people, and the private sector in the form of enhancing poverty reduction, facilitating basic education and improving community's health can also contribute to the DRR agenda. Commendable examples are seen through the commitments made by countries, such as those in the ASEAN region with the establishment of the AHA Center (ASEAN Coordinating Centre for Humanitarian Assistance on Disaster Management) and the conduct of joint disaster exercise through the ASEAN Regional Disaster Exercise (ARDEX), and implementation of AADMER (ASEAN Agreement on Disaster Management and Emergency Response).

Opportunities Created by Technological Advancement: One opportunity of utmost significance in recent times constitutes the ease and advancement of technological development in just about every sector imaginable. Through making use of the available technology, scientific and otherwise, the DRR system can be strengthened and taken forward much more effectively in modern days, for instance, through the uses of higher level of technology-based early warning systems. In general, technological enhancements can be utilized for a range of actions such as in identifying hazard risks as well as improving the processing techniques of properly identifying hazard threats related to earthquakes, tsunami and volcanic eruptions that may turn into disasters; and ensuring data and information are properly reflected and potential threats and their intensities to "at risk" population are properly estimated and conveyed. Similarly, advanced technology combined with necessary resources is more likely to pinpoint areas of high exposure, and vulnerabilities in areas that are more susceptible. Furthermore, the use of ICT-based technology and mobile devices facilitate the collection, analysis and dissemination of scientific information on risks and risk-reduction measures for an effective execution of the DRR agenda.

Mobilizing Private Sector and Devising ways of Risk Transfer Mechanisms like mass Insurance: Similarly, a compelling case for pursuing and sustaining a DRR development agenda, can solely be made on the basis of a business argument. The growing role of the private sector in modern times provides opportunities for all to extract the business argument such that, the shared risks of disasters can simply be converted into shared values. In other words, given the crucial role of the private sector in a highly globalized world in recent times, the increased investments in terms of trillions of dollars towards hazard exposed regions, will also enable the private sector to be able to extract tremendous opportunities to reduce risks and vulnerabilities through addressing underlying risk and exposure factors.

Along this line of thought, one aspect of risk mitigation and risk transfer, not discussed in this book volume, is the need for governments to explore and promote risk transfer mechanisms like mass insurance. As seen through various recent publications the gaps between insured losses and uninsured losses incurred as results of major disasters are too high (The World Bank Group, 2017; Aon Benfield, 2016). A greater mobilization of the private sector with active government support is required to design insurance schemes for the masses while promoting risk mitigation efforts at all levels. In general, the national governments need to devise a wide range of risk transfer programs, which reach the masses designed particularly to mitigate risks and avail the general public with various avenues of lessening potential adverse consequences of hazards and disasters.

5. CONCLUDING NOTE

National governments committed to mainstreaming disaster risk reduction into development planning and policy agenda and pursuing a sustained DRR development path should continually work on improvements in the way DRR-focused policies and activities are addressed, and also, undertake measures to ensure all stakeholders become more capable and more resilient to hazard and disaster risks. There may be times when as good as the DRR policies are, efforts must be dedicated to evaluating them in the case when modifications and adjustments are needed to make it timely. The 2004 Indian Ocean earthquake and tsunami and the 2011 Japan earthquake and subsequent tsunami and the resulting nuclear meltdown threats, for example, proved to be good lessons for demonstrating how risks and threats can cascade into very complex disasters. The growing and continuously evolving nature of disaster risks and threats, consequently, has heightened the need to devise DRR-focused development planning and policies followed by corresponding actions aimed at risk mitigation and resilience building. It is essential that measures to lower risks are accompanied by measures to strengthen resilience, such that the affected nation (or a community) is not only able to withstand or resist disaster impacts and bounce back following the event but also able to modify behavior and structure to adapt to future disaster threats. While examining disaster resilience precisely can be complex — through establishing factors and identifying appropriate indicators contributing to building resilience-, will policymakers be able to properly manage the disaster risks and threats, potential as well as imminent, and thus, strengthen resilience. Understanding disaster risks and devising policies and actions aimed at risk reduction, risk mitigation and resilience building are challenges that all countries face; how each country responds to these challenges and addresses the underlying risks and threats and pursues a sustainable development path determines the level of success.

REFERENCES

Alexander, D and I Davis (2012). Disaster Risk Reduction An Alternative Viewpoint (editorial). *International Journal of Disaster Risk Reduction*, 2, 1–5.

Aon Benfield (2016). The One Brief, *The Cost of Catastrophe Assessing the Impact of Natural Disasters*. Available at http://www.theonebrief.com/the-cost-of-catastrophe-assessing-the-impact-of-natural-disasters/.

UNISDR (2014). Progress and Challenges in Disaster Risk Reduction: A contribution towards the development of policy indicators for the Post-2015 Framework on Disaster Risk Reduction. Geneva, Switzerland. The United Nations Office for Disaster Risk Reduction (UNISDR).

UNISDR (2015). Sendai Framework for Disaster Risk Reduction 2015–2030. The United Nations Office for Disaster Risk Reduction (UNISDR), Geneva, Switzerland. Available at http://www.preventionweb.net/files/43291_sendai frameworkfordrren.pdf.

UNISDR (2015b). Making Development Sustainable: The Future of Disaster Risk Management. Global Assessment Report (GAR) on Disaster Risk Reduction. The United Nations International Strategy for Disaster Risk Reduction (UNISDR), Geneva, Switzerland.

UNISDR (2017). UNISDR Annual Report 2016 In support of the Sendai Framework for Disaster Risk Reduction. The United Nations Office for Disaster Risk Reduction, Geneva, Switzerland. Available at http://www.unisdr.org/files/52253_unisdr2016annualreport.pdf.

The World Bank Group (2017). Unbreakable Building the Resilience of the Poor in the face of Natural Disasters. Climate Change and Development Series. World Bank Group, International Bank for Reconstruction and Development, Washington DC.

INDEX

AADMER, 200
Afghanistan, 65, 75
AHA Centre, 200
ASEAN Committee on Disaster
  Management, 200
Asia-Pacific region, 186, 192
Asian Floods, 187
Asian tsunami, 88
Australia, 9, 147, 148, 152, 153, 155,
  156, 163, 164, 173
Australian Bureau of Statistics, 164
autocorrelation, 162

Bangladesh, 5, 7, 18, 24, 26, 75, 86,
  88, 91–93, 96–99, 101, 102, 105,
  194, 196, 210, 232, 258
Bangladeshi households, 32, 35
Bhutan, 75
binary response model, 88, 97
BNPB, 198, 199, 214
Bolivia, 20
BPBDs, 198, 214
Burkina Faso, 26

Chile, 224
China, 2, 67, 72, 75
Climate Disaster Resilience Index,
  220
Côte d'Ivoire, 22
community concept, 228
community resilience, 227, 229

computable general equilibrium
  model, 58, 122, 219
covariate weather risks, 34
Cyclone Aila, 32, 258
Cyclone Nargis, 17, 199

Democratic People's Republic of
  Korea, 65
DesInventar, 63–66, 78, 79
disaster insurance, 34
Disaster Management Agency, 239
Disaster Management Law 24/2007,
  197
disaster micro-insurance, 34
disaster resilience, 216, 218, 221–225
Disaster Resilience Scorecard for
  Cities, 222
disaster risk governance, 192
disaster risk index, 221
disaster risk management, 36
double counting, 57, 61, 62
droughts and rainfall fluctuations, 21
DRRM, 203

early warning systems, 191, 229, 240
earthquake resilience, 220
East, South, and South-East Asia, 62
ECLAC, 16, 56, 58
economic resilience, 218, 221
Ecuador earthquake, 199
El Salvador, 28, 30

EMDAT, 19, 50, 53, 56, 61–66, 73,
   75–79
Ethiopia, 22, 23, 25, 30, 31, 34
Ethiopian famine, 24
ex ante private coping strategies, 35
ex ante risk, 31
ex post covariate risks, 31
ex post public responses, 35
ex-ante disaster management plans,
   38
ex-ante mitigation strategies, 85
ex-post coping mechanisms, 85
exogenous shock, 124
extended insurance, 36

Family Life Survey, 91
fat tail disasters, 17
fat-tail events, 18
female-headed households, 35
Fiji, 28, 200
Fiji tropical cyclone, 199
flood Levees, 10
formal insurance policies, 34
Frenchville, 9

global financial crisis (GFC), 151,
   152, 171, 172
good governance, 224
Great East Japan Earthquake, 231
Guatemala, 19, 20, 24

Haiti, 224
Haiti earthquake, 17, 199
hazard rank, 92, 93
HFA, 191, 194, 196, 197, 200, 201,
   203, 212, 229, 230, 235
Honduras, 31
Hotspots Project, 221
household panel dataset, 30
Hurricane Andrew, 122
Hurricane Iniki, 122
Hurricane Katrina, 88, 119
Hurricane Mitch, 29, 31, 32, 88
Hyogo Framework, 190

Hyogo prefecture, 7, 37, 123, 125,
   127, 130, 131, 137, 138, 142, 143

index insurance, 34
index- or micro-insurance products,
   34
India, 2, 22, 24, 33, 34, 67, 194, 195
Indian Ocean tsunami, 236
Indonesia, 2, 5, 7, 12, 21, 23, 37, 67,
   73, 79, 86, 88, 91–93, 96–99,
   101–103, 105, 192, 193, 196, 199,
   200, 210–214, 225, 226, 230, 232,
   235–237, 244
input-output (I-O) modelling, 58,
   120, 122
insurance and re-insurance markets,
   28
insurance companies, 175
International Monetary Fund (IMF),
   65
Intergovernmental Panel on Climate
   Change, 16, 51, 80
International Food Policy Research
   Institute (IFPRI), 91
intra-regional linkage, 141
Iran, 65

Jamaica, 30
Japan, 7, 72, 73, 79, 119, 125, 128,
   157, 191, 193, 231, 232
Jordan, 20

Kobe earthquake, 7, 8, 29, 119, 121,
   123, 124, 126, 128, 132, 134, 137,
   139, 142, 143, 193

Lagrange Multiplier (LM), 162
Local Disaster Management Agencies
   (BPBDs), 198, 237, 239

macroeconomic indicators, 120, 138
Making Cities Resilient Campaign,
   235
Malaysia, 194, 231, 232
market-based impacts, 54–56

maximum likelihood estimates, 96
Mexican, 23, 25
Mexico, 28, 33, 34
Millennium Development Goals
    (MDGs), 16, 197, 201
Mongolia, 22, 72
multi-stakeholder platform, 232
Myanmar, 65, 199

NatCat SERVICE, 63
National Disaster Coordinating
    Council, 201
National Disaster Management
    Agency (BNPB), 198, 237
National Disaster Management
    Authority, 239
National DRRM Plan, 202
National Panel Survey, 91
NDRRM, 212
NDRRMC, 204, 206
Nepal, 23
new political equilibrium, 27
New Zealand, 163
Nicaragua, 29, 88
Nigeria, 30
nonmarket-based impacts, 55, 58, 59,
    61, 78, 80

ordinary least squares, 161

Pacific island of Samoa, 32
Pakistan, 194, 195
paradigm shift, 187, 212
Paris Agreement, 4, 16
Peru, 20, 23, 28
political will, 246
property market, 9, 147, 149
ProVention Consortium, 221

Republic Act (RA) 2010, 201, 205
Republic Act 10121, 204, 212, 240
resilience concept, 12, 186, 215–219,
    221, 223, 224, 226, 227
resilience index, 219–221

risk mappings, 236
Rockhampton, 10, 147

Sendai Framework for Disaster Risk
    Reduction, 16, 191, 194
shift-share analysis, 139
Sichuan earthquake, 199
Sigma, 63
social accounting matrix, 122
Social Vulnerability Index, 218
spatial dependence, 162, 163, 169
Sri Lanka, 88, 194–196
Sustainable Development Goals
    (SDGs), 16, 197
Syria, 20
systemic and structural factors, 242,
    243

2004 Indian Ocean earthquake and
    tsunami, 17, 21, 187, 197
2004 Tsunami, 197
2004 earthquake/tsunami in the
    Indian Ocean, 17
2007 Law, 197, 198, 212, 237
2010 Act, 202
2011 Great East Japan Earthquake,
    1, 193
2011 Thailand flood, 1, 22
2011 Triple catastrophe in Japan, 187
2013 Typhoon Haiyan in the
    Philippines, 187
2015 Global Assessment Report
    (GAR) on Disaster Risk Reduction,
    257
2015 Global Climate Catastrophe
    Report, 2
2015 Nepal Earthquake, 187
2016 Annual Global Climate and
    Catastrophe Report, 2
2016 United Nations Report on
    Disaster Risk Reduction, 258
2016 earthquakes (Japan and
    Ecuador), 187
2017 Asia-Pacific Disaster report, 2
Taiwan, 75

Tanzania, 5, 7, 86, 88, 91–93, 96–99,
    101–103, 105
Thailand, 120, 193, 194
Thailand Floods, 187
the Philippines, 2, 12, 18, 22, 35, 67,
    192, 193, 199, 201, 203, 206, 209,
    211, 212, 214, 232, 235, 236, 240,
    241, 243–245, 258
Timor-Leste, 65, 232
Tokai flood, 157
Typhoon Haiyan, 199, 258
Typhoon Lando, 214
Typhoon Nina, 214
Typhoon Pablo, 241
Typhoon Yolanda (Haiyan), 189, 203,
    211, 214, 245

Uganda, 25, 33
Ugandan household, 33
UNDP, 28, 221
United Nations, 199, 218

United States, 2, 119, 220
univariate time-series model, 125
USA, 88

Vanuatu tropical cyclone, 199
Vietnam, 24, 25, 29, 75, 231
Vietnamese, 23
volunteer response squads, 199, 239

weather risks, 34
West Africa, 33
wildfire insurance policy, 10, 175
World Bank, 17, 65, 221, 258
World Conference on Disaster
    Reduction, 190
World Risk Report, 91

Yemen, 20
Yogyakarta earthquake, 230, 237

Zimbabwe, 23

Printed in the United States
By Bookmasters

Printed in the United States
By Bookmasters